THE BLACKSMITH

Robert Serocki, Jr.

ONE WORLD PRESS
Chino Valley, AZ

Copyright © 2022 by Robert Serocki, Jr.

www.robertserockijr.com
robert@robertserockijr.com
800.410.9012

All rights reserved. No part of this book may be reproduced in any manner without permission of the author, except in the case of quotes used in critical articles and reviews.

Cover design: One World Press
Text layout & design: KuberaBookDesign.com

ISBN: 978-1-938043-23-9
eBook ISBN: 978-1-938043-24-6

This book was printed in the U.S.A.

One World Press
890 Staley Lane
Chino Valley, AZ 86323
928-848-6550
printmybook@oneworldpress.com
www.oneworldpress.com

Table of Contents

Foreword   v

Introduction   xiii

Part 1   The Blackening: Learning that I need to live life from my unconscious guidance   1

Part 2   The Whitening: The reunion of my spirit with my body beginning an elimination of the impurities of my life   63

Part 3   The Reddening: Uniting Conscious Life with Unconscious Life   119

Part 4   The Whole Complete Self   207

Final Thoughts and Results   248

My Four Steps to Begin a Journey of Healing, Developing Spiritually, and Attaining Your Dreams   255

My Game Plan Going Forward   257

About the Author   260

Other Publications   262

Foreword

This book is a must read for anyone trying to overcome the difficulties that are inevitable in our lives.

The author explains how he overcame PTSD and was able to finally put to rest events in his past that had emotionally scarred him, such as multiple instances of bullying in his childhood and being disregarded by his own family. The author also dealt with life threatening situations on many occasions while serving in the Marine Corps and being deployed during the first Gulf war. He also had to deal with being homeless and losing everything he had except his truck. Imagine the feeling of having no one to turn to for help and feeling like you are an outcast in society.

Using the multi-step process outlined in this book, an action plan for his life, the will to overcome all the obstacles that were before him, and inspiration from an old Civil War photo that looked uncannily like him, the author overcomes all of the difficulties described. Rob set out to research reoccurring dreams he had throughout his life. He then began to make note of his other dreams to derive meaning from them that could be applied to future actions he would take to improve his life.

This book clearly lays out how the author learned to follow the messages he received from his dreams. Using his unconscious mind as a guide and ignoring all the noise in the world, he was able to follow his instincts. This allowed him to make great strides to improving his life.

The author walks you through exactly how he analyzed his dreams and kept detailed notes of them. He was able to extrapolate the messages his unconscious mind was giving him. Using them as a guide he was able to put behind all the traumatic events from his past. He willed himself out of his wheel chair and was able to discard the unnecessary medications that he was taking. Using meditation and dream analysis he was able to self heal. By incorporating a healthy diet and a set of goals, his life would start to move in a positive direction.

This book lays out a detailed plan that the reader can incorporate in their own life. They can use this process of self awareness to overcome whatever obstacle or difficulty they are having. It shows you with examples how your dreams can be analyzed for the special message that your unconscious mind is trying to make the conscious mind aware of.

The author put an incredible amount of research and effort into this project. It is his gift to all those who feel hopeless or need to overcome traumatic events that have negatively impacted their lives. It is his hope that with the plan laid out in this book, that the reader can overcome the suffering that so many go through in life. He uses his life as an example and his plan as a template for you to overcome all that holds you back in this world.

Start your journey. Discover what your dreams may be trying to tell you and follow your instincts. This book will be the guide to a better life. Put the past behind you and remove the negative energy from your life. Look inside yourself for the answers along with spiritual guidance, to make your life more fulfilling and meaningful.

Don Vetter – Lifelong friend of the author.

"The purpose of life is to achieve success through analysis of the past, awareness of the present, and using that to develop into the future."

By
The Author

** The author of this book does not dispense medical advice, spiritual advice or prescribe the use of any technique as a form of treatment for physical, mental, emotional, or medical problems without the advice of a physician, either directly or indirectly. The intent of the author is only to offer information of a general nature and to provide some insight. If any individual uses any of this information in this book for yourself, which is your constitutional right, the author and the publisher assume no responsibility for your actions. **

"Your passion is the vehicle that takes you from pain to peace!"

By
The Author

Acknowledgements

First of all, I would like to thank Don Vetter for sending me the cropped photograph of the Civil War soldier which inspired me to write and complete this book. Secondly, I would like to thank him for writing the forward for this book, and for his continued friendship over the past 40 plus years. Next, I would like to thank Thomas Pilcher for answering my phone call and connecting me with the ladies who helped me in my research. Thank you also for your enthusiasm and efforts in regard to my book and for helping me with my research. Thank you also for your new and continuing friendship. Thank you to Susanne Greenhagen of Morrisville State College in New York and to Sandy Wilsey with the Town of Canastota, NY for much needed assistance and untiring efforts with my research, documents, emails, and phone calls regarding the Civil War soldier John Hart. Thank you to the lady from the National Archives, who answered my message on the general mailbox and gave me my message to continue interpreting my dreams and for your prayer (you know who you are). Continue to serve your personal, divinely inspired, soul mission. Thank you to the National Archives for your time in responding to my letter. Thank you to the Library of Congress for providing me a copy of the full Civil War picture that I had obtained a cropped picture from. A special thank you to Bianca Hernandez for all of your help, for listening to all of my long winded, and sometimes angry, ramblings about life, and most importantly, for providing me the "space" to complete my work.

Last, but not least, thank you God, Lord Jesus Christ Son of God, guardian Angels, Archangels, and Ascended Masters for all of your guidance and assistance, for everything you have taught me, are teaching me, will teach me, and most importantly, for always being in my life. I could not have done it without you all. Thank you, thank you, thank you. God bless…

Introduction

In my beginning, there was war. A war for freedom. War was the theme that would repeat itself throughout my entire journey. Perhaps, in the human perception of time, it was a journey that took an exceptionally long time. As I look back upon my life, I cannot help but wonder why I waited so long to see, to realize who I was and to be that which *I am*. However, I suppose that is partly the way it was supposed to happen, and at the same time, it was partly my responsibility that it took so long. Many battles were fought, both physically and mentally. This journey of mine has left me in great awe. I look upon it with amazement, and at the same time, I think, "Yes, of course it happened that way."

Throughout history people have disagreed about change and what we should do about it. They debate and fight over whether we should hold onto the past or spread our wings and be free. It is analogous to a caterpillar who has crawled into its cocoon to metamorphose into a butterfly. Should we all be controlled and told what to do as a mass, or should we each be allowed the freedom to take our own individual, personal journey and develop as we see fit?

It was a tough time for me. You see, war is what I have known most of my life. I finally broke the chains that were binding me by finally believing that there had to be more to life than this, than war, pain, suffering and death. One day, many years later, still in the pits of what I perceived as hell, I woke up. I began to realize that there had to be much more to my existence. I began to have faith in the fact that I was here and went through all of this turmoil and chaos for a specific reason. This reason revealed itself to me by becoming a student of my life. Once I knew what I needed to do, and how to do it, I experienced true freedom. This idea of freedom is what all wars are symbolically fought for in one capacity or another, whether it is a war between nations, or a war between a person's soul and their mind.

War is the symbol that awoke this ideal in me. After all, I surmised that if I sought my own personal freedom and found it, I would no longer live war and it would no longer exist for me. It would not exist for me because I would not be at war with myself any longer. I knew if I sought out and found my own personal freedom, I would be complete. I would be whole again.

Before I went any further, I knew I had to understand the "cycle of life" as I like to relate to it. This is my own theory that I developed. I use it to describe my life in its totality, so that it all makes sense to me. It all begins at the point of that from which I came. The famous psychoanalyst, Carl Jung referred to this as the "Prima Materia", or literally translated from Latin: First material. In other words, my beginning state before I came into this physical existence. The next state is kind of obvious, being born into "this world". While in this world, I saw how my life was broken into two parts: My conscious and unconscious life. For me, the object of life is to connect those two aspects of my existence together. Hence, making the two parts a whole. Once this has been accomplished and that state practiced through my individual work, I would then be complete. To me, it is a cycle of birth, life, death, and re-birth throughout my life, until I reached wholeness. When wholeness is achieved, the cycle would be complete. Then, at that point, I surmised I would be ready for a higher, or more evolved state of existence, whatever that would be.

This all caused me to ponder for a moment, and I was left contemplating several things. Is it the object of human life to overcome all our pain and suffering, our dependency on material things for relief and joy from those tragedies, maladies, and dependencies? Is the object of our suffering to force us to turn within for relief, salvation, success, and the answers to our questions? Thereby, rejoining the conscious life with the unconscious life. Is it that we each personally contain the answers to our own questions? Is it by doing this that we create a conjunction of the two, which takes us back to that from which we came (Prima Materia)? Thus, having been transformed, are we then able to live in both worlds (conscious and unconscious) at the same time, and be able to see it all as one, without any separation?

Is it this separation of the two parts of our lives (conscious and unconscious) that causes so much mental and emotional trouble for us? Is it that we have been trained throughout our life by our parents, society, and the government that the unconscious part of life is nonsensical absurdity when it is not? Is this done so that we can be controlled? Is this the hell that is spoken of? Is it created by man himself?

It seems as though we are born here perfect, from the perfect "Prima Materia," and then subjected to corruption by man-made ideologies and materials. We as human beings have the ability to choose to, or choose not to, partake in these corruptions. By choosing to partake in these man-made corruptions, does it signify a separation within ourselves? If we choose to reject these man-made ideologies, materials, and corruptions, does that then solidify our union with our own inner self? Thereby, using our own inner self as a form of personal guidance. Furthermore, what happens if we choose these corruptions and don't ever choose to make the union of the conscious and unconscious parts of our lives? Do we suffer repeatedly until that decision to "become whole" is made and lived?

Is this the point of the story of Adam and Eve and the choice to eat the forbidden apple in the bible? Is this the whole point of life? If so, where, and how did we go wrong to get born here? Or were we sent here to learn how to overcome these corruptions and all our suffering for some higher purpose? Is it that we are here to take what we have learned, create something, and live a certain way to inspire others to achieve that same thing? Is it by doing this, that we then enjoy our success? In other words, is our success for creating such a thing to inspire others, for "volunteering" to partake in such a mission, our reward? Is our physical life here on earth a developmental stage, which once properly completed, opens up a whole new way of life?

So, after contemplating these questions I had, I became a little frustrated and was really questioning what I am supposed to be doing in this life. Part of that frustration was due to the fact that at this point in my life I had healed my Post-Traumatic Stress

Disorder (PTSD), I had published three books and yet I still did not have any success. I had not achieved what I perceived as success for me and that was frustrating. So, I was also questioning whether I should keep writing books, doing my radio show and YouTube channel, or should I move on from that to something new. Maybe I had accomplished what I was supposed to with this? I seemed to be even more confused. So, that evening I vented my frustrations. I needed to let it all out so that I could release it, obtain some mental clarity, and move on from it. After venting that evening, I had a dream. The dream inspired me to continue my path of personal growth and the evolution of my whole self. I realized what was going on here. I had not completed my work yet. I will accomplish what I want to accomplish, and acquire what I want to acquire, if I do my work. I perceived that these goals and desires I had were like carrots being dangled in front of the nose of a famished rabbit in order to entice me down the proper path towards achieving my soul purpose.

My perspective on life has changed based on the personal evolution of self I have achieved. I used to believe that life was being born, living your life, dying, then going to heaven, or hell, based on how you lived your life. Now, I see life as two-fold. What I mean by that is that "my life" and "myself" are comprised of two parts. One being conscious, daily life. The other part being unconscious/internal life. These two parts of my total life affect and influence each other based on how I interpret them, react to them, deal with them, and incorporate, or dismiss them into or from my life. I believe that I must incorporate both parts into my life and connect the two into a whole. Hence, creating a whole self, or a whole person. I postulate that we as human beings have trouble dealing with life, with the things, events, and people we encounter daily, because we are only acting, or living, in half of our capacity. We are living life in a deficit so to speak. To me, it seems that this is the root of our troubles here on Earth. However, before we can incorporate our unconscious life into our conscious life, there must be a developmental period and then a shedding of the past. Hence, a purification of the present. Once that process is complete, the two parts (conscious and unconscious) can be combined into a whole. It is analogous to a Blacksmith taking a piece of steel, sticking it into a hot fire, pulling it out, putting it on an anvil and beating it. Then, repeating the process until the proper form is achieved. Then, and only then, can it be used for the purpose it was intended.

Therefore, I began working on developing a deeper understanding of my nightly dreams, how they could possibly give me insight into who I am as a person, and what I need to work on. In the past, I wrote down most of my dreams when I awoke from them. This was something I did religiously when I was dealing with and healing from my PTSD. I describe it all, and those dreams in detail, in my second book, *"The Chrysalis: A Metamorphosis has begun."* However, I knew that I needed to improve upon how I was interpreting these dreams on a deeper, more intuitive level, and how to incorporate them into my conscious life. Thus, bringing the two separate lives together (conscious and unconscious) into a complete, whole self.

I also understand that I as a "complete" being influence people by how I live my own personal life. All the people and events in my life are there, or happen, for a reason. They are meant to teach me something, as I am to do for them. There is a Latin phrase that is applicable here: *Cum Grano Salis* **(We always see our own mistakes in our opponent)**. There is a duality to everything. There must be. Because without that, there would be no balance.

This led me to the next necessary step, or stage, in my development. Now that I understood the external stimuli in my life, which caused me to act in ways that are not desirable, I must also look at my life overall. I figured a purification of my life must be completed to provide me with a clarity, so that I can complete my work. I had to remove everything from my life that distracted me from doing my work. I felt this step could not be done until I had completed the purification of my mind by retraining my brain to have different reactions to new stimuli in my life. This cleared the way for me to perceive my signs and apply them properly. This allowed me to see things which I could not see before, to learn things I did not yet know. I accomplished this by conducting a detailed analysis of all the major events of my life from birth to present. I categorized them all into related even or odd groups based on the addition of each of the digits of the dates of each event into a single digit. Then, I was able to ascertain an understanding of my life. It propelled me to be aware of, and pontificate on, what I went through and why. This pointed me in the direction I needed to take going forward.

Once my mind and life were purified, the next step would involve making the things I learned a reality. I had to make those amendments in my conscious daily life. This solidified the union of my unconscious and conscious. Hence, forming my whole self. It is here where true peace and happiness is experienced. This is born from my philosophical awareness and its implementation into my conscious life. To deepen my explanation a little more, lets discuss three things that influenced my life. I call these three things my conscious, sub-conscious and my unconscious.

Basically, all of my learned behaviors and experiences are stored in my sub-conscious. It is the center from which I operate. It influences my conscious, everyday life in either positive or negative ways based upon what I have stored in it. The contents are relative to what I have learned and experienced in the past. My subconscious attempts to control me. It does very well if I let it. That depends on my awareness of my unconscious and whether I understand it or not.

It is my perception that my unconscious attempts to give me messages in the form of riddles told through symbols in my dreams, and in my daily life, in order to influence or mold my subconscious in a positive way relative to who I really am, and not who my ego-conscious says I am (i.e., who I think I am based on external circumstances, material possessions and physical attributes.). The messages are given to me in the form of riddles and symbols because they contain things that I have repressed. Those things can be quite shocking. Therefore, if the messages were clear right from the start, I would probably reject them as nonsense, and/or make up an excuse for why "it" happened. I would subconsciously try to ignore such shocking things. Instead, the messages are crafted in the form of riddles. They pique my interest and inquisitiveness so that I will work through them. If the information was given to me bluntly it would cause shock. Then I would disregard it all as nonsense tricking myself into believing none of it was true or possible. My brain works as a filter for me so that this does not occur. My messages are filled with symbols construed of people, places, things, colors, numbers, animals etc., and often resemble symbols from throughout the past of human life since its inception. They form a continuity of man throughout time. They connect human unconsciousness with human consciousness forming a whole of humanity, a symbol for the whole self. These symbols of people, places, and things I know are designed to evoke a specific feeling within me that I need to pay attention to. It is as if that feeling plays an important role in the interpretation of my personal messages. For me they are not meant to be taken literally. Instead, they require study and analysis on my part. How do they make me feel? How do they influence me? From this point, I could begin to comprehend the true meaning of the message. Then I could apply it to my life accordingly. Thus, the sub-conscious and unconscious influence and affect my life in negative, or positive ways, based on my interpretation and reaction to them.

I call the subconscious negative because I feel it stores guidance for my conscious life based upon external influences such as society (i.e., consciousness). I call the unconscious positive because it gives me guidance from internal influences (i.e., who I really am, not who someone or something else influenced me to be). Now, the conscious is like the car that runs either poorly or greatly based upon the type of gas, oil and maintenance that is put into it (by the subconscious). It is either negative, and takes the course of a mental, and hence, a physical breakdown, or it is positive and affects my growth and the evolution of my total, true self. Then, life is taken to a whole new level. Therefore, I was confronted with the question of which influence, the external or the internal, am I going to follow? To answer this question correctly, I had to have an "awareness." By awareness I needed to be aware of what was going on in my life and why. I also had to be aware of the other half of my life, my unconscious. I had to be aware of its messages, interpret what they meant and incorporate their guidance into my life. Then I could become my real self. I was then aware that all the prior events of my life were designed to aid in my development. To facilitate my evolvement into who I really am. That is the work I must do to complete that.

My desires, ambitions, interests, and hobbies came back into play. I have them for a reason. However, during my development they had been stripped from my life because I had not learned how to live properly yet. Otherwise, it is like putting the cart before the horse. Once I had developed and completed this process, and had become a whole self in proper, intended form, I brought those desires, ambitions, interests, and hobbies back into my life. I now knew the proper way to behave. This gave me a maturity and moral aptitude that allowed me to act in a higher, more socially acceptable way. In other words, I would not act corrupt, deviant, or unscrupulous in order to accomplish my goals. Especially in achieving my success. I would do good with it because I would know how to properly behave.

Currently, we live in a society that has a specific system for survival. In the past, some cultures were nomadic, hunter-gatherers, or sedentary farmers. Whichever "system" they were in guided how they acquired the things they needed for survival. Our current system requires that we have jobs, or perform services, to obtain money so that we can acquire what we need for survival (i.e., shelter, food, water, etc.).

I figured once I had become my whole self, my desires, ambitions, interests, and hobbies would become the way in which I got "rewarded" for completing this process of making myself whole and living in my proper, intended form. Within the current "system" we live in, my desires lead me down my own individual path to my own individual paradise. There must also be a balance to this. This "freedom" to pursue this path to paradise is balanced with "responsibility." My "responsibility" at this point, is to be an "inspiration" to others by showing them what I achieved by completing this process of attaining wholeness. I knew the way to do this was by telling my story.

Therefore, I ask that you open your heart and mind so that you have no restrictions, no obstacles, no pre-conceived notions, preventing you from truly understanding what I am about to tell you in the following pages. This book has found you, or you found it, for a reason. Your responsibility is to figure out what that reason is. Everything is perfectly planned out. There are **NO** coincidences. With this book I am attempting to fulfill my "responsibility." It is truly my goal to "inspire" you.

PART I

The Blackening:

Learning that I need to live life from my unconscious guidance.

Chapter 1

My journey began with the onset of three dreams I had repeatedly from the age of seven until the age of 18. The first dream I began having was about the Revolutionary War. I was in a battle where our front lines had been broken and we were overrun. In the dream It was around evening time, and the sun was getting low on the horizon. I was running from some British soldiers who were chasing me through trees and over rolling hills. The air was filled with copious amounts of smoke from cannon and gunfire. There were things burning. The smell of gunpowder thickened the air even more. It was as if I was trying to get back to somewhere and reunite with the rest of my unit. It was like we had all been separated and hence, retreated. The British soldiers were gaining on me. I was very tired. I felt like I could not run any further. As I got behind a hill, I heard a crack in my right ear. Just then, a bullet struck me in the middle of my back to the right of my spine and to the left of my right shoulder blade. Then, it exited through the middle of my chest where my heart would be located. I could feel the searing pain from the impact and heat of the bullet. I could even hear bone cracking from the musket ball travelling through my body. At this point in the dream everything would go black, and I would wake up.

I also had another Revolutionary war dream subsequent to the first. In that dream, I was meeting with other military officers on top of a small hill. The area was comprised of entrenchments and breastworks. I was a Sergeant training a unit of men and giving them instructions. While I was conducting my training, the officers were watching me and assessing me just like they would normally do with a senior enlisted man in real life.

In the second dream I would have, I was in the Civil War. I was in a battle in which the battle lines had been broken after fierce fighting. Kind of like we were retreating. I never could remember which side I was on. I just remember that in the chaos, I ran down a dirt road towards this wagon. There were some trees around and a mountain in the background like a big rock ridge or cliff. I got to the wagon, opened a storage area under the wagon and I crawled in to hide there. While I was hiding in there, someone got into the wagon, opened the door to the storage area I was in, and stabbed me with a bayonet in the middle of my chest right where my heart would be. It was in the same exact place as the first dream. Only in the first dream the bullet went in my back first and then out through my chest instead of the other way around. At that point of the dream, everything would go black, and I would wake up. In this dream I never knew what rank I was either. I don't ever remember seeing any rank on my uniform in the dream. So, I always assumed that in this dream I was a Private. In that case, the uniform would have no rank insignia.

In the third and final dream I had repeatedly, I was in Vietnam. Again, as in the Revolutionary War dream, I was a Sergeant (Typically, one has to re-enlist to acquire the rank of Sergeant). I was walking through a field of tall brown grass with my radio man. We were the only two left in our platoon after a battle. Everyone else was dead, wounded, or separated from each other. There was a small thatch hut in the distance. The hut and the grassy area we were walking through were surrounded by a tree line. It began to rain heavily. I told my radio man to follow me to the hut so we could get out of the rain. Just then, I heard a crack in my right ear. Suddenly, a bullet went through the upper right side of my back, in between my spine and shoulder blade, and then out the center of my chest where my heart would be located just like in the other two dreams. Then, everything would go black, and I would wake up.

It was in 1988, at the age of 18, that I stopped having these dreams. At that point I enlisted in the United States Marine Corps. Since then, I never had those dreams again. I was in the Marine Corps for four years, from 1988-92. In 1990, I was sent to Saudi Arabia, and I fought on the front lines of the first Gulf War. I was a demolitions expert and when I got back from the war, they sent me to Sniper School. I graduated first in my class. I got out at the rank of Corporal. It is a senior rank in the sense that I was in charge of my own squad. They wanted to promote me to Sergeant and send me to the drill field to be a drill instructor and train other Marines only if I chose to re-enlist. I did not. I got out in 1992. I wrote and published three different books about my service, having PTSD from my service, and how I overcame it all.

Ever since the publication of my first book, *A Line in the Sand: The True Story of a Marine's Experiences on the Front Lines of the First Gulf War* in 2006, and my second book, *Chrysalis: A Metamorphosis Has Begun*, published in 2014, I had contemplated writing a book about my three childhood dreams. It was not until after I published my third book, *The Sword and the Anvil: A Definitive Guide for Natural, Healthy Healing from Post-Traumatic Stress and Trauma*, which was published in 2016, that I gave writing this book some serious thought. However, I still approached the subject with trepidation. I wondered what the heck would I really write about? My three dreams would not even fill a chapter, let alone a whole book. But, as Carl Jung stated in his book, *Modern Man*, a person's dreams provide them with a historical continuity of their consciousness. Sort of like historical documents do for society and individuals alike. As I contemplated this theory of his in relation to my own existence and how my life has turned out, I instantly knew I had to do something with these three dreams. I figured that since I had those dreams repeatedly for 11 years, they must have at least some significance for me personally. They must have something important to teach me.

As my luck would have it, one day a friend of mine, who I had been friends with for over 40 years, sent me a picture of a fellow from the Civil War. He said, "Rob, you've got to check this out!" So, I looked at the picture. It was a photo of a young man's head and shoulders. Upon seeing it, I realized it looked exactly like me! I mentioned this to my friend, and he said, "I know. That is why I sent it to you. It looks just like you without your glasses when you were about 13 or 14 years old."

I received the first picture of the two soldiers from the Library of Congress (LOC) from their files. The second picture is a cropped from

6 | PART I: THE BLACKENING

the first one. It is cropped from the guy on the left. The cropped picture of the head and shoulders is the one my friend sent me. **No copyright infringement is intended.** The last picture is mine. It is a picture of me currently. I include them here to show the similarities between the man in the Civil War photo and myself.

This was all too uncanny for two reasons. One, my friend knows about my three dreams. I told him about them repeatedly since we were seven or eight years old while sitting on my front porch. The second reason is that in the second dream I repeatedly had, I was in the Civil War.

Because this photo of the Civil War soldier looked so much like me, and because of my childhood dreams, my interest in it had significantly peaked. I thought that I should try and track this photo down and see if I can find out who this person is and what happened to him. But just as quick as my interest had peaked, reality set in. I thought, "Eh, I will probably never be able to track him down."

At this point in my life, I had figured my writing days were over and that I had probably accomplished what I needed to with it in terms of releasing my trauma and healing myself. I figured it was time for me to move on to other endeavors. I was investing in the stock market, doing my radio show, fixing up a new house and trying to sell the books I had written. I did not have time to do the research or write this guy's story, even if I ever could find out who he was. So, I put the picture away.

I spent the next few weeks doing my thing, stock market, radio show, selling books and working on my house. In particular, I was building a concrete cobblestone patio in front of my house. Over the course of several days, I poured around 1200lbs of concrete and about half as much mortar. It was grueling work as it was, let alone doing it in the heat of the full sun. I eventually finished and a few days later, upon waking in the morning, I rolled out of bed, my feet hit the floor, I felt a sharp pain go from my lower back down my right leg all the way to my toes, and I fell on the floor and could not get up. My back went out and I spent the next two weeks bedridden in immense pain.

After about a week or so had passed and the pain had subsided enough that I was not screaming all day and night, I began to think that this must be happening for a reason. This must be a sign. As I have done in the past during bad times, which I describe in detail in my first three books, I took the opportunity to re-evaluate my life and what I was doing with it.

I had realized that everything I was currently doing must be taking me further away from what I was really supposed to be doing. This must be why this was happening. The reason must be to get me to stop and re-focus on what I am doing. My intuition was telling me that my journey was not over, my work not complete. Now was not the time to just go on living a normal life. I had the sense that more personal development was needed and that I had a lot more to say about it all. Perhaps, I had more to contribute the world as well.

At that precise moment I was reminded of something my psychiatrist had told me many years ago while I was trying to heal my PTSD. I was in a bad frame of mind at the time, I was ready to just give up on everything, including my writing. At that point I had only written and published my first book, *A Line in the Sand*. I had told the doctor about those feelings and that I was no longer going to continue writing. I also told the doctor that I had nothing else to write about. The doctor then said, "On the contrary, I think you have a lot more to write about and say!"

Now, here I was lying in bed contemplating all of this, and I had realized that the doctor was right. At this point in my life, I had written and published three books about my life journey, the war, PTSD and how I healed it. Now, I was contemplating writing a fourth book. Just then, I was overcome with a sense of energy and excitement in a sort of esoteric way that I felt in my belly. I knew what I had to do. This was a sign. I had to discover what I was now supposed to do with my new life and how to do just that. I had to write this book. I intuitively knew that through the journey of writing it, the answers I was seeking would be revealed to me. So, upon healing up enough to get out of bed, I pulled out the Civil War picture and I began my search.

I began by emailing the Library of Congress (LOC) to see if I could even track down this photo, where it was taken and possibly who it was. Then, I called the National Archives. They told me to send them a letter in the mail outlining my request, which I did at a later date. They informed me that it would take approximately four weeks for me to get a response. The LOC asked me to send an email to them with a file of the picture I had. I did that right away as that could easily and quickly be done.

Within a day or so the LOC responded to me. The picture I had, which was the head and shoulders of a Civil War Soldier, was cropped from a larger photo. They had this photo in their archives. It was labelled as having been taken in 1862 at Harpers Ferry, Virginia (later West Virginia) and was of two Union Soldiers who were supposedly of the New York 22nd State Militia.

I now had to learn about this regiment. I found a book on Google that was photocopied and put online, and it could be accessed for free. It was titled, "**History of the 22nd Regiment of the State of New York from its Organization to 1895.**" It was written by General George W. Wingate [1896]. There were a few typos in it that led to some rather frustrating research; however, the book was fantastic and quite useful.

Now that I had learned about the unit, I was still left with the problem of tracking down this person in the photo who looks like me. I had no clue how to do that or where to start. So, I just started making phone calls to museums, historical societies, etc., trying to get any info I could. However, to my dismay, everything cost too much money for me to pursue. Or, I would have to go to these places and conduct the research myself. This I could not afford either. It seemed like I could not get anyone to help. That night when I went to bed, I said my prayers and asked for help finding out who this person was.

That night I had a dream. As I was waking from the dream, I heard a voice say, "Company I." When I woke up, I wrote it down. I began thinking about my dream. I thought about it all day. However, I was still frustrated as I could not do anything with just "Company I." That could mean anything. That night when I went to bed, I prayed and said, "I need a name!"

That night I had a dream again. As I was waking up form it, I clearly saw an older man who appeared to be hovering above and in front of me dressed in Civil War era business clothes. He was wearing a long grey coat, grey top hat, grey pants, and a long, black bow tie. He then says, "J.W. Harp," At least I thought that is what he said. I was not sure if it was Harp or Hart. After I got up that day, I began to do more research on trying to find out who this guy in my picture was.

One day I was checking some statistics on the website I had at the time. I noticed I had some visitors on it from Stone Mountain, Georgia. I never heard of it. So, I looked it up. I saw a picture of it online. I thought it looked similar to the place in my Civil War dream. I also found out that there was a small battle there during the Civil War, which was part of Sherman's march on Georgia. It was fought in front of a big rock mountain and there was a dirt road. Both things were similar to my dream.

So, I was thinking about my dream from the previous night and the name that was spoken to me. All I had was this name (Harp or Hart) and an infantry company name. I also had a picture of someone who looked exactly like me. If you recall, the file said that picture was from the 22nd New York State Militia Unit during the Civil War. I went back online and started researching the unit. I started by looking through the online book by Wingate again. At the very end of it I found a bunch of roster lists and tables of the companies that comprised the unit. So, I thought, "I'm going to give it a shot and see what happens." I looked up Company I and I found the soldier roster. I looked for the name (JW Harp or Hart). Bam! Freakishly enough, there was the name J.W. Harp on the 1862 roster. However, it was missing from the 1863 roster. Now, I obviously wanted to know what happened.

Now, recall the letter I also sent to the National Archives after I contacted and heard back from the LOC. In that letter I had mentioned the Stone Mountain, Georgia area. I finally had received a letter back from the National Archives. Unfortunately, they could not locate the photo. In the letter, the National Archives had suggested I contact this museum in Georgia. By the time this had occurred, I had forgotten that I mentioned Stone Mountain in my letter. So, having forgotten that, I was intrigued that "Georgia" showed up again! I proceeded to call the National Archives because

I wanted to find out why they mentioned this museum in Georgia out of all the different places they could have mentioned. When I called, I got an answering machine to a general mailbox. I left a message asking for someone to call me back.

The very next day, a woman called me back from the National Archives. She proceeded to explain that they mentioned the museum in Georgia because I had mentioned Stone Mountain in my letter. Then, I remembered I did that. Since I needed some help in conducting my research and where to start, I began to explain my book and that I now knew where the photo was taken based on what the LOC had told me. I was being vague about my book because I did not want this person to think I was nuts because a lot of my book has to do with my dreams. She kept saying, "I get it," when I would discretely explain some things. I really did not know what she meant, but at that moment I felt compelled to just spill my guts about it. However, before I could say anything, she said, "God just told me to tell you to keep writing down your dreams and to continue doing what you are doing, and everything will be fine." I was stunned! I almost dropped the phone. I could not believe it and she was completely serious. So, as you could imagine, we had quite a conversation at that point. She said she "wrote down the date" and that she would keep me in her prayers. She also told me that she gives messages to people from God. She said God puts her in contact with the specific people that need to hear whatever message she has for them (given to her by God). She does not question why or how. She just does it. She told me that throughout the day, there are at least five people that check the answering machine I had left my message on. She said that she just happened to walk by the machine that day. She saw a message on it, so she checked it.

The actual day the woman from the archives had called me back was 6/6/2017. Intuitively, I was compelled to add those numbers up, which comes to 22. I felt that this number also needed to be added together in order to get some sense of finality. So, I added 2+2, which equals 4. I then pondered if the number 22 and four mean anything. I got on my computer and looked it up. I came across several websites that explain numerology. I happened to click on ***angelnumbers.com***. I read the description for both numbers. Basically, they symbolize support, guidance, and strength given to an individual by their guardian angels. The numbers are also said to be messages of encouragement to work hard on one's goals and that the time is right to accomplish them. They carry the advice to believe in oneself, your intuitional guidance and to focus on your work because it is time to show the world what you know. It also stated that the most ambitious of dreams can be turned into reality and that one needs to see the larger picture and work with the details provided to complete this larger picture. And finally, freakishly enough, it gave a message of encouragement to bring things to completion with the help of spiritual and material guidance.

So, it was at this point in June of 2017, I began to re-evaluate things, deepen my studies, go into a very deep contemplation about life and what it means to be human (a question I have grappled with since one of my college professors posed it to me a few decades ago). I now knew I needed to complete a comprehensive, in-depth analysis of my three childhood dreams, my regular nightly dreams, and of my life up to this point. I wanted to combine the results hoping that it all would help me to make sense of out of my life and my development. I knew somehow that the answers of what to do next would be revealed to me through this process. At that moment, the phrase, "One must become a student of his life," popped into my head.

Since I had come this far with the Civil War dream, I decided to look deeper into it even though it was the second of the three dreams I had as a child. At this point all I had was the picture of a Civil War soldier who was supposedly in the 22nd New York at Harpers Ferry, WV coupled with the discussion I had with the woman at the National Archives. These two things were not a lot to go on and they did not match up. So, based on everything, I decided to look deeper into the individual J.W. Harp in Company I that I got from my dream.

I began my search by going back to the 1896 book by Wingate I had printed off from Google. I had the information that there was a JW Harp on the Regiment's roster in a Company I. Next, I wanted to see if they were at the battle of Harpers Ferry, and I was looking to somehow connect that information with the picture I had from the LOC.

As I previously stated, while this was an excellent book by Wingate, it was full of typos and mistakes which made for some extremely frustrating research. I also soon found out that this was not just an issue with this book but was also quite common with information from and about the Civil War. I came across many articles from Historians who expressed their frustrations about this matter.

I went back to the beginning of the book and began reading it with great fervor. The unit was formed because of the Civil War. Companies A-H were formed in New York City in May of 1861. However, Company I was not formed until the 22nd was beginning its campaign of 1862. Companies A-H were preparing to leave for Baltimore, M.D. Upon hearing the news, many individuals rushed to sign up to do their part in the war. Hence, Company I was formed. However, they did not have supplies, gear, or rifles for them. So, the rest of the Regiment departed. Company I received their gear and rifles the following day. The rifles issued to them were different than those used by the rest of the Regiment. Their rifles had shank bayonets instead of the sword style bayonets the others had. The others also had Enfield rifles. All the book said was that the rifles of Company I were different but did not say which kind they were. Company I then departed and joined the rest of the Regiment in Baltimore, MD.

On June 20, 1862, the 22nd NYNG received orders and departed for Harpers Ferry. At this point, I was thinking so far so good. However, in the picture I have of the soldier that looks like me, he had an Enfield rifle with a sword bayonet. So, the picture could not be of soldiers from Company I. I then thought about how the lady at the LOC told me this picture came from a personal collection that was obtained. She had mentioned that a lot of the pictures in collections like these are mislabeled and they did not know for sure if the label on my picture was correct. I dug a little deeper into the book and found a description of the 22nd NYNG's uniforms, along with a picture of them. On page 19 the book stated:

PART I: THE BLACKENING

"They adopted as their uniform a single-breasted frock coat, cut in the French style, with the skirt reaching to the knee, made of grey cloth, with red collar and cuffs, trimmed with white piping. The trousers were of gray, with a red stripe edged with white piping down the sides; the cap was a gray kepi, with red band and top, each edged with white piping."

Based on this information in comparison with the Civil War picture I had from the LOC, I concluded that this could not be a picture of the 22nd NYNG. The uniforms of the two soldiers in my picture were completely different than the description given in Wingate's book. I was still positive it was at Harpers Ferry as I have a hard time believing the original photographer had no idea where he was at when he took the picture. So, I believe that was at least labeled correctly. Then, I thought maybe there was some confusion about the exact unit he was photographing. Maybe the units were just so close together in certain locations, or situations, that the photographer got them mixed up somehow. My research on the uniforms along with the pictures would certainly collaborate this and it is most certainly plausible. Therefore, I continued my research and looked for more evidence one way or the other.

As I was saying, the unit left for Harpers Ferry on June 20, 1862. The Regiment was on three months enlistment (part of these three months was already used up from enlistment through Baltimore, etc.). They were encamped along a breast work. The unit was placed on picket's duty, which is being out forward of your units' position in order to watch for an advancing enemy, etc. It is like being a forward observer. This was the first time they had this duty. One of the men picked for picket's duty was Harp. The book said he was a big boaster and talked about what he would do if he encountered the enemy. So that night his friends pulled a prank on him. They tried to scare him in the middle of the night like he had been found by the Confederates. Harp fired his rifle. No one was hurt, which was good because the pranksters were his own men.

I soon found out that on August 25, 1862, Harpers Ferry was reinforced with the newly raised regiments of the 111th and 126th New York Volunteers (NYV). These new regiments did not have the men experienced enough to drill themselves. So, the Corporals of 22nd NYNG were sent to instruct the men of the 111th and 126th NYV. This obviously could have led to the confusion of the photographer thinking he was taking a picture of the 22nd NYNG, but it was really the 111th and/or the 126th NYV. The book also went on to mention that a lot of the officers of the 22nd NYNG accepted commissions in the 111th and 126th NYV shortly afterwards. Obviously leading to even more confusion on the photographer's part who would not be privy to such information and/or not understand what was really going on.

On August 24, 1862, which was the day before they were to be reinforced, the enlistment of the 22nd NYNG had expired. Therefore, on the 28th of August they were ordered to return to New York. The Regiment finally arrived back in New York on September 2, 1862. The unit was mustered out of service on September 5, 1862. The battle of Harpers Ferry took place from September 12 to 15, 1862. Therefore, based on all of the aforementioned evidence about the uniforms and what actually occurred with the 22 NYNG, I concluded that the picture of the soldier that looks like me could not be of the 22nd NYNG. However, I do believe that the picture was taken at Harpers Ferry. I think it is safe to say, the photographer got confused about the units since they intermingled for training. It appeared that he mislabeled the photo in that regard. Based on this conclusion, I began researching the 111th and 126th NYV. There were no Harp's in Co. I of the 111th NYV. So, I checked the 126th NYV. There were no Harp's there either. If you recall, I mentioned earlier that I wasn't sure if the name I heard in my dream was Harp or Hart. Since there were no Harp's, I decided to check for J.W. Hart. There it was, John Hart in Company I, 126th NYV. He enlisted in Fayette, NY August 8th, 1862, at the age of 22. I then started looking up Historians, researchers, Historical Societies, Museums, etc. so I could obtain more information. I was led to a lady in Lennox, NY, which is about 72 miles or so east of Fayette, NY.

She was listed as the town Historian for the town of Lennox. There was a number listed there for her. So, I called it. However, I got an answering machine. The voice on the answering machine was a male. So, I hung up without leaving a message figuring it was a wrong number and the list was out of date. A few minutes later my phone rang. I did not recognize the number. I was not going to answer the phone, but my gut kept telling me to. I thought maybe it was the person's phone I called earlier when I had the wrong number. I thought I should at least answer and let them know that I had called the wrong number. So, I answered the phone.

It turns out that I did have the right number. The person who called me back was this lady's nephew. His aunt had recently passed away. So, he had her phone calls routed to his phone. I explained why I had called and that I was writing this book. He was a genuinely nice man, and we became friends and have kept in touch ever since. He was interested in what I was doing and volunteered to help me with my research locally there in Canastota, New York (it is remarkably close to Lennox). He then gave me the name of a lady who worked for the town of Canastota, NY, and her number. She had experience doing volunteer work on the history of the Civil War in New York. I called the number and explained what I was doing and asked for help conducting my research. This lady was truly kind and helpful. She said she would look into John Hart for me of the 126th NYV and get back to me via email.

This lady also put me in touch with another lady who also did work on Civil War Veterans history and records in New York. Over a series of emails and weeks, I obtained a good deal of information. It was rather difficult research because of the fact that there were a few local John Hart's. Some of their records had been mixed up together because of the confusion I spoke of earlier in regard to research and Civil War records. So, I had to dig deep and look for clues and put all the pieces of the puzzle back together. It was like trying to translate a paragraph written in Latin into English. After months of painstaking research, contemplation, and numerous headaches, I was able to get the right records for the right person and put the story of John Hart of the 126th NYV together. All of this seemed quite synchronistic to me. There is no way it could have been coincidence. It all came together to perfectly.

Here is how the story goes according to the research I conducted. John Hart enlisted in Fayette, NY August 8, 1862, at the age of 22. He immigrated here from Germany with his parents, which was listed on the 1850 Federal Census for Sullivan, Madison County, NY. It indicated John was 10 in 1850 and born in Germany in 1840. His sister Harriet was listed as born in Madison County, NY in 1842. Hence, they must have come to America after John's birth in 1840. Or perhaps in 1841 before Harriet was born in 1842. From Fayette the men went to Waterloo, which was the next town to the north of Fayette. Then they travelled west to Geneva where the unit was organized by Colonel Eliakim Sherrill. Then they travelled east to Troy, NY, and the unit was mustered in there on August 22, 1862.

They left the state on September 2, 1862, and went to Baltimore, MD. From there they moved to Martinsburg, VA. Then on September 11, 1862, they retreated to Harper's Ferry and were attached to General Miles' command. Between September 12-15, 1862, they engaged in the unit's first fighting during the siege of Harper's Ferry by the Confederates. The 126th NY took the brunt of the enemy's attack at Maryland and Bolivar Heights. Colonel Eliakim Sherrill, who organized and commanded the 126th NY, was wounded during the battle and carried off the field. This caused the men to scatter and retreat in confusion. They were ordered to return to the fight. They lost 16 men dead and 42 wounded during the actual fighting. Because of an ineptness of command to properly fortify and defend Harpers Ferry, the Union, including the 126th NY, surrendered to the Confederate Army on September 15, 1862. Here is a quote from a wayside marker at Harper's Ferry that was taken from a letter written by Lieutenant George York of Company I (John Hart's Company):

"On Sunday evening, the second day of our fight, I was ordered out in front of our camp to skirmish as the Reb's were getting rather thick. Now just keep in mind that I had been up for three nights before. You can imagine how pleasantly I must have felt. It was a dangerous position, but I felt as if I did not care whether the Reb's had me or not. Our hundred men were detailed and put under Lt. Munson and myself. You ought to have seen us hunting our way down Bolivar Heights for the front of our camp. At last, we reached our position." Because of their

surrender by the inept command of senior officers, the entire unit was labelled as the Harpers Ferry cowards even though they withstood the largest portion of the attack.

Next is a picture of the area where the battle took place in Harper's Ferry. Both the picture and the description of the battle I just gave are eerily familiar to my Civil War dream!

*This looks exactly like the rocky cliff with trees and a dirt road in front of it from my dream.

Google Search: https://www.google.com/search?source=univ&tbm=isch&q=pictures+of+maryland+heights+civil+war&sa=X&ved=2ahUKEwjvvfmxgZ7rAhUzKX0KHXXAAHcQ7Al6BAgKEDo&biw=1360&bih=625#imgrc=1RrIx7xYHiC-pM

Pinterest. Saved by Irina Shriver

Harper's Ferry, WV. View of Maryland Heights. *No copyright infringement is intended.*

https://images.app.goo.gl/FX6XKNCbpAtnfi2S8

Chapter 1 | 19

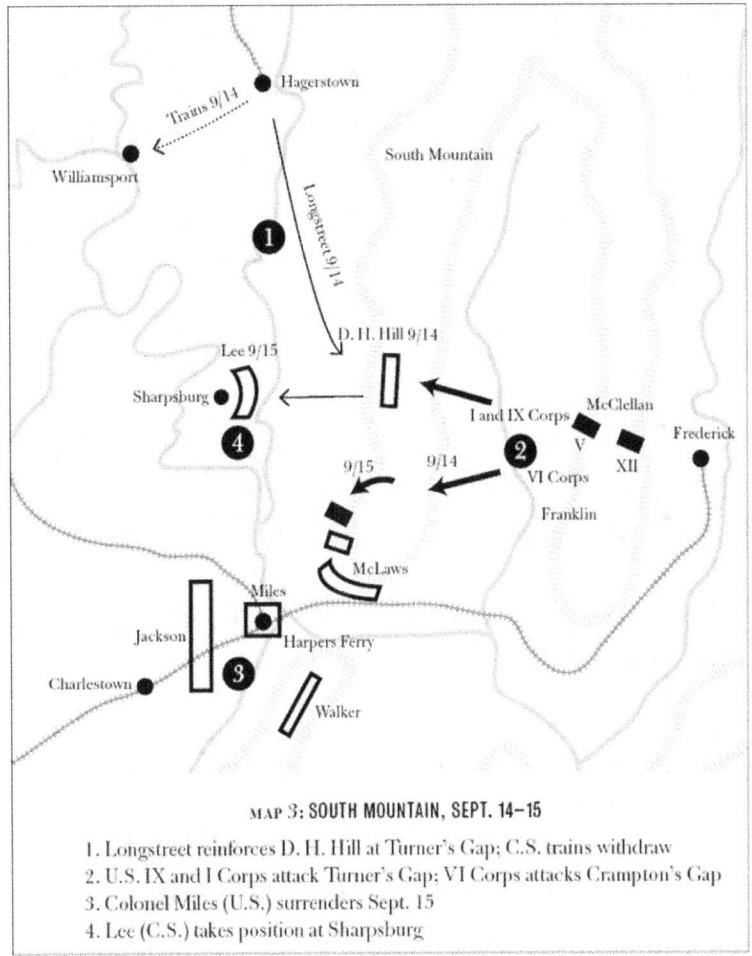

MAP 3: SOUTH MOUNTAIN, SEPT. 14-15
1. Longstreet reinforces D. H. Hill at Turner's Gap; C.S. trains withdraw
2. U.S. IX and I Corps attack Turner's Gap; VI Corps attacks Crampton's Gap
3. Colonel Miles (U.S.) surrenders Sept. 15
4. Lee (C.S.) takes position at Sharpsburg

Google search: https://www.google.com/search?source=univ&tbm=isch&q=pictures+of+south+mountain+harpers+ferry&sa=X&ved=2ahUKEwjQ3s73gZ7rAhV-GDQIHbdDDOoQ7Al6BAgKEDw&biw=1360&bih=625#imgrc=7FIQU6YSa5wwjM

Erenow.net https://erenow.net/ww/the-long-road-to-antietam-how-the-civil-war-became-a-revolution/11.php
No copyright infringement is intended.

20 | PART I: THE BLACKENING

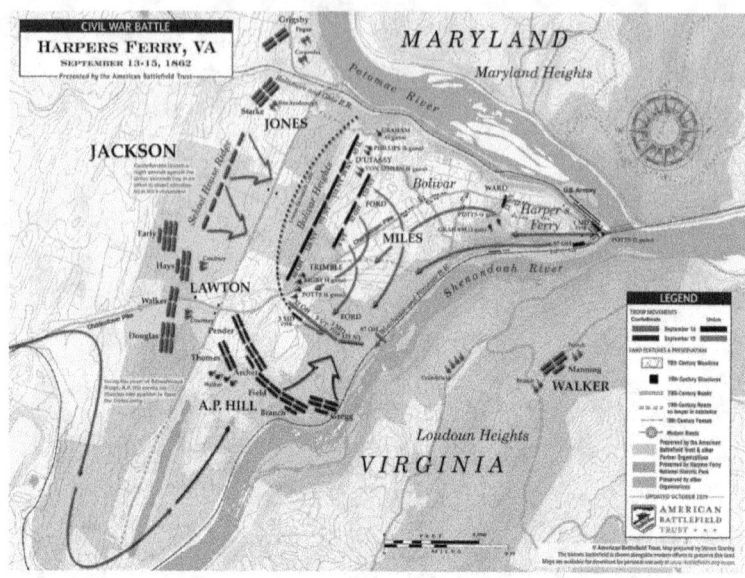

Google Search: https://www.battlefields.org/learn/maps/harpers-ferry-september-13-15-1862

American Battlefield Trust: Harpers Ferry - September 13-15, 1862 (October 2019). *No copyright infringement is intended.*

After surrendering, the 126th NY was paroled and sent to Annapolis, MD and then to Camp Douglas, Chicago, Ill. Here's a quote from Wikipedia about Camp Douglas:

"Later in 1862, the Union Army again used Camp Douglas as a training camp. In the fall of 1862, the Union Army used the facility as a detention camp for paroled Confederate prisoners (these were Union soldiers who had been captured by the Confederacy and sent North under an agreement that they would be held temporarily while formal prisoner exchanges were worked out)."

They spent two months there awaiting to hear of their exchange. They would be exchanged for Confederate prisoners. Again, from Wikipedia:

"Union soldiers who were paroled after their capture by Confederate Lieutenant General Thomas J. "Stonewall" Jackson at the Battle of Harpers Ferry, Virginia (later West Virginia) on September 15, 1862, were sent to Camp Douglas for temporary detention. Under the terms of the prisoner cartel, they had to await formal exchange before they could leave the camp. These 8,000 paroled Union soldiers began to arrive at Camp Douglas on September 28, 1862. Brigadier General Daniel Tyler relieved Colonel Tucker of command of the camp. Under Tyler's command, these Union soldiers had to live under similar conditions to those endured by the Confederate prisoners from Fort Donelson. The conditions were worse because the camp had become filthy and even more run down during its occupancy by the prisoners. The paroled soldiers were fortunate to have only about a two-month stay. They were able to tolerate the conditions somewhat better than the previous Confederate prisoners could because the Union parolees were more warmly dressed and in better physical condition. The damp conditions and bad food still took their toll. By November, forty soldiers of the 126th New York Volunteer Infantry Regiment had died and about another sixty were ill with fevers."

"Under these oppressive conditions, the Union Army parolees became mutinous, set fires, and made many attempted escapes. On October 23, 1862, General Tyler brought in regular U.S. troops to stop parolee riots. Secretary of War Edwin Stanton also ordered Tyler to relax his strict discipline, which helped calm the parolees. Most of the prisoner of war exchanges between the Union and Confederate armies under the cartel were completed by the end of November 1862. All the parolees left the camp by the end of that month except for Colonel Daniel Cameron and his 65th Illinois Volunteer Infantry Regiment, who were held until April 19, 1863, and put to work as guards. Thirty-five men of this regiment also died of disease at the camp during their confinement."

The 126th was declared exchanged on November 22, 1862. From here they went to Washington, D.C. and camped at Arlington Heights, VA to help defend Washington, D.C. from the threat of a Confederate attack. They were here from November 23-25, 1862. On December 3, 1862, they moved to Centerville, VA and were attached to the 3rd Brigade, Casey's Division, 22nd

Army Corps in the defense of Washington, D.C. This would conclude their activities for the year 1862.

While conducting research on Google about Centerville, I came across an old newspaper article in the Fare Facs Gazette Volume 9, Issue 4. It was the fall 2012 issue. It is the newsletter for the historic Fairfax City, Inc. It was about the conditions in Fairfax, VA. at this time during the Civil War. Fairfax is only a 16-minute drive from Centerville present day. So, it is close. Also, a lot of sick and wounded were transferred back and forth between the two places at this time. So, I read the article to get a glimpse of what things were like for John Hart during his stay here in the defense of Washington D.C.

Both places were reserve hospitals for the sick and wounded. The article had mentioned that of the 623,000 + soldiers who died during the Civil War, 2/3 of them died from disease. So, I did the math. That is roughly 411,180 soldiers! The article also goes on to mention that the most prevalent illnesses were that of chronic diarrhea, typhoid fever, other types of fevers, and of course dysentery. Here is a quote from the article:

"The featured ailment listed during this time period was rheumatism (305 patients). Given the physical strains of walking an average of 13 miles a day in mud, heat, and cold, and sleeping with and without tents outside in various conditions, it is not surprising that arthritic complaints abounded. There was no cure for the rheumatism, but rest and pain relief were prescribed. Fevers-intermittent (coming and going) and typhoid-along with diarrhea and dysentery were the most prevalent diseases. The sheer number of soldiers who became ill for a few days, or for weeks and months at a time, put a stress on the regiments and on the entire, still developing medical system. Organization, surgeons, nurses, supplies, food, transportation, death were many of the issues to be dealt with in a temporary hospital situation. And, for local inhabitants, whose homes and land were overrun by soldiers, well and sick, they had to continue to learn how to survive during hostile times."

It is interesting to note that all of these diseases, physical strains and living conditions of the soldiers during this time period sound almost exactly the same as the conditions my fellow Marines and I had to endure during the first Gulf War. For instance, we all had dysentery for several months. I discuss all that in greater detail in my first book, *"A Line in the Sand: The true story of a Marine's experiences on the front lines of the Gulf War."* It was published in 2006.

John Hart and his unit remained in Centerville until April 1863. At which time he was attached to 3rd Brigade, Abercrombie's Division, 22nd Army Corps. Then on June 25, 1863, his unit was ordered to join the Army of the Potomac in the field attached to 3rd Brigade, 3rd Division, 2nd Army Corps for the Gettysburg Campaign.

On July 1, 1863, John entered the battle of Gettysburg. His regiment was commanded by Colonel Eliakim Sherill until he took command of the entire brigade on July 2. Lieutenant Colonel James M. Bull took command of the regiment. If you recall, the 126th NY was formed by Colonel Sherill in NY where John Hart had enlisted. Colonel Sherill was mortally wounded during the battle on July 3, 1863.

I had obtained a copy of John's Civil War Muster Roll abstract for 1861-1890 from the historian ladies in New York that I previously mentioned who were helping me with research there locally. According to his muster roll John was wounded at the battle of Gettysburg on July 2, 1863.

So, I started to try and track down what happened. I looked up the New York State Military Museum's website and found a history page of the 126th in Battle. They had links to click on for newspaper articles that were written during the Civil War about the Unit (https://dmna.ny.gov/historic/reghist/civil/infantry/126thInf/126thInfCWN.htm) and (https://dmna.ny.gov/historic/reghist/civil/infantry/126thInf/126thInfMain.htm).

I found an article titled, *"The 126th in Battle! Heroic Valor and Its Fearful Cost! Three Hundred of the rank and file killed and wounded!"* The article went on to say that there were about 5-600 soldiers in the unit who participated in the battle of Gettysburg. The article stated that they would be known as the heroes of

Gettysburg and that they had redeemed themselves from the surrender at Harpers Ferry where they were labelled the "Harpers Ferry Cowards."

Morris Brown of Company A had captured a rebel flag that had Harpers Ferry on it. General Hayes read the line saying, "Boys, do you see that name? Now, - - them, forward on the charge!" The article stated that, "such a charge was never made." He was speaking about Pickett's Charge in which John and his unit participated in during the battle of Gettysburg. Further on in the article I found a list of all the killed and wounded in the regiment during this battle. I found John Hart of Co. I listed as wounded, slight in the side.

I soon found another article dated July 10, 1863, from Baltimore, MD. It stated that the wounded soldiers had all been sent to various hospitals on July 6, 1863. Incidentally speaking, I had quit taking all of my PTSD medications cold turkey on July 6, 2013. For some reason, I was very compelled to do it on that day. It was a feeling I could not shake. So, I did it. I had tried to quit my meds two other times but could not hack it. This time, somehow, I knew I would be successful, and I was. I discuss it all in my last two books, *"Chrysalis: A metamorphosis has begun,"* and *"The Sword and the Anvil: A definitive guide for natural, healthy healing from Post-Traumatic Stress and trauma."* I found John listed as being sent to the hospital at Fort Wood Bedloe's Island, which is currently Liberty Island and where the Statue of Liberty now stands.

As I have mentioned, a lot of these Civil War hospitals and prison camps had serious problems with diseases, such as chronic diarrhea, typhoid fever, other types of fevers, dysentery, and various arthritic conditions. I had also stated that of all the soldiers that died during the Civil War 2/3's of them died from disease. I went back to John's Civil War Muster Roll Abstract. Some of it is so obscured due to the ravages of time, etc., I could not read it. However, there was several things that I could ascertain. John had been sent back to his unit. But, in August of 63, just another month or so later, he was absent and back in the hospital again. Then he was sent back to his unit and was absent yet again on August 23, 1864, because he was sick. On December 25, 1864, he was transferred from Company I to Company B by his regiment. A lot of the men had been wounded and killed by this point, so the Regiment was consolidating a lot of the companies with very few men into others. I believe John was probably stuck in a Company that functioned more to the rear or had some kind of administrative duties due to his illness.

Most of the 126th was mustered out of service on June 3, 1865, in Washington D.C. as was John. Some Veterans and recruits that remained were transferred to 4th New York Heavy Artillery. After John's original wounds from Gettysburg healed his unit was in many notable battles. Such as, The Bristoe Campaign, Battle of the Wilderness, Spotsylvania Courthouse, Cold Harbor, Siege of Petersburg, Deep Bottom, Ream's Station, and Appomattox Court House where General Lee and his Army surrendered April 9, 1865 (https://civilwarintheeast.com/us-regiments-batteries/new-york-infantry/126th-new-york/). John did miss some of these battles, or portions of them, due to his sickness no doubt. However, he would have seen action in most of these famous, historic battles.

So, now that I had this straightened out to the best of my abilities, I went back to the records that the historian ladies had emailed me. I found John's Home for Soldiers Record (Home's for Soldiers were government run institutions for sick and wounded soldiers during the Civil War) and his Index Card. According to John's Home for Soldier Record he had gone there in 1890. Then that date was crossed out and the date of June 27, 1906, was written in. His Index card states that he had applied for, and got, a pension on January 24, 1894. After being readmitted to the Soldiers Home in June of 1906, he died on October 11, 1907. His record states that he had Locomotor Ataxia since the war, which is a degeneration of the posterior columns of the spinal cord, or the peripheral spinal sensory nerves, or both. This disease can be caused by syphilis, but also by injuries to the spinal cord or nerves, overexertion, exposure to cold and wet, acute rheumatism, typhoid, and typhus fevers, diphtheria, pneumonia, influenza, alcoholism, sexual excess, sever hemorrhages, and prolonged labors (https://jamanetwork.com/journals/jama/article-abstract/422950) and (https://jamanetwork.com/journals/jama/article-abstract/458077). All of these are the diseases that were killing the soldiers during the civil war and obviously John had been affected by these since he was sick in the hospital during the war. Also, a lot of the people that contracted this Locomotor Ataxia, or Tabes, suffered from chronic gastrointestinal disorders before the onset of this disease.

John left a widow who was living as a border with her daughter and her son-in-law at a farm. She apparently was walking across the street to deliver some bread she had just baked to a neighbor, when she collapsed in the street from an apparent heart attack and died. This was May 27, 1910. They both were survived by four children who lived in the surrounding areas of Oneida, Cazenovia, and Syracuse, New York.

The next dream that I want to discuss is the one I had first about the Revolutionary War. Many years later, as I was conducting research and writing this book, I came across a letter written by an American Militiaman who was in the battle of Bunker Hill on Saturday June 17, 1775. It was copied as written and contains typographical errors and misspellings.

Saturday June 17. The enemy appeared to be much alarmed on Saturday morning when thay discovered our operations and immediately began a heavy cannonading from a battery on Corps-Hill, Boston, and from the ships in the harbour. We with little loss continued to carry on our works till 1 o'clock when we discovered a large body of the enemy crossing Charles-River from Boston. They landed on a point of land about a mile eastward of our intrenchment and immediately disposed their army for an attack, previous to which thay set fire to the town of Charlestown. It is supposed that the enemy in the wind favouring them in such a design; while on the other side their army was extending northward towards Mistick-River with an apparent design of surrounding our men in the works, and of cutting off[f] any assistance intended for our relief. Thay ware however in some measure counteracted in this design and drew their army into closer order.

As the enemy approached, our men was not only exposed to the attack of a very numerous musketry, but to the heavy fire of the battery on Corps-Hill, 4 or 5 men of war, several armed boats or floating batteries in Mistick-River, and a number of field pieces. Notwithstanding we within the intrenchment, and at a breast work without, sustained the enemy's attacks with great bravery and resolution, kiled and wounded great numbers, and repulsed them several times; and after bearing, for about 2 hours, as sever and heavy a fire as perhaps ever was known, and many having fired away all their ammunition, and having no reinforcement, althoe thare was a great boddy of men nie by, we ware over-powered by numbers and obliged to leave the intrenchment, retreating about sunset to a small distance over Charlestown Neck.

N.B. I did not leave the intrenchment until the enemy got in. I then retreated 10 or 15 rods; then I receved a wound in my rite arm, the bawl gowing through a little below my elbow breaking the little shel bone. Another bawl struck my back taking a piece of skin about as big as a penny. But I go to Cambridge that night. The town of Charlestown supposed to contain about 300 dwelling-houses, a great number of which ware large and elegant, besides 150 or 200 other buildings, are almost all laid in ashes by the barbarity and wanton cruelty of that infernal villain Thomas Gage.

Oh, the goodness of God in preserving my life althoe thay fell on my right hand and on my left! O, may this act of deliverance of thine, Oh God, lead me never to distrust the[e] and put confidence in no arm of flesh! I was in great pane the first night with my wound.

Farnsworth, "Diary," Mass. Hist. Soc. Proc., 2nd Series, XII, 83-84.

This letter was from Amos Farnsworth who was a Corporal in the Massachusetts militia. I retrieved it from the book, **The Spirit of Seventy-Six: The story of the American Revolution as told by its participants.** Edited by Henry Steele Commager and Richard B. Morris. *No copyright infringement is intended.*

28 | PART I: THE BLACKENING

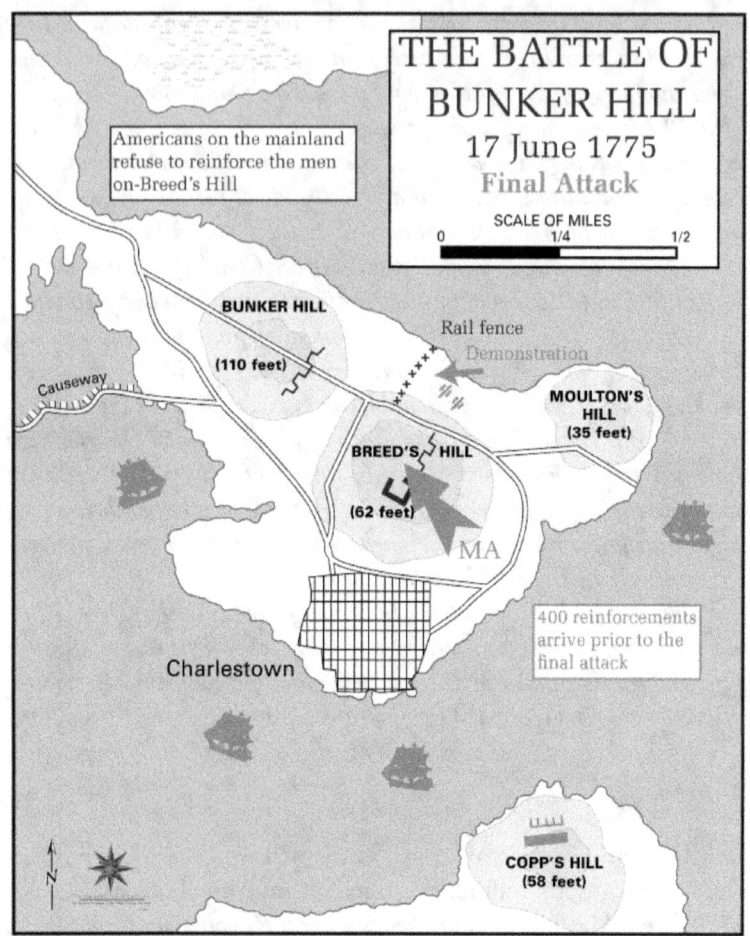

Public Domain, https://commons.wikimedia.org/w/index.php?curid=34971438

No copyright infringement is intended.

These pictures show the hills of the area where the battle was fought, and the avenue of retreat Corporal Farnsworth would have taken to get to Charlestown. It also sounds and looks eerily like my Revolutionary war dream from childhood. Everything sounds the same except for the exact location of the wounds. Not only is

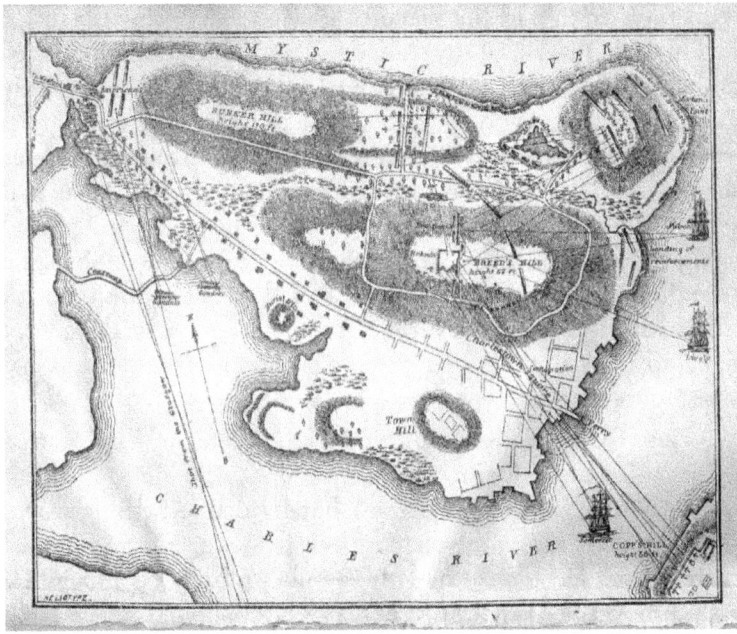

By George E Ellis - US Army images, Public Domain, https://commons.wikimedia.org/w/index.php?curid=2249084

No copyright infringement is intended.

that ironic, but so is the fact I had the book that I got the letter and information from. I bought the book back when I was in college in the early 2000's. It just kind of jumped out at me in the bookstore, so I bought it. I put it on my bookshelf and never read it until I started doing research for writing this book almost two decades later. When I came across that letter by Corporal Farnsworth, I could not believe how similar it was too my dream!

Lastly, I want to discuss the third and final dream I had about Vietnam. I had a weird experience with this dream. It was in the late 90's and I was elk hunting with a friend. We were in this area of tall brown grass (like in my dream). We had been pursuing this herd of elk for about three miles when some people in a truck drove by and scared them off. So, we had no choice but to return back to camp. As I was walking back through the tall grass with the tree line in the distant (also just like in my dream), I had my rifle slung over my shoulder. I was dressed in camouflage and a boonie cover (also just like in my dream). I had suddenly got this really strong de ja vu feeling like I had done this before. Then, at that moment, I had got very anxious. I had this ominous feeling. It was at that point I remembered my dream. It was as if I was reliving it in that present moment. This voice in my head said you have done this before. It almost freaked me out because the whole experience felt so real. I swore I had done this before. I shook my head to clear my mind and I just kept on walking back to camp. I never mentioned it to the friend I was with. It was just way too weird.

I also conducted some research on the Vietnam War. I started by searching to see if any U.S. units were wiped out during any of the battles (because of my dream), hoping that something would pop up to help me on my search. There is a lot of information out there on the war and I knew this would probably be a daunting task. I moved forward with my search, and I found information about the Army 1st Cavalry during Vietnam. They took most of the casualties during the war. So, I searched "were any 1st Cavalry units wiped out during the Vietnam war?"

The search brought up a battle in which a 1st Cavalry Unit was ambushed in the La Drang Valley on November 17, 1965. After the initial battle at Landing Zone X-Ray, 2nd Battalion, 7th Cavalry was ordered to move cross country to Landing Zone Albany. There they would be picked up by helicopter. They were moving through the jungle when they were ambushed from all sides. Companies C and D took the worst of the ambush. Most of the men in both companies were hit. The casualties were quite large. Specifically, 93% of Company C were wounded or injured, half of those died. This battle was the first significant contact between the U.S. and the Vietnamese. The way the Vietnamese attacked then became their standard for engaging U.S. troops the rest of the war *(1st Cavalry Unit Ambushed in the La Drang Valley* https://www.history.com/this-day-in-history/1st-cavalry-unit-ambushed-in-the-la-drang-valley).

Also of note, during the war that I was in, I fought on the front lines. I was in "C" company, 1ˢᵗ Battalion, 7ᵗʰ Marines. Two weeks before the ground war was supposed to start, I was transferred to 2ⁿᵈ Battalion, 7ᵗʰ Marines. We were sent on a suicide mission five days before the actual ground war was supposed to start. We were tasked with a night infiltration of two Iraqi mine fields while the Iraqi's were watching on the other side. Our unit was also the first to make contact with Iraqi forces and engage in combat on the ground. My experiences during the war are described in greater detail in my book, *"A Line in the Sand: The True Story of a Marine's Experiences on the Front Lines of the First Gulf War."* This battle in La Drang Valley sounds eerily like my Vietnam War dream. My dream, coupled with my hunting experience and my personal experience in the Gulf War, is now even more eerie indeed.

Chapter 2

At this point, based on all of this research on my dreams and my life experiences, I decided to complete an analysis of all the major events of my life. I figured I needed to do this in order to make some sense out of my life and the direction I must take it. This would give me a basis, or a foundation, to begin analyzing my regular, nightly dreams properly. It would also help me understand them. I made a list of all the major events that comprised my life to this point. I also wrote down the dates of each event. I wrote the dates down because numbers are a way of connecting matter to the psyche. Numbers have been used by all cultures throughout the continuum of time in some capacity or another to achieve this connection. So, I did the same.

There was a total of 35 major events and their associated dates. This number is significant for me, and we will discuss that a bit later. I added the numbers of the dates up and got either a single digit number or more than a single digit number. In the case of the latter, I added those numbers together as well to get each event in my life down to a single digit. I did this because that shows a finality or an ending. Whereas, a double-digit number, or a string of numbers, suggests that the computation is not complete (i.e., just as a mathematical equation denotes). If you recall, I mentioned earlier that Carl Jung said we all come from one single thing (Prima Materia). That singularity, that oneness, also influenced me to add all the numbers up until I got a single digit. In some cases, I only had the year recorded and in others I had the entire date. In the latter case, I assumed that this was fine. I was sure that I remembered only the numbers I was supposed to, according to a divine plan. Then, all the events that contained the same number were grouped together accordingly. By doing this, I was able to break down the extensive list of events in my life into smaller, related groups, which facilitated a more streamlined analysis. Thus, it allowed me to put the events of my life together like a puzzle into a form that has meaning.

Therefore, I was able to ascertain some semblance of meaning to my individual life. This analysis allowed me to put my life into context so that I could understand my life better. It also helped me to understand my dreams and the guidance they gave me down my path of obtaining wholeness, or oneness. This analysis was the foundation to begin this last part of my developmental journey. I felt that this part of the journey needed to be completed so that I could then begin to do the work I was put here on earth to do.

This is a process in life that I believe we all are supposed to go through. To me it is a process that is part of the purpose of life for everyone. It is something that must be completed in preparation for the real work one was put here to produce, to give form to, and to make permanent in the world for the benefit of others who need it, search for it, and find it. It is a process Carl Gustav Jung called, *The Process of Individuation*, where we learn who we really are. Not just physically, but spiritually. It is Where we learn that each of us is an individual with an individual and distinct purpose for being here. That is what I believe, and I felt compelled to complete this process.

The first three stages of this process, as I understand them from Jung, which I may add are symbolic of the Holy Trinity (i.e., The Father, The Son, and the Holy Spirit), are called the **Blackening**, **The Whitening** and **The Reddening**. The first of these stages, The Blackening, is where a mental union is obtained in the overcoming of the body (i.e., childhood). The second stage, The Whitening, is where there is a reunion of the spirit with the body beginning an elimination of the impurities of one's life. It is where there is a changing of spirit into body. In other words, a transformation is completed (young adulthood). The third step, The Reddening, is where there is a binding of the soul to either the good or the bad (middle aged adulthood). Here, the choice is ours and it is this choice that I believe clearly defines what it means to be human. What it means to be human, as I mentioned earlier, is something I have been trying to define for about three decades, ever since that question was first posed to me by one of my Anthropology Professors in college.

This one simple question from that professor sent me on a lifelong journey. It had quite an impact on my life. The Reddening portion of this process is where soul and spirit are separated from the body and instinctual impulses are repeatedly modified into a higher, or socially more acceptable activity. This is done until a "pureness of one's life" is obtained. You either choose to live the right way, or the wrong way. Hence, you are then bound to either Heaven, or Hell. In other words, by our own choice we live in paradise, or we create our own hell. We are free to make the choice. Just like the story of Adam and Eve in the Bible describes.

Once these first three stages are completed, a fourth arrives where the individual lives a distinct life as a complete person (i.e., the whole self as Jung so aptly put it). This usually occurs in middle aged adulthood to old age. As I mentioned earlier, the first three stages are symbolic of the Holy Trinity. Keep in mind that when one symbolically completes the trinity, such as in performing the sign of the Cross, he makes "four" as a "Cross" clearly delineates. This "four" represents the fourth and final stage of living life as a whole-self and of the quaternary (recall I mentioned that the date the woman from the archives called me back added up to four). It also symbolizes what the Greeks call "Temenos", or safe space. This is symbolic of where one's mental work is to occur in a safe, secluded, and isolated environment until the cleansing of the ego is complete, and then one is living as his or her whole self. This is usually symbolized as a circle inside of (or assimilated into) a square throughout history.

The symbol of three is everywhere. It is in the three stages of individuation, the Holy Trinity, the saying that all bad things come in threes, that three is an evil number, or in the number 13 where three by itself relates to the first three stages of individuation and the one represents the final stage where one lives as a whole self. Thus, symbolized by adding the one and the three together and getting four (i.e., completeness). The number four is also found everywhere. As I just mentioned, it is a symbol for completeness and as a "temenos" in the form of a square, which is depicted with four sides. Without four sides, it would not be a square. Thus, it would not be complete. This squareness is everywhere. It is in houses, buildings, back yards, rooms in a house, etc. All of which are typically seen as "safe spaces" where some sort of work or activity is conducted, such as me writing these words down on a safe space (i.e., a square piece of paper) and in a safe space (i.e., my square office).

Here is my list of the 35 events in my life:

1. I was born: 1/30/1970=21(2+1=3):**3**
2. My parents got divorced: 1980 = 18 (1+8=9):**9**
3. Trouble with bullies in junior high: 1983=21(2+1=3):**3**
4. Moved to a new state with my mother: 1984=22(2+2=4):**4**
5. Graduated High School: 1988=26(2+6=8):**8**
6. Joined the Marines: 1988=26(2+6=8):**8**
7. Left for boot camp: 10/10/1988=28(2+8=10) (1+0=1):**1**
8. Got to Saudi Arabia for 1st Gulf War: 8/12/1990=30(3+0=3):**3**
9. Battle of Khafji/My 21st Birthday: 1/30/1991=24(2+4=6):**6**
10. Got Married: 1991=20(2+0=2):**2**
11. Wife left me/Got divorced: 1992=21(2+1=3):**3**
12. Got out of the Marines: 7/27/1992=37(3+7=10) (1+0=1):**1**
13. Got home to live with my father: 8/1/1992=30(3+0=3):**3**
14. Moved back with My mother/Dealt with Ex-wife and her baby who she lied to me about and I found out later was not mine: 1993=22(2+2=4):**4**
15. Went to jail for the night because of a girlfriend's lies: 1994=23(2+3=5):**5**
16. Started community college: 1996=25(2+5=7):**7**
17. The day my heart stopped for a whole minute: 1997=26(2+6=8):**8**
18. Started college at a University and that is where I met my next long-term girlfriend: 1998=27(2+7=9):**9**
19. Graduated from College/Got full time job as assistant archaeologist/bought 1st home: 2001=**3**
20. Broke up with long-term girlfriend: 2004=**6**

21. Met my next girlfriend who would become the mother of my son: 2004=**6**
22. God spoke to me and told me I would lose everything, but it would be ok: 2004=**6**
23. My son was born, and I met next girlfriend: 2/6/2004=14(1+4=5):**5**
24. Published first book, *A Line in the Sand: The true story of a Marine's experiences on the front lines of the first Gulf War*/Bought a historic 2nd home: 2006=**8**
25. Lost the historic home and 1st home/ Moved to an apartment/My PTSD became full blown: 2007=**9**
26. Went to hospital for first time due to my PTSD/Began working on healing PTSD: 3/2009=14(1+4=5):**5**
27. Got out of hospital/Lost apartment/ My girlfriend and I moved in with her dad: 4/2009=15(1+5=6):**6**
28. Went to hospital the 2nd time due to PTSD: 2010=**3**
29. Ended up in wheelchair due to PTSD: 2010=**3**
30. Got out of my wheelchair: 2/2013=**8**
31. Quit taking my PTSD medications on my own/ Began healing PTSD in healthy, natural ways: 7/6/2013=19(1+9=10) (1+0=1):**1**
32. Left girlfriend's dad's house and moved to new apartment/Healed PTSD: 10/13/2013=11(1+1=2):**2**
33. Published my 2nd book, *Chrysalis: A Metamorphosis had begun,* chronicling my PTSD: 5/2014=12(1+2=3):**3**
34. Published my 3rd book, *The Sword and the Anvil: A Definitive guide to Natural, Healthy Healing from Post-Traumatic Stress and Trauma*, describing how I healed my PTSD: 3/2016=12(1+2=3):**3**
35. Moved to a new home and began writing this book: 1/4/2017=15(1+5=6):**6**

I took the total number of 35 significant events in my life and added them together which equals eight. Also, I was compelled to add up each number of every event of my life (1 through 35:

1+2=3+3=6+4=10, etc.) to obtain a grand total. Then I added those numbers to get a single digit: 630(6+3+0=9). Therefore, I now have a complete numerical accountability of my life. Then, I put the groups of events together that contained the same single digit number and interpreted the significance and meaning of those specific groups of events. Thus, showing symbolic, developmental periods of my life.

Events with the number one (Period of volatility):

- The day I left for boot camp
- The day I got out of the Marines
- The day I quit taking my PTSD medications and began healing on my own in healthy, natural ways.

The day I left for boot camp was the refining of, or adding too, the development of my manhood (ego-consciousness). It was a transition from my teenage years into young adulthood. The Marine Corps is where I was built into a tough, young man that could handle anything that life could throw at me. It began in boot camp and continued through my four years of service, including the year I spent on the front lines of the first Gulf War. This was a time where my mind was forced to overcome my body. I had to heal all the ills of my past, from my childhood, where I was picked on, ridiculed, and consistently beat up. At that time, I thought I was a skinny whimp and weak. The Marine Corps was the final stage of my preparation to handle what I would go through in my future, as part of the individuation process and the real work I was put here to do. Without this development, I would not have been able to accomplish this process, and thus, my work. I sort of think of it as an athlete abuilding his or her body so that he or she can perform at the highest level.

The day I got out of the Marines is where I transitioned into another part of the development of my ego-consciousness. It is where I met my dark shadow, the evil side of me so to speak. The thing that I would eventually have to overcome. My dark shadow being my PTSD and all the damage my life had caused me, both mentally and physically. It was something that would come to the forefront of my life. It would have to be dealt with in order to obtain a "mental cleansing", so that my mind would be prepared to receive my unconscious guidance (i.e., my messages and instructions for my life). I think perhaps that it also, in an esoteric sort of way, started forcing me to rely on my internal guidance more, and to ask for "help" from my spiritual source when I needed it instead of turning to society for this guidance.

The day I quit taking my PTSD medications, I transitioned into the ending of the development of my ego-consciousness. I was now turning inward for help on a consistent basis instead of outward to society, or man in order to heal myself and solve my problems. Therefore, I can surmise, and be quite sure, that these three events belonging in group number one, are symbolic of the first stage of the individuation process (*The Blackening*). They give meaning to the first part of my life, or what Dr. Wayne Dyer would call, "the morning of my life."

Events with the number two (Period of volatility):

- When I got married, the last year I was in the Marine Corps.
- When I had left a girlfriend's dad's house, moved into a new apartment, and finished healing my PTSD.

The first event where I got married, symbolizes a section of my life where I had moved on from the guidance of my mother, the guidance of my father and the Marine Corps. Symbolically, all of their jobs were done. The Marines and my father being my ego-conscious guide (my manhood) and my mother being my unconscious guide, the feminine side of my whole-self (my intuition, nurturing and caring side). Jung stipulated that for a man his ego-conscious is represented by a male and his unconsciousness by a female, both in his dreams and in his physical life. This is reverse for a female. It was at this point of my life that I was ready to go out into the world on my own and experience life for myself, based on what I had been taught thus far by the Marines, my father, and my mother. I was basically on my own emotionally and living totally from impulse (i.e., consciousness), which led me to marry my ex-wife. I was now ready to be my own ego and find my own unconscious guidance, which is symbolized in physical life by marriage, or a union, and also by a female in my unconscious by my dreams as I previously stated.

After I got married and divorced, I went through several girlfriends. Subconsciously, I was looking for my unconscious (female) guidance in physical form in order to balance out my life. At that point, I was living totally in my ego consciousness (what society, my parents and the Marines taught me to be). It was not until my girlfriend and I moved out of her dad's house into a new apartment, that I found what I needed in terms of my unconscious female guidance. She was clearly what I needed. She was the epitome of exactly what I needed to develop within myself (i.e., my internal unconscious guidance from my dreams). Before I met her, I was living in my ego and trying to control the outcome of my life. I kept picking women who were a symbol of that and living completely out of conscious/unconscious balance. It was not until "things" were cleared out of my life, so to speak, that I was able to see the forest for the trees. That is precisely how it had to happen. I needed to learn to interpret those dreams in terms of messages guiding me on what to do in my life without trying to reason with them. I also needed to learn to act based on my intuition and instincts.

I needed to quit living based on what my father and the Marines had taught me about going out into the world, conquering it, and physically making my own life. Her and I leaving her dad's house and going out on our own, symbolizes the part of my journey where I learned to do just that. It is where I learned that life for me needed to be lived with a balance between the conscious and unconscious, and guidance was given to the conscious by the unconscious through dreams. For me, they needed to be interpreted properly through their symbolism (not literally), and then the knowledge learned from the symbolism in my dreams applied to my conscious life.

Events with number three (Beginning of a positive period):
- I was born
- Trouble with bullies as a child
- Got to Saudi Arabia in 1st Gulf War

- My wife left, and I got divorced
- Got home to live with my father

(The five events below are a transition from one phase to another.)

- Graduated college and got full time job as Assistant Archaeologist
- Went to the hospital the 2nd time for my PTSD
- Ended up in a wheelchair
- Published 2nd book, *Chrysalis: A metamorphosis has begun*
- Published 3rd book, *The Sword and the Anvil: A definitive guide for natural, healthy healing from Post-Traumatic Stress and trauma.*

The very first event in this group is obvious, I was born. Except for the events concerning me graduating college, getting my full-time job, and publishing the books, these events represent further development of my ego-consciousness/manhood through a series of physically and mentally tough events. A good way to explain it I suppose, is that these events are analogous to putting steal into a hot fire, pulling it out, putting it on an anvil, beating it, and repeating the process until what is no longer needed is stripped, and the proper form is developed for its intended use (i.e., like a blacksmith; hence, the title of this book).

The other three events concerning my education, a job, and the publishing of books, symbolize my training for what I was sent here to do (i.e., my real work). It is where I began to develop my unconscious or reunite with it. This is where I learned how to read, research and study in a more professional manner. Then I learned how to write properly, and I was introduced to the work of Carl Jung by my old boss. It is also where I was presented with the idea to write my first book. This began my work of going through the individuation process (with the help of Jung's work and my unconscious), and then write about it to give it permanent form in the world, and thus, solidifying what I have learned in my mind. This led to me publishing three more books since the first, including this one, equaling four books in total. Therefore, this group of events represents a transition from the Blackening to the Whitening part of the individuation process. As I stated earlier, the second stage, The Whitening, is where there is a reunion of the spirit with the body beginning an elimination of the impurities of one's life. It is where there is a changing of spirit into body. In other words, a transformation is completed (young adulthood).

Events with number 4 (Beginning of a negative period):

- Moved to a new state to live with my mother.
- Moved back to that same state, as a young adult, to live with my mother and deal with my ex-wife and her baby that was not mine.

There are only two events here; however, they are significant ones indeed. This is the part of my life where my unconscious guidance was developed. However, it was developed in a dark way. I am a male, so as I previously stated, my unconscious is symbolized by a female. This is a male's inner intuitiveness, instinctiveness, and nurturing capabilities. In other words, my guidance. Which, when living as a whole self, my guidance comes internally from within myself. Not externally from my man-made environment.

Both of my experiences with my mother and ex-wife had left me dealing with abandonment issues in that they both literally abandoned me (ultimately my whole family did as well). The two things that were sacred to me, my mother and marriage, left me alone in the world and feeling ill treated. Thus, leaving a bad taste in my mouth towards women (i.e., towards my unconscious guidance, and hence, I repressed it).

As time passed this attitude changed, but we will discuss that later. I was mad about that for quite some time; however, I no longer am. The reason being is that I now understand why those things happened to me. It is quite simple really. My unconscious had to be developed in the same manner as my conscious in preparation for what I must do in life. It is like the analogy I just used in describing my conscious development and how it was similar to putting steel into a fire and beating it on an anvil like a blacksmith. For me, this process was completed by the age of 49.

Therefore, based on the analysis of my life events thus far, I have a much clearer understanding of the processes at work here and the purpose of the ego-conscious and unconscious. These two halves of me must both be developed into their proper forms respectively, in preparation for the work that must be completed afterwards in merging the two selves together into a whole self. Then, that work that was just completed, must be put into form by giving it permanence in the world for the benefit of others. That completes the cycle.

Events with number five (Period of volatility):

- I went to jail for the night based on a girlfriend's lies **(a developmental transition of my unconscious occurred after this event and is described below).**
- My son was born, and I met my next girlfriend.
- I went to the hospital for the first time due to my PTSD and I began working on healing it.

The first of these three events, I believe, represents a transition into a new phase of my unconscious development. After the event where I went to jail, several things were purged from my life. A girlfriend (a symbol of my unconscious) who was no good for me, a house I was living in (I moved to a new house) and the situation I was in. For me, that all was an ending of a portion of my unconscious development. Then, the next phase of my unconscious development began. After my unconscious had been beat up, stripped of the un-necessary parts, and then molded into proper form, I started to work on accepting my unconscious guidance and trusting it.

The birth of my son, who was moved to a different state by his mother, is a long-term part of a phase of my life. The culmination of this phase must occur at the precise time and will come to fruition later. I believe this will come about when he is in his high school years, or shortly thereafter. By that time, I will have been done with completing my individuation process. This, I believe, will be part of a phase where he will need me for guidance through his development into young adulthood in preparation for his real work. I also believe this will be part of my "reward" for completing the individuation process. After he was born, I met a new girlfriend who I am still with today. This started a new phase in the development of my unconscious guidance. At this point, there were several different parts of the development of my unconscious occurring at the same time. I began learning about it, trusting it, and following it through all the things that occurred to us during that time. I did it without trying to physically force an outcome in my life through a system of ego-conscious reasoning (although, there were times I got off track). It was like I had no choice to do that, like I was being forced to do so. It was as if it was the only way to make it through all of this. She was the perfect person for this developmental phase, and I believe I am what she needs for her development. She handles the intuition and nurturing side of our life together and I handle the conquering of things side of our life together. Thus, we are in perfect balance. Together we are a complete being. We are also a symbol to each other of what we each need to work on within our own selves, internally and externally.

The last event of this group was where I went to the hospital for the first time due to my PTSD and where I began to work on healing it in earnest. It is where my mind was cleansed of all of its baggage. It was all purged from my life. It is where my mental work was completed in my safe spot, my "temenos", as we discussed earlier, (i.e., my safe spot was with my girlfriend). This was the beginning of the phase where my mind was cleansed and healed, so that I could then begin to get my messages from my unconscious guidance clearly. Then I was able to follow that guidance through the rest of my individuation process. This specific period of events that I have been talking about where my son was born, and I met my girlfriend, began in 2004 at the age of 34. The PTSD began to develop in earnest shortly thereafter. It continued for the next four years, getting worse and worse until I could no longer ignore it and I had to succumb to its powerful effects. In 2008, I gave in, and I started seeing a doctor for it. I was prescribed medicine to calm me down. It was not until 2009 when the doctor finally got me to talk about the war, and because of opening up that can of worms, I ended up in the hospital for the first time. It is here where I began to cleanse and heal my mind from its baggage. I was 39 years old. I did not complete that work until 2013 at the age of 43. That whole process took nine years to complete. Remember the number nine. It is an extremely important number in the events of my life, and we will discuss it shortly.

Events with number 6 (Period of volatility):

- The battel of Khafji on my 21st birthday.
- When I broke up with a long-term girlfriend.
- Met the woman who became the mother of my son.
- The time God spoke to me just days before my son was born, telling me I would lose everything, and that I would be ok. It was necessary to clean the past and make room for the new.
- Got out of hospital the first time, lost my apartment, moved in with a new girlfriend and her father.
- Moved to a new house with same girlfriend of nearly 14 years.

There are six events that belong to this group. During the first event, I really turned inward and started praying religiously. I was looking for help to save my life because I feared dying in the war (we were told that 90% would die the first day of the ground war and also because I remembered my three war dreams). This one specific event began a long transition period where I worked on completely trusting and listening to my unconscious guidance, without second guessing it.

Me breaking up with my long-term girlfriend occurred because I was focusing internally. I understood why I had to break up with her. My unconscious told me I needed to do it, so I could move on with my development and so could she. I knew that if we stayed together, I would be responsible for keeping her from developing. I could not do that. That was not up to me. If I thought it was, that would be totally egocentric. That would be living the old way in my ego conscious.

That now leads us to when I met the woman who became the mother of my son. We have previously discussed the importance of my son's birth. However, choosing his mother as my partner was a bad choice for me because it was made through my ego. My unconscious had been telling me to stay away from her, but I did not listen to it, and it turned out horrible between her and I. After that, I told myself I would never ignore my instincts again (i.e., I would never ignore my unconscious guidance again). This is where, right before my sons' birth, God spoke to me and told me I would lose everything, but it would be ok. It is necessary. It is discussed in my first book, *A Line in the Sand: The true story of a Marine's experiences on the front lines of the Gulf War*. However, this all came to fruition several years later. It took time for it all to unravel.

The last three events in this phase of my development were comprised of my complete emersion into my unconscious to get through all of this. The last event is where I completed my individuation process, which is symbolized by writing this book. For me, it is like a summary of everything, so that I have a complete understanding of my life and the reason for it. It is how I personally learn. Then what I learn is made permanent in the world for others, so that they may benefit from the knowledge I have attained. Therefore, this book completes a cycle. The writing of this book had begun shortly after I moved to the new house in January of 2017.

Each of these six events began with something being stripped from me, followed by a period of healing, maturity and above all, spiritual growth. However, if I divide these six events in half and look at the first three, I see that the first three events in this group were concerned with the stripping of ego-conscious ways of thinking and the physical things these ways of thinking produced. Each time this occurred, a period of mental healing and maturation followed.

Therefore, following my line of thinking, I looked at the last three events of this group and I saw where things had been stripped from me mentally and physically. Then, that was followed by a deeper, spiritual growth. In other words, the ego-conscious mental and physical barriers had to be released first (which were created through living in my ego-consciousness). Then, the process of healing those wounds began and ended. This process cleansed all the mental baggage that was created by all of this. Thereby, allowing a much deeper type of growth to occur internally (i.e., spiritually). Thus, these events paved the way for the development of my unconscious and the adherence to its guidance. Hence, providing me the opportunity for a whole new way of life. In other words, I was now ready to begin my transition into the reddening phase of my individuation process.

Events with number seven (where I transitioned into the Reddening phase of the individuation process [Period of volatility]):

- I started college at a community college

There is only one event in this group, but it is highly significant in that this is where my entire life began to change. I started down the path of learning everything I needed to know to do my real work, complete it, and give it proper form in the world. Then I could live my life as a complete, whole-self and receive the rewards for doing so.

At this point of my life, I had a landscape maintenance business. I wanted to expand the business. So, I decided to go to college to get a degree in landscape architecture. However, in my first week of classes, I made a huge decision. One of my courses was an art history class. In it, we were talking about Egypt and all its artifacts. I decided right then and there that I wanted to be an Archaeologist. After class that day, I headed to the advisor's office. I changed my class schedule and my degree path to Anthropology, with an emphasis on Archaeology. That one single decision changed my life forever and sent me down the path I needed to be on.

Events with number 8 (where my ego-conscious was developed [End of period of negativity]):

- I graduated high school
- I joined the Marines
- The day my heart stopped beating and I was clinically dead for a minute

- I published my 1st book, *A Line in the Sand: The true experiences of a Marine on the front lines of the first Gulf War*
- I got out of my wheelchair after being in it for three years
- There is a total of 35 significant events in my life which adds up to eight (35:3+5=8)

The last event of this group (35 total events [3+5=8]) says it all. These events were all big decisions I had to make, which shaped my entire life. Each decision began a period of enormous growth for me and changed the direction my life was going in. Thus, ending periods of negativity.

Graduating high school and joining the Marines symbolized me leaving my childhood phase. Thus, I was entering young adulthood and beginning my manhood so to speak. This toughened my ego up so that I could handle all the things I would face from here on out. It is also where my PTSD came from. It gave me the material from which three books came. Writing those books allowed me to mentally cleanse the damage these experiences of developing my manhood and toughness caused. Basically, I went through phases where I was physically developed. Then, the negative effects of that development had to be cleansed, or cleaned up, so that I could move forward to the next phase. It is like when I sculptor carves a statue out of stone. When he is done, he must clean up all the debris so that the statue can go on display for all the world to see in its pure form. The same happens to the unconscious.

When I was 27, I was at a Denny's with friends. They were Paramedics and EMT's. While there, my heart stopped. I was technically dead for a minute. While I was "dead," I was floating in this blackness up towards this bright light. I remember feeling the most intense sense of peace I had ever felt in my life. I told myself, "This isn't so bad. I don't know what I was so scared of (regarding death)." I then awoke on the floor with my friend standing over me, ripping a large adrenaline needle out of a plastic bag and getting ready to stick it through the middle of my chest into my heart. After that, I really focused on college and building my career, as I had just acquired an entry level position in the field of archaeology.

Nine years later, I wrote and published my first book, *A Line in the Sand: The true experiences of a Marine on the front lines of the first Gulf War*. This kicked off my writing career, as well as the beginning of me facing my past, and my PTSD, so that I could heal from them.

The day I got out of my wheelchair after being in it for three years was a huge decision. Up to that point, I had lost everything in my life (remember I mentioned what God told me before my son was born about losing everything). I even lost my ability to walk, and ultimately, my ability to live my life. I remember sitting there in my wheelchair on all the PTSD medications they had me on. I was thinking to myself that this was no way to live my life. This could not be my life. I knew that I was supposed to accomplish something with my life. So, I decided enough was enough. I was going to get out of my wheelchair, and I was going to get my life back. Indeed, another decision that changed my life forever. This began the final stage of my healing process. I healed my PTSD in healthy, natural ways. That phase ended with me having published three books on the entire ordeal. With that, this phase was completed.

Events with number 9 (my unconscious development where I was guided to focus on looking internally for direction and to heal the mental damage the events of my life caused [End of a positive period]):

- My parents got divorced (caused me to become an introvert).
- I transferred from a community college to a university to finish my degree (Where I had to learn to focus internally for answers and direction because of my schoolwork).
- I lost both of my houses that I owned and moved to an apartment where my PTSD got worse (This is where I turned completely internally to heal and where I began to focus on using my unconscious as a guide not only in my healing process, but also in my writing).
- I added together all the numbers of the list of 35 events of my life, one through 35 (1+2=3+3=6+4=10+5=15, etc.)

Chapter 2 | 49

and came to a total number of 630, which I added together (6+3+0=9) for a single digit number of nine.

This group of events is incredibly significant, and they coincide with the events in group eight. Each one of these events represents a phase where ego-consciously created material things were lost, whether they were ways of thinking, living, feeling, or material possessions. This had to happen to "make room" for the growth I needed to achieve and the work I needed to complete. In other words, I would have a clean slate to begin from. I had to release myself from my personal history, so I could become who I really was. Obviously, this had to happen in stages, occurring concomitantly with the events of my life. If it all had happened at once, it simply would have killed me. I do not think any human being could handle something like that. Hence, the saying, "God only gives us what we can handle."

The 35 events of my life add up to eight. Eight is also the last single digit even number. Each number of the 35 events added together equals 630 (1+2=3,3+3=6, 6+4=10, etc.). This then adds up to 9 (6+3+0=9). Nine is the last single digit odd number. Hence, these two numbers, eight and nine, show a finality. Therefore, I decided to take all the even events prior to group eight from groups two, four and six, and combine them. Then, I took all the odd events prior to group nine from groups one, three, five and seven, and combined them. In each of the two groups the events were put into chronological order. Thus, I had a series of events under group eight, and a series of events under group nine. I did this to ascertain any relationships and/or significance between each of them (i.e., the even events before group eight and the odd events before group nine). This then showed that each of the events in group eight and nine began new phases of my development throughout the course of my life. That information also showed me how my ego-conscious (under group eight) and my unconscious (under group nine) were each developed and how each was divided into pertinently related sections. What follows next is a detailed description of exactly what I did and the results I obtained by doing so.

Group #8 (End of a negative period, i.e., the development of my ego-consciousness):

- Moved to a new state with my mother (even event from group #4).
- Graduated high school (event from group #8).

At age 14, I moved to a new state with my mother and stepdad for a new start because the prior experiences were so horrible for me. In other words, those experiences provided guidance that influenced me to move, along with accomplishing a portion of my ego-conscious development. This set the stage for me to join the Marines. The place I joined was important. If I had joined the Marines from where I was living with my father, I would have been stationed somewhere other than Camp Pendleton. Thus, I probably would never have been in the First Gulf War. Or, if I stayed with my father, I may not have joined the Marines at all and that would have altered the course of my life entirely.

- Joined the Marines (From group #8)
  - I was in the battle of Khafji on my 21st birthday (From group #6)
  - I got Married (From group #2)
  - I moved back with my mother to deal with my ex-wife and a child who ended up not being mine (From group #4)

Joining the Marines led me to war where I became a man. It is where my "toughness" was honed. This was in preparation for all that would befall me upon returning home from the war. It was the final preparation for what I was going to have to deal with physically and mentally for the next 20 years, which brought me to the point I am at today.

The next event is when I got married. Marriage was sacred to me. Especially having been raised Catholic. However, my ex-wife had treated me horribly and left before I got out of the Marines. This really shook me up. Especially, on top of the war. This process took about a year to unravel. However, it was an especially important event for a few reasons.

First, because of how the government had treated me during the war and how my ex-wife treated me, I decided not to re-enlist. The Marines were constantly bugging me to re-enlist for about the last six months of my career. They were promising me the rank of Sergeant upon re-enlistment, and they wanted to send me to drill instructor school. My ex-wife wanted me to accept the offer and re-enlist. So, because of how badly the government and my ex-wife had treated me (two very sacred things to me), I decided to get out of the Marines. Those things guided me to make the proper decision. I say proper because, as you may recall, I had the three same dreams repeatedly as a child. Those three dreams stopped when I joined the Marines. Remember that in each of those dreams I was in the military and went to war and had been wounded in the same spot all three times. I was also a Sergeant in two of the dreams. Clearly, these three dreams were a reminder to me to not make the same mistake again. They were a warning that I should not re-enlist and take a higher rank, which would mean staying in the military. Hence, I would have been stuck in a phase of development never able to complete it and move on. Therefore, if I re-enlisted, I would receive the same fate yet again (i.e., the war/military would break my heart, wound me, in other words kill me both physically and spiritually). It was a message to me that I am here to do something important. The Marines were only supposed to be part of my life, a developmental phase of my life, not my life's work. I needed to get out in order to break the life cycle I was in so that I could move on with my development. In other words, I had some "karma" to heal so that I could finally move on unencumbered from my past.

I never had realized the significance of these dreams before I conducted this analysis. I knew they were important, but I did not know why. I have spent the last 26 years of my life trying to figure out what they meant. I only knew that they were important. Now I know why. Keeping in line with my methodology, 26 would equal 8 (2+6=8). As I mentioned earlier, eight is the last even single digit number, which shows a finality. Thus, after these 26 years of development, I am at the end of all this negativity, and the culmination of all those events shows the ending of my ego-conscious development.

- Day my heart stopped beating and I was clinically dead for a minute (From group #8)
  - Broke up with my long-term girlfriend (From group #6)
  - Met my next girlfriend who became the mother of my son (From group #6)
  - Day God spoke to me and told me I would lose everything but that I would be ok (From group #6)

The day my heart stopped, where I was clinically dead for a minute, kicked off a series of events where I had relationships with women who were not incredibly open emotionally. They all had their own personal issues to deal with but were refusing to work on them and it was causing issues in the relationships. These relationships had a purpose. They were supposed to be symbols to me of how I was handling my own business. In other words, I had issues I was supposed to work on that I was repressing and ignoring. It is like the Latin phrase I mentioned earlier says, "Cum grano salis"— we always see our own mistakes in our opponent.

During the relationship I had with the mother of my son, because I was trying to make it work, I respected her request to deal with the PTSD she said I had. I did not think anything was wrong, but I thought I would try for her sake anyways. I saw a counselor who said I was fine. However, at the time, I was contemplating writing my first book about the war. My boss had been pushing me to do so. I discussed that with the counselor who helped me make the decision to write it. This then led, over the course of the next eight years, to me facing and healing my PTSD, and publishing three books about all of it.

So, these three relationships led me down a path to the doorstep of dealing with the issues that were within me. It was at that point, a few days before the birth of my son, God spoke to me and told me that I would lose everything. He said it would be ok. It was necessary.

My first book was published in 2006. The day I finished writing the book, I was standing in my kitchen, and I told God that I was ready to do his work, whatever that may be. Over the course of the next four years, I lost everything. I lost two homes, my career of nearly 20 years, filed bankruptcy, lost my family and all my friends in the sense that they no longer talked to me, saw me, or even checked on me to see if I was ok.

Then my work began. As part of this work, I met the woman I have been with for the last 14 years (1+4=5: Falls under group #9 of my unconscious development). This we will discuss after we are finished with group #8 (i.e., my ego-conscious development). You will see how groups eight and nine are so closely related (my ego-conscious and unconscious development/negative and positive respectively).

- I published my first book (From group #8).
  - Got out of the hospital/lost my apartment. My girlfriend and I moved in with her dad (From group #6).
- I got out of my wheelchair after being in it for three years (From group # 6).
  - My girlfriend and I moved out of her dad's house and into an apartment and I finished healing my PTSD (from group #2).

The last two events of this group happened concomitant to each other resulting in the healing of my PTSD. Writing my first book and publishing it began the process of dealing with my PTSD, which was caused by my childhood, the war, and the subsequent events of my life. Writing the first book accomplished the goal of releasing all of the emotionally charged memories the events of my life had created. A few years subsequent to this, I was in and out of the hospital twice and put on several different types of medications at once.

The woman I have been with for 14 years was with me through all of it. We lost the apartment we were living in after losing my houses, job and beginning the bankruptcy process. We moved in with her dad and during that time, I had begun writing my second book. However, I stopped writing it as my PTSD got worse. I was put on even more medication, seven different ones in total, and all that culminated in me ending up in a wheelchair for several years.

After being in that wheelchair for three years, I got to the point where enough was enough. This was no way to live. My life must be about something more than being a doped-up Veteran in a wheelchair. I decided that I was going to find a way to heal on my own. First, I forced myself out of the wheelchair. Then, six months later, I quit all seven medications I was on cold turkey. It had to happen that way. What I mean is, that once I wrote the first book and let all that mental baggage out, it took several years for it all to unravel. Me deciding to heal and be done with all that stuff was a symbol that I was done releasing and experiencing all those emotions, and I was now ready to heal the damage all that trauma caused. As I mention in my third book, healing takes time, so give yourself that. It took time to get that way, it will take time to heal. I can see all of this now. It is obvious to me now that my mind is clear and not encumbered with "baggage." However, when I was going through all of that, I could not see it. That is why I say in my third book, *The Sword and the Anvil: A definitive guide for natural, healthy healing from Post-Traumatic Stress and trauma*, that one of the things I needed to do to heal, was to become a student of my life. Everything was there that I needed to heal, to understand what I had been through, and why. That was key for me to heal and develop properly.

This is where my current girlfriend and I moved out of her dad's house into a new apartment, and I healed my PTSD. It was during that time that I finished and published my second book. Then I wrote and published my third book about healing from PTSD in healthy, natural ways in 2016 (2+0+1+6=9: The ending of a positive phase and the ending of my unconscious development). I had always thought afterword's, that those two books should have been one book. Thus, this book would have been my third book and not the fourth. Before I wrote my first book about being in the war in 2006 (2+0+0+6=8: Ending of a negative phase and the ending of my ego-conscious development), a psychic told me that I was going to write two or three books. However, she was not sure which. She also had mentioned that because of the last book, people would go back and buy the first two books, and someone would make a movie about me and my life. She then said that they would want me to be on set to make sure it was accurate and that I would become very wealthy and famous.

- Moved to a new house with my current girlfriend (From group #8).

All the previous events in their entirety brought me to this point where my current girlfriend and I moved from our apartment into a new house in January of 2017, and that is where I completed my individuation process. The culmination of this is symbolized by the completion of this book. All of this leaves me pondering just what is going to happen next and it leaves me in great awe. I approach this portion of my life with excitement and confidence that it will all happen perfectly, the way it is supposed to, and that it will all be ok.

- Total of 35 significant events in my life which adds up to 8 (3+5=8).

Now, I have a complete understanding of the development of my ego-conscious and its purpose. You can clearly see, based on the events of group #8, how I was able to label it as the development, and ultimately the cleansing of, my ego-consciousness (i.e., my manhood and what society made me). Therefore, we will now discuss group #9 and the odd numbered events associated with it.

Group #9 (End of positive period, development of my unconscious)

- My parents got divorced (From group #9).
  - I was born (From group #3).
  - Trouble with bullies in school (From group #3).
  - Left for boot camp (From group #1).
  - Arrived in Saudi Arabia for the 1st Gulf War (From group #3).
  - Wife left/Got divorced (From group #3).

- Got out of Marines (From group #1).
- Got home to live with my dad (From group #3).
- Went to jail because of a girlfriend's lies (From group #5).

Obviously, I had to be born for any of this to occur. My parents got divorced when I was about 10 years old. This began my unconscious development. It caused me, or perhaps I should say guided me, to become introverted, to live within myself. As I got older and into junior high, I began to have problems at school and at home. I used to get beat up and picked on all the time, and then when I went home, I would get yelled at some more. All of this forced me to live even more introvertedly within myself, as this was the only way I could escape the trauma I was going through daily.

After I moved to a new state with my mother to escape all of this, my interest in the Marines developed. Because these traumatic experiences were now gone from my life, I had space to think with no distractions. These experiences also helped me to think from within, to "trust my gut" so to speak (i.e., my intuition and instincts). I began seeing commercials and advertisements in magazines, etc., about the Marines and how they were the best, how tough they were. I felt like I had something to prove to myself. I had to prove to myself that I was not a skinny, little whimp.

As time went on the desire to join the Marines became stronger. It was so strong that I had to do it. In fact, I still remember being in high school before I joined the Marines and telling my mother that we were going to have another war. It would be 15 years after Vietnam ended, which would be 1990. Vietnam ended in 1975. I told her that I was going to be in the Marines, and I would be in that war. Sure enough, in 1990, the first Gulf War started. I had been in the Marines for two years at that point and I was sent to fight on the front lines of that war.

I also remember watching the movie, "**Rambo First Blood**," co-written by Sylvester Stallone, and watching how he was a loner who had problems from the war. I knew I was going to be like him in the movie. There was also a song from Huey Lewis and the News (my favorite band), *"Walking on a thin line,"* that was about PTSD. I instantly liked it and somehow resonated with the words in it. It was like I knew I would completely be able to relate to it someday, that I would live it. Therefore, on February 10th, a few days after my 18th birthday in 1988, I joined the Marines. Several months later, after graduating high school, I left for boot camp.

Because of my experiences in the war, the fact that we were told 90% of us would die the first day of the ground war, and the memories of my three war dreams, I became very spiritual. I prayed relentlessly. I had turned inward again even more deeply than before. Thus, the experiences of the war guided me into a deeper development of my unconscious.

During the war, I had met my future ex-wife through a series of letters she anonymously began sending me. Here, another side of my unconscious was developed in terms of cultivating the intense, internal emotions that are associated with being in love. This was a first for me. Hence, this very nurturing, caring side (or feminine side) of a male, had begun to be developed with this event of my life.

A year after we got married, she left me and subsequently, we got divorced. This hurt me and caused me to live within once again. Only this time, it began an introverted process where I did not care about anything or anyone. This is where my unconscious was getting "beat up." I was being prepped and stripped for yet another series of events in the further development of my unconscious.

After my ex-wife left me, I got out of the Marines in 1992 and moved back home with my father. This is where I began to turn within even more, looking for direction on what I wanted to do with my life. I was working at a robotics factory and taking machine shop/engineering classes at a community college (not the one I attended years later for Anthropology). I had found out my ex-wife was pregnant when I got home from the Marines. I knew it was not mine. However, over the course of a few months while I was working and going to school, I began to feel guilty. I had this strong urge to move back to where my mother and ex-wife were. That way I could take care of business. My ex-wife had convinced me during this time at my fathers, that the baby was mine and I blindly believed her without really knowing for sure. So, I had to follow my internal intuition and go.

Several months after moving back to my mothers, the baby was born. I helped deliver it. Then, two weeks later, my ex-wife called me on the phone and told me the baby was not really mine and that she did it just to make me angry. I never saw or heard from her again. This then led to another series of events down a new path. Now I can see that the purpose for her being in my life, was to get me to move back to the state where I lived when I had joined the Marines. Obviously, as if I even need to say it, there is a reason I needed to be there.

Shortly after all of that, I was kicked out of my mother's house. I had a low paying job as a waiter and a cook at a restaurant. I had no money and nowhere to go. So, I lived in my truck while working there and eventually saved enough money to rent a room in a house. The house was filled with people who were addicted to crystal meth. At this point, I got a second job working at a bank to make more money. While doing all of this, I started dating a new girl. She was a completely different person from someone I would normally associate with. Before this, I was very judgmental about appearances. However, there was a change in my unconscious thinking based on these past events and I began to think, "You can't judge a book by its cover. Maybe I should be more open minded."

This relationship ended upon me going to jail for the night based on lies she constructed and told the Police. Upon getting out of jail, I got the matter resolved appropriately and the charges were dropped. However, there was a reason for this relationship. During this time of dating her and working two jobs I had another strong intuition to start my own business. It just so happened that her mother had a landscape maintenance business and was selling it. So, I followed my unconscious guidance yet again, and bought it from her. This led me to a community college because I wanted to expand my business by getting a degree in Landscape Architecture. However, upon beginning, I had an art history class. We started talking about Egypt and all its associated artifacts. It was like the class had put a fire in my belly. My intuition (i.e., my gut) was telling me that this is what I need to do for a living. So right after class that day, I changed my degree to Anthropology with an emphasis on archaeology.

- Transferred from community college to a university to finish my degree (From group #9).
  - Graduated from college, got a full-time job as an Assistant Archaeologist for a local city government and bought my 1st home (From group #3).
  - My son was born, and I met my next girlfriend (From group #5).

At this point, I had finished my community college education and I transferred to a major university where I obtained a bachelor's degree in Anthropology with an emphasis on archaeology. Because of that, I obtained a full-time job as an Assistant Archaeologist to my boss. He is the one who started teaching me how to write and introduced me to Carl Jung. As I was working on my writing skills, I started acquiring all the books about Carl Jung and his methods that I could. At the time, I did not know why I had such a strong feeling to buy those books. I just knew I had to do it. I somehow knew that I would need them later. There on my shelf they sat, for the next several years.

Also, during this period, I met the woman who would become the mother of my son. That ended horribly as well. However, it led to the "stripping" of everything in my life as God had told me would happen. It also taught me that because of her and my past relationships, I was never going to handle another relationship the same way.

About six months after she had left me, I met another woman through work. When we started dating, she would call me every two weeks and want to go out. So, I would oblige. I had decided I was not going to force things. I would just go with my "gut" (unconscious guidance). I figured I would let it go wherever she wanted to take it. That way, the worst thing that could happen is that I could end up with a friend, and who could not use that. Here we are, still together after nearly 16 years. She has been by my side throughout my entire PTSD and healing journey. If it wasn't for her, I would've been living on the street homeless, and finished for sure.

- I lost both of my houses and moved to an apartment where my PTSD got worse (From group #9).
  - I went to the hospital for the 1st time for my PTSD (From group #5).
  - I went to the hospital the 2nd time for my PTSD (From group #3).
  - I ended up in a wheelchair (From group #3).
  - I quit taking all my medications cold turkey (From group #1).
  - I began to heal on my own in healthy, natural ways (From group #1).
  - I published my 3rd book (From group #3).

As I have stated, losing all the things in my life had cleared the way for me to move forward and heal. Hence, my healing process began. I was provided with the opportunity and the space with which to complete it in. Earlier in the book, I mentioned the Greek word, "Temenos," meaning safe spot where one could complete their mental work safely. This is what my girlfriend was for me. She provided me with my safe spot where I could conduct my work.

Obviously, with me being in the hospital a few times, being in a wheelchair and on all kinds of medications, I needed a safe spot to conduct my mental work. This gave me the opportunity to concentrate on writing my next two books, which allowed me to release all this trauma and damage in constructive ways. This completed my mental cleansing and gave form and permanence to everything I have learned. Now that literally ***everything*** was cleared from me and healed, I was ready to move on to somewhere new and complete my individuation process. At this point, we moved into a new home in January of 2017 (2+0+1+7=10:1+0=1: Period of volatility).

- All the numbers of the 35 events add together (1+2=3+3=6+4=10+5=15, etc.) to get a total of 630, which added together equals 9 (6+3+0=9: Ending of positive period).

These events in group #9 and the odd numbered events prior to nine comprise the development of my unconscious. You can clearly see how both groups eight (ego-conscious: Negative) and nine (Unconscious: Positive) are closely related and both necessary. It is at this point, over the course of the next two years, I completed the work of my individuation process where I worked on incorporating my unconscious guidance (dreams and intuition) into my conscious life and living it accordingly. This culminated in form and permanence with the writing of this book.

What occurred simultaneously throughout my life is that my ego-consciousness was developed and stripped. My unconscious was developed and stripped. Therefore, a pure ego-conscious body and a pure unconscious spirit were left and now completely developed. This was done so that I could now carry on with living my life as a whole self. In essence, I was being prepared throughout my life to be able to complete the individuation process in middle aged adulthood. This last phase began with me taking the time to study my entire life.

Me writing this book is the completion of not only the reddening phase of the individuation process, but the completion of the individuation process itself. As a matter of fact, the day I finished writing this section of the book was 2/14/2018, which added together equals nine (2+1+4+2+0+1+8=18, then 1+8=9). Now, remember nine is the group of events that transpired in relationship to the development of my unconscious and ended a positive period. I also find it highly ironic that during the entire time that I was writing this book, I was waking up at either eight or nine o'clock every single morning!

While I was writing this book, I was given guidance by my unconscious on what to write, how to write it and when to write. I gave my unconscious my complete attention and I adhered to each one of its instructions. Then, there were periods where I would put everything away for a while so things could sink in. My life experiences created this book. This book represents the final stage of my development. I am giving it permanent form in this world. By doing this, I am taking what I have learned and putting it into an art form (a book), which Jung says is supposed to occur. This is how we finalize our individuation process and solidify what we have learned (i.e., giving what I have learned permanence in the world). That precipitates a total and complete understanding by the individual concerned.

Therefore, a numerical system has revealed itself to me through this analysis of my life, which seems to connect matter with my personal psyche. This system is particular to my individual life. However, I surmise that everyone has their own particular system present in their own lives. Those same numbers may show up for you, but their symbolism and meaning will be different for you than they were for me. Or, one may find a completely different set of numbers, or system, relative to their own individual life. After all, this is called the individuation process. I believe the numerical system and its meaning would be revealed to each person who takes the time to study and analyze their life as I have conducted with mine. It's all relative to the individual you are, which is revealed at the culmination of the "individuation" process. And, at that point, one is able to move on and live as a whole self in proper, intended form. This is what I believe I have ascertained from analyzing my own very individual, personal life.

PART 2

The Whitening:

The reunion of my spirit with my body beginning an elimination of the impurities of my life.

CHAPTER 3

In this chapter, we are going to discuss what I call my "guidance" that I received in the form of dreams. This all took place from 8/31/2017 to 1/13/2020. In January of 2017, my girlfriend and I moved into the new house we just bought. Moving into the new house was part of group #6 and ultimately fell under group #8. If you recall, all the even events prior to group #8 represented the development of my ego-consciousness. It also represented the ending of a bad phase and the beginning/transition into a new phase of my life. This new phase was comprised of me understanding and incorporating my unconscious guidance into my life. Then, conducting my conscious life accordingly. That is what moving into the new house symbolized and began.

I will analyze these dreams and discuss what they meant to me personally. Remember, that while there are general explanations to dreams and their symbolism, I had to consider my own individuality, who I am as a person, the circumstances of my personal life and what exactly these dreams and symbols meant to me. As I meditated on the meanings of my dreams and their symbols, I used general explanations to guide me through the process. Quite often, they have several different meanings to them. So, what I did was read them all and focus on the one definition that meant something to me, that stood out to me, and/or gave me that feeling in my gut, my intuition, that I had to learn to completely trust. I also had to focus on the people, places, and things in my dreams because they were specific to me. In other words, they meant something to me only. Or they stirred up a feeling, thought, or emotion that was personal to me. These symbols were also there because they would help me remember my dreams.

For example, say I dreamt about an ex-girlfriend. The dream is symbolic and not meant to be taken literally. So, it requires meditation and careful thought about its meaning. If the process were too easy, we would never learn the important lesson, or be able to properly interpret its message. Also, when we interpret our dreams, we sometimes learn unnerving and or unwanted things about ourselves. If we were just given this information all at once, we would either ignore it or it would shock us and derail our development. We are human. That is the way we are built and the bane of our existence. So, in this dream example, the fact that my ex-girlfriend is female is important. That symbolizes my unconscious (i.e., my inner self, my female side). Everyone and everything must have proper balance. This is what the yin and the yang symbolize. There is pretty and ugly, fat, and skinny, rich and poor, male and female, good and bad. It is the way of the Universe. Therefore, to have that proper balance as a male, I must have a female side as well. This would be represented by my unconscious. It is the reverse for a female.

The fact that the female in my dream is an ex-girlfriend also means something especially important. Therefore, I would have to meditate upon what she meant to me, who she was as a person, etc. Then, I would have to put the two symbolistic meanings together and come up with an answer on what the dream means to me and the message therein. From this point, I would then follow the guidance of my dream by incorporating its meaning into my physical life. Thereby, making the unconscious guidance conscious, and thus, being in proper balance. Remember, the Universe requires that everything be in proper balance. When it is not, that's when problems occur. Study history, politics, society, religion, etc., and you will see what I am talking about.

Therefore, say that in real life my ex was very closed and unemotional. Say, she was domineering and had to be in charge and then we had a hurtful breakup. These are all male traits per say. So, to interpret this properly, I would have to surmise that my unconscious (my female side) is telling me not to live out of balance, not to live from one side more than the other. Also meaning that if I live out of balance in this way, bad or unwanted things will happen. Also, by my unconscious using my ex-girlfriend as a symbol of this in my dream, it will help me to remember it in the morning as it would have an effect on me. Dreaming about my ex-girlfriend is not meant to be taken literally. In other words, it does not mean I am going to see her again. It does not mean that I still have feelings for her, or that she does for me. It is all symbolic.

Before we discuss my dreams, let us first recall that previously I mentioned the three stages of the individuation process outlined by Jung. These are related to the three stages of the alchemical process of modification as outlined by Jung in his book, "*Alchemy*". Those three stages are:

1. "***The Blackening:*** *The mental union in the overcoming of the body; the healing of all ills.*" This relates to the first stage of my development and all the things I went through as a child and how I dealt with it, how I overcame the limitations of my body regarding the bullies and my family by joining the Marines and making it through the war, thereby healing those ills of my youth. In order to accomplish this, I had to use my mental strength to overcome the limitations of my body. This all resulted in my first book (i.e., giving permanency to it in an art form so that I completely understood what I had just learned as we just discussed and also to inspire others).

2. "***The Whitening:*** *Reunion of the spirit with the body; elimination of impurities; changing of spirit into body.*" This relates to the second stage of my development where, because of the PTSD and all that I had been through, I was trying to heal by finding myself, finding out who I really was, and I began to do this through spiritual means. In order to get in tune with my spirituality, I realized I had to eliminate the impurities in my life, such as using prescription medications to cope (i.e., reunite my spirit with my body). Those things place a barrier between spirit and your body. In other words, fix the separation of the parts of my true self and make myself whole again. During that period of my life, I felt completely isolated and separated from everything. During this whole time, I felt lost. It was like I was just a face in a sea of people, and I did not know who I was. This all resulted in my second and third books be published,

which I thought should have been one book. I felt I rushed them, and I just did not quite completely understand what was going on yet. I did not understand the much bigger picture of life yet, and I thought I was done with my work when I healed the PTSD. I did not yet understand that I had only completed two phases of a three-phased developmental process.

3. *"**The Reddening:** Binding the soul to either good or to evil, the soul and spirit are separated from the body and instinctual impulses are repeatedly modified into a higher, or socially more acceptable activities."* This relates to the third stage of my development, which is what I have completed now. This was where I either bound my soul to good and my true self, or to evil and materialistic things of this world, which all have results that are fleeting. In other words, it is a way of acting. It is where I learn to either trust my unconscious guidance and follow it, or physically try to control the outcome of things in my life myself through my ego. This is where I must continually modify my instinctual impulses for the physical things of life that Society has taught us, we need, must do, or think. In other words, eliminate any sort of dependence on physical/material external things. Instead, I needed to evolve, or perfect myself, so that my instinctual impulses are to turn within, to spirit. All of this resulted in my fourth book being published, which you are reading now, and hence, I am free to live my life as my real, whole self. Thereby, conducting myself and my activities in a higher, more socially acceptable way and conducting the work I was put here to do in order to inspire others.

These three stages of the individuation process also are related to the three dreams I had throughout my childhood about me being in the Revolutionary war, Civil War and Vietnam. All of which resulted in me being wounded in the same three places in the chest where my heart is located. This all was not only to symbolize that this time (i.e., in this life), if I did not advance and overcome my past and evolve, it would again destroy my heart (i.e., my center), metaphorically, and eventually, physically killing me. Also, they were to remind me of Jung's three stages of individuation and how to overcome all of this to get to my true self.

Therefore, my revolutionary war dream relates to stage one: **Blackening**, in the sense that the Revolutionary war was really the mental union of all the colonies in physically overcoming the body of England. The Civil war dream relates to stage two: **Whitening**, in the sense that the Civil war was about reuniting the bifurcated country into a whole again, eliminating the impurities of society and signifying a transformation. The Vietnam dream relates to stage three: **Reddening**, in the sense that the Vietnam war was about binding the soul to either good or evil (i.e., freedom or communism) and modifying people's instinctual impulses to blindly serve a country/military, or doing copious amounts of illicit drugs and alcohol, to achieve a state of peace, which is all everyone really wanted in the true form of the word. However, they were having problems throughout society and turning to the wrong physical, material things to achieve a state of peace, happiness, and freedom. In other words, it was about eliminating all those socially unacceptable activities, behaviors, and social policies to a point where a new, clearer, purer, more socially acceptable society could be formed.

Within the last few months of writing this, I had several dreams. In these dreams the usual suspects of colors, numbers and symbols appeared. My unconscious was providing me with more insight into my conscious life and what I needed to be doing and focusing on. On the one hand, I had been grappling with the activities and ideas of the conscious and unconscious parts of my life. On the other hand, I was struggling with the process of joining the two together and implementing them into my life.

I was walking up and down the beach by the blue ocean, then walking up the sidewalk against a steady flow of clear water. Then, I saw Frida in a red dress. Next, I was falling asleep in a class at school. Finally, my father was telling me he spent 760 bucks and only had 750 left.

For me the sea, or ocean, symbolizes the connecting of the unconscious and conscious mind. Something that I had just explained my mind had recently been occupied with. After realizing this, I began to think about this affinity I have had ever since I could remember with being on the water, especially the sea. A lot of my conscious "awake" time has been spent dreaming of living by the sea, or on a big boat on the sea in a harbor somewhere. I have always longed to live in San Diego, or in San Clemente, California right next to the water so I could see it and experience it every day. The Ocean to me represents total peace and relaxation. Something I just explained we all crave. Obviously, I have been craving this connection of my conscious and unconscious much, much longer than I had suspected. The joining of the two is where total peace, relaxation and true happiness come from. Not from material, physical things produced by man here on earth. Those are all fleeting and leave us craving more and more. That is where addiction and abuse steps in.

The blueness of the water suggests I have unconscious emotions that are heavy and deep, which I clearly did. The clear water, which I am walking against the flow of on the sidewalk, suggests my emotions are clear, I am in touch with them, my true nature, and my spirituality, which I was. However, the fact that I am walking against the water flow is quite important. To me, this suggests that I am going against my intuition, instincts and experiencing difficulties because of that. In other words, I am making things harder for myself than they need to be by physically trying to force the outcome of things instead of trusting my unconscious guidance and following it. This must be done with the understanding that whatever I need in life will be provided for me, without me trying to force it, as long as I complete the work I am supposed to complete (i.e., the individuation process).

In the last part of this dream, I dreamt of Frida in a red dress. This red dress relates back to the three phases of individuation and specifically the third phase: **Reddening**. If you recall, this is the final stage where the binding of the soul to either the evil or good occurs. This is where the soul and spirit are separated from the body and an instinctual impulse, such as a behavior or routine, is repeatedly modified until it is a higher, more socially acceptable behavior. This occurs until we are rid of the impurities and a clarity, or pureness, is achieved. Red is also a known symbol for one's passion. This represented my passion for writing, which I was getting away from because of all the things I was doing in my daily life. I obviously needed to modify my behavior and routine so that I could obtain a clarity and a pureness. In other words, knock off what I was doing, obtain a clarity about what is going on and get back to writing so that I can complete this process of individuation.

In the last part of my dream, I was falling asleep in class at college. This suggests to me that I am ignoring my training, my teachings. In other words, I am falling asleep on what I am supposed to be doing. Thus, ignoring it.

This all, leads me to realize that I have this need to join my conscious with my unconscious making a more complete self. I am in touch with my emotions and spirituality. I also know what I need to do, but I am going against the flow. I am making it harder than this really needs to be. Perhaps, and quite emphatically, I am operating from what society has taught me in my conscious life instead of what my unconscious is trying to teach me from within (i.e., my true self, who I really am). Therefore, it is blatantly obvious to me that a decision must be made here. Do I bind my soul to good and complete the Reddening phase and thus, the individuation process? Or do I bind my soul to evil and continue facing obstacle after obstacle until I "get it"?

Finally, there were two significant numbers in the dream, 750 and 760. In the dream my father was saying that he spent 760 dollars and all he had left was 750 dollars. If you add up each series of numbers, 750 and 760, you get 12 and 13, respectively. Then if you add 1+2 you get 3 and 1+3 you get 4. This is important because those two groups of events (3 and 4) led to the publication of my second and third books and the ending of a phase. Now, if you take 750 + 760 you get 1510. If you add 1+5+1+0 you get 7. Group number seven had only one event and it was a transition into a whole new phase of my development, the Reddening phase. The transition into this phase took 22 years to complete. So, my father (who represents my ego-conscious and to me stubbornness, meanness, and toughness) saying that he spent 760 bucks and has only 750 left, suggests to me that I have spent more than half my time on this phase. In other words, I have spent more time on this than I was supposed to because of my stubbornness, toughness, and meanness (i.e., my conscious being in control to long) and I had better get to it as my time to complete this is running short.

It was at this point that I also started looking up numbers online to see what they mean symbolically. Obviously, numbers were important to me because of the life analysis that I conducted, which drew my attention to them. So, I wanted to dig deeper, learn more and add to my knowledge. With that in mind, I looked up 750, 760, 12, 13, 1510, and 7. I went through several sites online, but one really resonated with me. So, I stuck with it. It is called Angel Numbers-Joanne Sacred Scribes. I will paraphrase what the site said these numbers mean.

750: *The important decisions you are making will bring positive changes, which will bring about great opportunities in your life. These changes will have a direct result on your daily activities because you will be devoting more time towards your spiritual endeavors and life purpose. You will have opportunities to expand your spiritual awareness because of these positive changes in your life. Be ready to receive messages and info from unexpected sources. Stay alert to any interesting new experiences, surroundings, and people. Remain open to interesting ideas, new revelations, and epiphanies. Listen to your intuition. These changes will align you with your soul purpose and they will make your life better. Continue along this path with passion and confidence. This is all happening for a higher purpose. Your angels are always with you and by your side.*

760: *Explore every part of yourself. Focus on yourself, your home, your family, and financial matters. You are being congratulated for so diligently working on your divine life purpose. Your strong connection with the divine realms has manifested great opportunities for you to quickly advance along your spiritual path. You are encouraged by your angels to continue to listen to your intuition and angelic guidance. Keep up the good work and all of your material needs will be met along the way. Now is the best time to expand your awareness through research, study, and learning. Now is the best time to look at classes, courses and books that resonate with your interests. The right avenues will appear at just the right time.*

12: *Do not be held back by old habits that need to be changed. Look to your new experiences optimistically. They will bring about positive changes and opportunities. These will help you achieve your goals. It also allows the old to be replaced with the new. Look for different ways to improve your home and surroundings. This also includes within your home. Surround yourself with love and happiness. Make sure whatever you put out into the Universe is of a positive nature. Stay on this positive path and use your natural talents to their best for the benefit of yourself and others.*

13: *There may be some upheavals happening in your life. This is occurring for karmic reasons and will break new ground for you, which will bring new opportunities for you to grow spiritually. Adapt to these changes with grace. It may be a blessing in disguise. You are being guided and assisted with your soul mission. Your angels and Ascended Masters are by your side as you go through all of this. This will bring you into alignment with your Divine life purpose. If you ever are unsure, ask your angels for help.*

1510: *Your positive thoughts and intentions are manifesting rapidly. This will bring about beneficial, important life changes for you. Stay positive, avoid negative situations and people. Your positivity will determine the outcome of the changes. Be positive and go in the direction of your goals. You will find success on all levels. Spend some time alone meditating. Take time to reflect, to develop your insight, your confidence and wisdom in regard to your own experiences. Living life involves learning, evolving, and growing through them.*

7: *This will be a beneficial time of you overcoming obstacles and realizing successes. Your angels are happy with your life choices, and you are on the right path. Keep up the good work you are doing successfully serving your soul purpose and mission. Your angels are supporting you all the way. Positive things will flow to you to help you along your journey. Look further into developing your spirituality and encourage others to do the same. Learn new skills, listen to your intuition, step out of your comfort zone in order to further develop and advance on all levels. You have an important soul mission and life purpose which involves communicating, teaching, and healing others all while serving humanity in a manner that suits you best. Set a positive example and inspire* *them to seek their own passion and purpose in life. Take up a spiritually based practice, profession, or career if you are inclined to do so.*

The very next night, as if my unconscious was not done teaching me about this, I had another dream. In the dream several significant things occurred and there was more color symbolism, but the dream focused more on specific events that would mean something to me personally. At one point in the dream, I had a plant that had bugs all over it. So, I did something to it to make it better and hornets flew out of it after me. I became enraged and said, "Now I'm going to spray it." Someone else in the dream then said, "no, it's only going to make it worse."

This was important as it also takes me back to the conscious and unconscious parts of life. In this case, I have a plant covered in bugs and I was trying to control the problem/force a result. That resulted in the situation only getting worse. Then, I wanted to spray it, which is me yet again trying to physically control the situation. I heard a voice telling me not to do it as it will only make it worse. This suggested to me that I need to quit trying to physically force things to happen in my life. I need to focus on listening to my intuition and go with the flow. I need to focus on and listen too, my unconscious guidance, not my conscious influences. This reminds me of the three stages of individuation.

In the next part of the dream, I took the plant over to the couch. It was in a green pot, which in the dream seemed to be the source of the problem. I then proceeded to yank the plant out of the pot by the roots and I dumped out the dirt. Then, the person who owned the pot walked by. I handed them the pot and I said, "It's over." The green color of the pot symbolizes my need to establish myself financially and professionally, wanting recognition and maintaining control. I had been doing exactly that. I have been trying to do things my whole life to establish myself financially and professionally, without being focused on what I was really supposed to be doing. I was living my life thinking *I was* in control. I have always done things and wanted recognition for them and never got it. This only upset me, so I would try to accomplish something else in hopes of getting that recognition. I have always tried to maintain some sense of control over my life and its results, as that is what everyone and society had taught me to do. This desire to get recognition was designed to take me precisely down this path so that I may learn.

The lesson here with all this, is that I am focused on all the wrong things, and I am trying to physically bring about a desired result. What I need to do is focus on what I am supposed to be doing, such as perfecting and evolving myself so that I can be my true self, to write about it to solidify the learning and publish it so that it is out in the world for others to become inspired. Quite often, I believe that what the soul, or individual needs, humanity needs as well. This is how we change the world. This is how we inspire it to be a better place. We do this by being the change we want to see. That is summed up by the Dali Lama when he said, "Yesterday I was stupid and tried to change the world. Today I am wise, and I changed myself." I have this quote hanging on my office wall at home.

Therefore, by focusing on that and what I am supposed to do, not only do I positively grow myself, but I positively affect the world. I stay focused by paying attention to my intuition, the guidance that is given to me and trusting that it is the right thing for me and my development. Again, this takes me back to the uniting of the conscious with the unconscious, the third stage of the individuation process of personal development (i.e., the Reddening).

After these series of dreams, I had a few more. They were a bit of a different nature in the sense that they were full of symbolism in terms of colors and things like water. They did not contain any numbers as one of the last ones did. The two colors in these dreams that appeared were black and red. Both of which again refer to the three stages of individuation in personal development, the Blackening (first stage) and the Reddening (the third and final stage).

I was in a heavy rainstorm and went into a tent. The second dream I had that evening had aliens in it who came here and were grabbing women and wanting to mate with them. The whole time they kept saying, "One woman, one man."

The heavy rainstorm represents a turmoil or conflict in my waking life. Me going into a tent represents to me that I am hiding from it and/or not acknowledging it. This second dream represents the total, or complete self. In other words, the joining of my unconscious and conscious parts of life to make a whole, or complete person, which is what I needed to do.

The dreams I had were a series. I would wake up, fall back asleep and the dream would pick right up where I left off when I had awoken.

I was back in an old bar I used to hang out in many years ago. I saw people there I once knew and hung out with. They were still there, still doing the same things, after all this time. They had not advanced, grown or accomplished anything positive. The only changes that occurred were that their bodies had been physically changing in a negative way and their personalities had gotten negative to the point where I had to leave. I no longer wanted to be around them. I was leaving, and I found an old jacket I had left there. Only now, it was all dirty, black, and smelly. So, I left and went outside into the parking lot. I could not find my truck and then it began to rain extremely hard. The rest of the dream contained heavy rain, flooding, rushing water and waterfalls.

These dreams are quite interesting to me. For a few weeks prior to having them, I was struggling with trying to figure out what I should be doing. I was wondering if I should set up a schedule and spend half the day writing and the other half marketing my books? Or, what about the stock market, my five-year plan, and taking care of the house? If I do nothing but writing and marketing, I will not have time for any of those other things I like to do. I did not want to give up doing them either. Then, I asked myself if I should I write out a schedule each week and schedule all these things?

I then asked myself, why must I change? Why do I have to quit doing some of these things I like to do and do other things I do not like to do. Then I had those two dreams. So, I began to interpret the dreams in the context of those questions I had asked myself, and with what was going on in my conscious life at that moment. These dreams were answering my questions. The heavy rainstorms suggest I have a conflict in my conscious life, which I did. The dream of me being in a bar where I used to hang out, seeing people I used to know, who had not progressed, was telling me that I have changed and moved on. It also symbolizes me letting go of my past and my past ways of living. The dream is telling me it is time to let go of it all and leave it where it belongs, in the past. It was time for me to move on to something else. It is also telling me that those who ignore the path of self-evolution never progress. Moreover, those people simply digress (symbolized by the people I knew in the bar). This also caused me to pay attention to the people around me who have not progressed, who keep doing the same things over and over again. Then, I realized how their problems do not go away, how the quality of their lives deteriorates, and yet they still refuse to change. No matter what happens.

The turbulent water in my dream represents stress, emotional unbalance, or difficulties, which I was clearly having. The waterfall in my dream is remarkably interesting indeed. To me, the waterfall symbolizes letting go, releasing pent up emotions and bad feelings, which is what I was trying to do. It is even more apropos when I take it another step further in the sense that I am writing about all of this as I go through it. That is an extremely healthy, constructive way of releasing things, such as emotions that are attached to memories. This is something I have been doing since I first started trying to heal myself from my childhood and the war. That is when I wrote my first book, "*A Line in the Sand: The true story of a Marine's experience on the front lines of the Gulf War.*" I then continued that process and wrote my second book, "***Chrysalis: A metamorphosis has begun.***" Then I wrote my third book, "***The Sword and the Anvil: A definitive guide to healthy, natural healing from Post-Traumatic Stress and Trauma.***" My dream is clearly telling me to keep writing, keep developing and keep sharing it with the world in order to inspire people, in order to illuminate the way, so to speak. This is how I should deal with all of this and how I should proceed. This is the work that I currently need to be doing in order to release all my past ways of living and thinking.

The waterfall in my dream was crystal clear. This is significant because that represents a revitalization, regeneration, or renewal. My dream is telling me that by continuing to write about this, (i.e., finishing and completing my work) I will be "renewed." However, after coming to all these conclusions from my analysis, I was still left with this problem of trying to figure out if I need to make a schedule and sit down every day to write for eight hours. The problem is, I just cannot sit down and force myself to write. I must be inspired to do so. I must feel it, then do it. Sometimes, I write several days in a row and then take a break for a while. Sometimes I write one day and do not get back to it for a week. I must allow things to sink in and settle after I write about them. I then remembered that is how I wrote my first three books. The first one took six years, the second about four years and the third two years.

I quickly realized this is how I write. This is my process. This then left me to contemplate how long it would take me to complete this phase of my work, a year? I started working on this phase in earnest in June of 2016. I have a sticky note on my computer with the date 6/22/2018. I put that there two years ago as I was reading a book that led me down the path to completing the final portion of my individuation. The book said that if one embarks down a path, such as the one I am on, that person could completely change their lives in just two years. I put that date there when I still lived in my apartment and had begun studying for this part of my development. Only, at the time, I did not realize what I was actually studying for. I just knew I had to start doing it.

After these dreams and conclusions, I went back to my books, which I do anytime I am faced with any sort of dilemma or any question I need to answer. I came across some verses of the ***Tao Te Ching***, which at that time I was reading a verse of every day. A part of one of the verses talked about remaining hidden like a sprout and not rushing to an early ripening, which I now know is about the isolation of myself that was required to properly complete my development. I then came across another verse that talked about being less demanding of others and especially of myself, and that we are all free to work, play or not do anything.

The next few mornings, while I was having coffee with a friend, I noticed he kept asking me, "So what are you going to do today?" Write, research, yard work, stocks?" Then, those verses of the Tao hit me like a ton of bricks! That is the answer. I am free to do whatever I wish every day and that I should not rush anything. Just let nature take its natural course as the sprout does. I will accomplish what I need to accomplish, precisely when it needs to get done! My unconscious guidance will let me know what to do and when to do it. Just like when I become inspired to write and must do it. I decided right at that moment that I was no longer going to worry about the next day, the next moment, or what I was going to do. Time no longer really means anything. I declared to myself that I will no longer plan out a schedule or activities. I will simply do what I feel inspired to do that moment, that day. I will go with the flow of things. I will go with the flow of nature.

For the next couple months as I was practicing what I had learned from these series of dreams, I really did not have any dreams that I remembered when I awoke in the morning and had nothing to write down in my dream journal. Then, just after the beginning of December (about three months later), the prophetic dreams began once again, and I had to write them down as I remembered every detail when I awoke in the morning. Sometimes, I had to write them down in the middle of the night because I just could not fall back asleep if I did not do so.

I was outside in the white snow with a flannel shirt on and a black beanie cap. I was chopping down big, tall pine trees with an axe one by one, and the trees never seemed to end.

During the two days prior to this dream, I had been studying and learning about my personal development and growth. I was realizing that I must leave my personal story (the war, Marines, PTSD, old habits, and ways of thinking) behind me, so that I can make room for the next phase of my life at a higher, more socially acceptable level. Just like I had to lose everything to heal from my

PTSD. The purpose was that a clear, new slate would be prepared, which then would lead a to a new phase that was not encumbered by my past. However, I was not completely sure that I was supposed to leave all of this behind me this time, especially what I am doing for work (i.e., my book marketing and stock market). I figured the answer would be revealed to me at the appropriate time in just the right place. Perhaps, this dream is letting me know what is to come sometime in the future.

The black beanie on my head symbolizes my deep unconscious. The hat being round signifies the emergence of my unconscious. The hat on my head suggests that I should let my unconscious guide me, not my ego. The pine trees in this case, symbolize life and my connection to the upper and lower, my conscious and unconscious, my whole self. The fact that I was cutting down pine trees, one after another with an axe, symbolized that I was foolishly pursuing things that were a waste of my resources repeatedly, and that I was continuously cutting down my connection to my whole self by letting my ego rule my life instead of my unconscious. The snow I was standing in symbolizes the fact that I was frozen in time, in other words stuck. My development was at a standstill.

This was related to the things I was currently doing regarding marketing my books, social media stuff, radio show, etc. They were things that I was foolishly pursuing repeatedly through my ego, which were a waste of my resources. I am not able to progress to the next phase because I am wasting my efforts and resources on things I should not be. I need to let my personal story/past go. I need to detach from my ego, man's way of doing things, and regenerate and transform myself for the future. I must reunite my spirit with my body. In other words, focus on living as a whole self. I must live from my unconscious guidance. I must listen to and follow what it says via my dreams. That will bring the unconscious into my conscious life. Hence, being a complete self. In other words, my old habits, and ways of doing things need to be let go of so that I can develop spiritually and follow my proper path.

I was talking to my old boss. He was showing me these complicated diagrams, like engineering stuff that I did not understand, mostly because it was so small and blurry. I could not read it. I was worried he could smell alcohol on my breath because I had a few glasses of wine the night before. My boss kept coughing and complaining about having heartburn. He said it was his medicine that was causing it. I asked him if it was just his regular medicine. He said no, it was detox pills for alcohol and that he said he had been in jail all weekend.

Everything in this dream represents my past, old ways of thinking and acting, things that prevented me from moving forward. In other words, blockages. During that time, I did not have the courage to quit my job and pursue my dreams because I did not want to lose my job, which ended up happening anyways. Perhaps, this was to be a lesson to apply for the future. Through my unconscious I am letting go of my past/personal history and ways of thinking. It is as though my dreams are explaining to me not only what is happening, but what is going to happen in regard to the shedding of my past ways of thinking and acting. I need to make room for the next phase of my development to begin.

I ran this race where I had to climb this big greyish white hill made of rock for a mile and a half with tons of people. I had to climb on my hands and knees. I had to climb across these big ravines high up in the air using this white string and I used my fingers to do it. I was scared. Then I went to the museum and saw my old boss in his office. I was looking for folders for my papers. I laid down in a bed for a nap. When I woke up (in my dream) my penis looked sickly as it was sticking out of my pocket, and I was trying to hide it. There was this stuff on me and the sheets like blood, but I was not sure. When I saw all of this, I was scared. Then I went looking for my vehicle and could not find it. I ran into my boss again working in the snack shop. I kept running into people I knew but could never find my truck. I then woke up in the morning and recorded my dream.

This dream is telling me to remember all that I have accomplished and overcome in my past (the mountain I have climbed to get to this point). The next part of my journey at a higher level is all at my fingertips. I need to trust that higher guidance, my unconscious. It will guide me to success and completion of the next stage. It was showing me how my past has stifled me, blocked me, leaving me feeling anxious. I am running away from my real self, trying to hide my real self. Partly because I am growing in ways that scare or disturb me. Living from my unconscious guidance goes against everything I have been taught my entire life by my parents and society (i.e., ego). I am looking for the way to get there but because my past ways of thinking and behaving prevent me from doing so, I cannot find the way. In other words, if I do not let go of the past ways of thinking, behavior, activities, and ego, I will never find the way, I will never get there. I will be stuck. The fact that each time I saw my boss in the dream he was working, also symbolizes something. That boss in real life was always working. That is all he did was work on writing his books and publishing them. One after another. This means to me that I should be working relentlessly towards improving myself, towards my development like he worked towards the development of his career.

There was this red centipede that kept showing up in the house and raising its tail with its pinchers at me. Then I saw it attack this green grasshopper and eat its head. I also had to protect my dog from it, it almost stung him. At the end of the dream, I was having sex with my girlfriend. Her hair style was different, all frizzy, kind of like a perm and she was covered in oil and had lost some weight. I kept trying to have sex with her but never finished. I would start but then something would come up and I would not finish. Then when that incident was over, I would try again, and this would all repeat. I then woke up from my dream.

This dream symbolizes that I am letting my fears get the best of me and they are running my life. I just need to take that leap of faith and understand that I have the wisdom to meet any challenges head on. I just need to make the choice to make that "jump" and do it. If I do not do that, my fears and past will consume me and prevent me from becoming a whole self, my real self. I want fulfillment, stability, and balance in all aspects of my life. But if I do not make the necessary changes, I will never finish this transformational task. I keep trying, but I allow myself to get distracted by things. I also keep trying to physically force an outcome. I keep repeating that behavior. Then undesirable things keep happening. If I keep that up, I will never finish my individuation process. I keep repeating this ego conscious behavior. I am not progressing.

I must trust my higher guidance and listen to my messages from my unconscious. I must let go of the past. I need to focus on my transformation. Internally, I have everything I need to meet these challenges. I need to make the necessary changes and focus on the next phase of my life. Or I will never complete my task and live my soul purpose.

I had several more dreams after this, which continued along this same theme. All these dreams are saying the same thing to me repeatedly. I was supposed to be purifying myself, transforming myself, reuniting spirit and body now that the events of the development of my ego-consciousness were over. That part is complete. Now I need to start living purely from the guidance of my unconscious by bringing that into my conscious life.

I was also depressed during this time. Me constantly looking for things and not finding them or trying to do things and not completing them in my dreams, symbolized the anxiety of me not being able to find my way through my life. Or through my purification and transformation.

Interestingly enough, after all these dreams where my unconscious is beating me up trying to get me to make some changes, the message of my dreams began to change. As if I had begun to make those necessary changes in my conscious life, and I was now beginning to move through the rest of this process.

I was in my backyard and the people in the house behind me were having a party in their backyard. Only this time there were two big, square, red tents and a bunch of people and kids. They were making a lot of noise. I was getting really mad, and I wanted to yell at them, but something kept telling me to just let it go, it is only one night, and they will be over and done with it in a little while anyhow. It is not going to hurt anything.

Me being in my yard and surrounded by four walls symbolizes me trapped in my ego. The lady in the house behind our house is my unconscious. I do not know her, but I know of her. Her being in her back yard, which is square and behind four walls, symbolizes that my unconscious is separate from me. I am aware of my unconscious, but I am blocked from it. I am not accessing it. What I need to do is bring my unconscious contents into the light of my conscious, to join the two so I can be my whole self. I need to break down those walls.

Next in my dream, I hear a voice telling me what to do about her party and noise. I wanted to yell at her (my conscious trying to dominate); however, this voice (my unconscious) is telling me what to do. I need to listen to my unconscious and do what it says in order to de-potentiate my ego conscious. This will bring my unconscious guidance into my conscious life.

I was back in boot camp, but it was different, I was different. It was like I did not fit in, like it was not working out and I want to say I remember wanting or trying to bring alcohol with me to boot camp. The barracks I was in was square and filled with people.

This dream is telling me that the past is not who I am. It is time to move on from that part of my life. I need to quit trying to bring the past, false self with me. I have healed the mental damage from that part of my life. So, it is time to say goodbye to the past for good. That part of my life is over. My ego's development is complete. It is time to develop my unconscious.

After these dreams, I did not have any dreams for a couple of days. I was being given a couple days of rest to let these things settle in after my unconscious had beaten me up again.

I was in a restaurant in a square room again. I saw an ex-girlfriend outside. I opened the door to say hi and shake her hand. She said hi and gave me a hug and a kiss. It was kind of awkward. We talked. She said that she was running now. I got jealous and thought I should do that but realized that that was her path, her thing. I must follow my own path of transforming myself and do my own thing. Then there was this really loud noise and she left out the door. It got so loud I left to. I went to the restaurant next door. I went into another square room. My ex was sitting at a table with a woman I did not know. She sees me and looks to something else. So, I look to see what she is looking at. I see this guy I do not know walk up to me and hold out a white round plate with eight pieces of triangular, rust colored carrot cake on it arranged like spokes of a wheel. He says, "Here, try some." I declined and then I woke up from my dream.

This dream shows a shift in my unconscious in a few ways. Being in a square room symbolizes my inner self, my unconscious guidance. Walking up to my ex-girlfriend who is representing my unconscious, saying hi and giving her a hug and a kiss as she comes into the room symbolizes not only me acknowledging/meeting my unconscious, but also me accepting it into my conscious life. I was upset the day before about why some people work, have money, drink, treat other people badly, are egomaniacs and have no problems. Especially when I worked so hard all my life on all my books, made no money, had to get rid of my internet, cable tv, turn the heat off in the house, lost everything, etc. However, I realized that all that had to be done so my slate was clean from distractions, from all the ego things that had the power to influence and control me. That way I could concentrate on the next phase of my life.

The next part of my dream symbolizes just that indeed. When my ex tells me, she is running now, and she looked in shape, I got jealous and thought I needed to do that like her. Just like I do in real life. But then, In the dream, I realize that is her path and what she must do. My path is different, and I must do what I need to do and follow it. The next part of my dream symbolizes me realizing this and doing it.

In the next part of the dream the man symbolizes my conscious, the round plate is my center, it being white is the purity of it. The pieces of cake are a symbol of the quaternary (eight is double of four), which symbolizes the four stages of the individuation process. The fact that they are rust colored symbolizes the transformation of me into my real self. Rust is the material that is left over from the alchemical process of transforming stone into gold (i.e., oxidation). So, in my dream, rust is symbolic of the process of my transformation. The fact that they are triangular symbolizes the tendency of the universe to converge towards unity, towards a whole. All of this on the plate (including the plate) symbolizes the alchemical opus (i.e., the work/transformation into being whole). This all is a resemblance of the Triurti picture, which is a Hindu painting. It depicts all of this inside a square.

The last part of my dream is my unconscious guidance telling me that my conscious ego (the man) will try to tempt me to go back to my old ego conscious ways (the rust-colored carrot cake) and that I should "decline" that trick (me declining the cake). There are also four people in the square room at the end. My ex and the unknown woman both represent my unconscious because they are female. The unknown man represents my conscious and I represent myself. Because there are two women, one known and one unknown, the dream is telling me I have completed more work on my unconscious. However, I have more work to do transforming myself and becoming complete. Now, let's look at the numbers 4 (the number of people) and 8 (the pieces of cake) from my dream.

4: *This is telling me that I am supported in doing what I need to do to achieve my goals. When I act towards my goals things will work in my favor that will help me build solid foundations and give me guidance along my path.*

8: *Represents achievements, success and moving forward. I need to stay optimistic and listen to my intuition (unconscious guidance). I must have positive expectations for abundance in every aspect of my life. I need to work on setting foundations for myself and loved ones, so my future prosperity is ensured. I will always be supported, but I alone have the responsibility to make sure I do the proper work and put in the effort when and where necessary. I have to live up to my full potential. Financial abundance is on its way because of my focused and relentless work on achieving my goals and dreams. Just rewards will be mine. I need to be grateful for all my blessings and for those yet to come.*

In the last several dreams there were four people. Two were male (including me) and two were females. This is showing both sides of a person (conscious and unconscious), which are to be equal. However, a few dreams ago as I just mentioned, three of the four people in my dreams were unknown, showing that my whole self was way out of balance (i.e., the parts are there but I do not have a familiarity with them). I was living my life more on the conscious side. In this last dream, it is showing the proper balance in myself that should be attained between conscious and unconscious. This signifies that I have moved closer to an understanding, and completion of, attaining my whole self.

I was in the military trying to lead all the soldiers on an exercise through this hilly terrain. They would not listen and kept getting lost. So, I gave up and quit. Then I was climbing this giant stone staircase that led up above the rain forest jungle and mountains. They were calling off the names of people and saying where they lived at different stages. I told them to say I was living with my new girlfriend (she was an unknown, but exotic female). So, they did, and we went off to the right and we kept going even higher. I got to this one step, and you had to go around to the right. It was tight and scary. My girlfriend in the dream had turned into my mother. I ordered her to go first but she would not. She told me to go first, so I did. Then we were at the top and there was this fountain of water coming out of a pool of water and we were told the water could wash anything away and clean anything. So, I washed all the dirt off my hands and arms. Then, I pulled out a healthy sandwich with green lettuce and a red tomato on it. One of my nephews was there making fun of me. His father was there, and he said, "Everyone always makes fun of how much he eats, but he always eats the right stuff." Then I woke up from my dream. In the dream my nephew and his father were on my left.

The first part of this dream about the military symbolizes a collective thought (ego), which is what the military basically is. It also symbolizes me trying to control everything, force things, living totally in my conscious, and by living that way things will not work out. I will get lost, frustrated, and just give up. This was my old way.

Climbing the stone staircase above the rain forest and mountains shows a gain in depth and height in my understanding of my whole self. My girlfriend turning into my mother supports that, but also suggests that my understanding of my unconscious self has grown and that I need to listen to the guidance it gives. If I do, things will work out. This is symbolized by me listening to my mother when I went to the right instead of me forcing her to go first, which was me acting out of ego consciousness.

The fountain with water represents life, that magical elixir that is pure and can heal and clean all. My nephew represents the childlike behavior of my conscious life, and his father represents me overcoming that (based on what he said). He and my nephew were on my left, my mother on my right. That symbolizes the balance needed between my conscious and unconscious life in order to live in my center (i.e., being my whole self). The fact that in this dream I know all four people (including myself) also shows that I have a much deeper understanding of this proper balance, the whole self and the transformation that is taking place.

My current girlfriend and I were in a bar that was square, sitting at a square table. She was on my right. My mom and stepdad walked in and sat down with us. My mom across from me on the right and my stepdad across from my girlfriend on the left side. My girlfriend and I both had drinks in round glasses. Each glass had a big square ice cube in it. My drink was murky looking. I said, "Why is my ice cube black and yours white?" Then I said, "I guess mine is dirty and yours is clean." Then I woke up from the dream.

This whole dream symbolizes my much deeper understanding of conscious and unconscious life and uniting the two into a whole self and that my work is progressing. The ice cube being square symbolizes my gain in understanding and incorporating my unconscious into my conscious life; however, my ice cube being black and in murky water also symbolizes that there is still work to be done in this area and work to be done on balancing the two. It symbolizes I have unclear and confused feelings. That is symbolized by my cube being black and my girlfriend's being white (i.e., the yin and the yang [balance]).

I was having a lot of dreams and I was dreaming almost every night as if I was progressing rapidly and/or being guided at a faster pace. My dreams show a constant progression in my development and progress through my individuation process.

I was working in a restaurant. There were three guys working there with me who kept harassing me. I knew all three guys. Every time I did something back to them or said something to them, they got worse. I had a glass of wine, and I was climbing a ladder to go see my boss who was a woman I did not know. As I was climbing the ladder, one of the guys I knew tipped my glass of wine in my hand and spilled it. I told my boss what they were doing to me and what they just had done when I got to the top of ladder. She yelled at them and took care of it. They disappeared. Then I was busy working and she told me to make sure everyone got everything they needed. The restaurant was busy. Then I looked into this room, and I saw myself (like I was now out of my body looking at myself) and I was holding my girlfriend in my arms. She was lying flat and looking at me looking at her and myself. The me that was holding her was looking to the left, she was looking to the right at me. The me that was holding her was standing up vertically. My girlfriend was lying flat horizontally just about at my waste, forming a cross, and she was wearing a white dress like a wedding dress.

The first part of this dream symbolizes the fact that yes, I do have an understanding as I know all three men, but I have been living in my conscious life too much lately (all four of us are men) and that if I keep doing that, I will continue to get lost and frustrated and have problems. The middle of the dream with my unknown female boss, symbolizes my unconscious and that I need to rely on that and listen to it and if I do, everything will work out. In the last part of the dream where I am busy at work, I am outside my body looking at my physical self-holding my girlfriend in the room. That is saying that with everyday life, all the chaos that goes on, all the things that need to get done, I need to remember that balance between conscious and unconscious life and live accordingly. It will get me through everything, and it will all work out. The fact that together they form a cross refers to the quaternary and the balance between the conscious and unconscious that is needed to be a whole self and be complete. The fact that she is wearing a white wedding dress and I am looking at me holding her in a cross like pattern symbolizes that I need to make a union, a serious commitment with my unconscious guidance.

I was at my parent's house. My stepdad and mom were there. My parent's friend (a woman I know) tried to give me advice about dealing with my back. Another friend of theirs (a female I also knew) tried to rub it and my back was covered with scratches and scabs. My half-sister was there and told me my back was bad from stress and trauma. She said she knew because her friend's mom was some kind of doctor or something. I got mad at her and said, "What does your meth head friend's mom know." Then I peed blood on the floor and in the toilet. I then work up. In the dream, everyone at my mom's house was partying.

    This dream describes my unconscious trying to guide me. It is a warning that if I do not listen to my unconscious guidance and live accordingly, bad things will happen. It is telling me to listen to the guidance it is going to give me next. Me urinating blood is my unconscious telling me that waste and unfit substances are being removed from my body in order to maintain balance. In other words, my spiritual body is undergoing detoxification and purification. This detoxification is going on both mentally and emotionally.

In the first one, I dreamt that my girlfriend's work was doing a free procedure to get rid of skin cancer, so I told her to let me go first since I did not have insurance. So, I went, and I had to take eight pills, two were white, two were green, two were red and two were black. I had to take them and get every part of my body put under this hot bright light that burned all the pre-skin cancer spots off that were brown. Then I had to go back the next day and repeat it a second time for the final step. Then

Chapter 3 | 91

I was riding in a van with three other guys I did not know (four of us total), three of us were patients. The van stopped at the place we had the procedure. A woman got in and asked for payment for the treatment. The guys all refused to pay for it. They disappeared. I paid and got out of the van. There was a ladder leading up to the next floor where this woman was. I had to carry this square cardboard box up to her. I was very sore, but I did it. Then I went inside. Everyone was dressed in white, and everything was white. They said they would make me feel better. They gave me pills to take in order, but I could not remember what order, so I just took them all.

I was on some farmland, and I walked away from my truck and then I went back for it, it was sinking in this dark black water. I got in my truck trying to save it. Then suddenly, the truck was driving backwards, and I was in the driver seat driving. Then my sister and her ex-husband came up behind me in a truck. Her ex was driving, and he rear ended me. My truck spun around the right way. I was still driving but the truck was uncontrollable. So, I took the key out of the ignition. Just as I did that, I heard my ex-girlfriend's dad said, "take it out now! It's the only way to save it." I said, "Already done." The truck stopped, and he showed up. He had three red scratches on top of his bald head. They looked fresh. He grabbed the truck key which was gold but bent a little. He then said, "It's bent some, but it should be ok."

The first dream is again reiterating that my spiritual body is undergoing detoxification and purification and it is occurring during this dream. In my second dream, my ego fights back. In the beginning I try to find my way on my own by leaving my truck, but I realize this is not right and I go back to my truck. My ego tries on two occasions to trick me into thinking, or believing, that it knows the way, that it is my true guidance, that it holds the "golden key" to life. However, in the dream I figure it out by listening to my unconscious guidance telling me I was not going the right way and to remove the thing that was controlling it or running it (the key). Then my ego try's yet again by showing me the gold key (i.e., the way), but I realize again he is wrong when I see the bent key and call my ego on it. Then my ego says, "it'll be fine." I still did not believe my ego, and I woke up

2: *Have courage, faith, and trust. The answers to your prayers are manifesting for you. It just may not be obvious yet. It may be a test of your patience, but rest assured that all will come to pass at the right time. Exhibit compassion, diplomacy, consideration, and adaptability as you serve others in your daily life. You are encouraged to pursue your life's work with faith and trust.*

3: *Follow your intuition so that you are able to take the appropriate action. Use your creative skills and abilities to manifest your desires and to enhance your life and that of others. Follow your path and mission with optimism and enthusiasm. Your prayers and positive affirmations have been heard and are being responded to. Have faith that your goals and desires will manifest in your life at the right time. Trust your skills and talents. Be communicative and social with others and live your life with joy, optimism, and spontaneity.*

I was in an office building, I walked down a hallway to a square office room. My old Boss and a female co-worker were in the room. The female co-worker said something to me about not to listen. I then left the room and walked down some hallways in my clean, white socks. The hallways had formed a square. My socks felt comfortable. I went into a bathroom and the floor was all dirty and I was worried I would get my clean, white socks dirty. I was looking for a urinal that had a clean floor in front of it. I found one and started to urinate but there was a guy washing his clothes in the urinal and he got dirty water everywhere and messed up my socks. I got mad and beat him up. There was another guy in there who started talking bad things about Marines, I beat him up too and I left. Both of those guys were older and unknown to me. I went back to a room where my old boss and female co-worker were again, and I went over by this round table and sat down. There was a big green scorpion there who had a head like a praying mantis. I said, "What the hell is this doing here?" I thought I better kill it before it bites me. It then jumped on me, and it ran down my leg trying to get under my pant leg. I was scared it would get me and I panicked. My old boss said, "Don't touch it or it will bite you." I grabbed it and it stung me on my thumb. It hurt and drew a little blood. Then I killed it. I smashed its head. Then I saw another regular looking, tan scorpion but smaller, on the floor and I killed it. Then my old boss had a small scorpion. It was tan, curled up in a circle on his wrist and he flung it on me. I killed it. I then left the room and went into another square room which had chairs lined up against the wall to the right of me like a waiting room. The guy I beat up in the bathroom was there. He was dressed in black, and he had his shoes off. He had black socks on, and his feet stunk really bad. His feet also appeared to be swollen. I remembered the guy and I was mad he was doing that with other people around. I thought that he was an idiot. I mumbled something to that effect under my breath as I walked by him but did not say anything to him. He then got up and left. I thought, "Thank God" and I woke up from the dream. My old boss was always on my right and the female co-worker always on my left in the dream. There was a total of three scorpions in the dream and I killed them all.

The hallway in the beginning of this dream represents the path I must take. This path leads to the discovery of my inner self, my unconscious. In other words, this is the journey I was on at that moment. My boss and the female co-worker represent my ego and my unconscious guidance. I am being instructed not to listen to my ego. Me walking down the hallway in clean white socks represents me taking the path to the purification of my way. Me urinating also represents me cleansing myself, or that a cleansing of myself needs to occur. Me beating the two guys up represents me conquering my ego. Me going back to the room with my boss and female co-worker and then sitting down at the round table is telling me to find my way back to my unconscious guidance, to my center.

The scorpions represent the painful things and situations in my life. In my past I was engaged in things harmful to my well-being. My old boss also represents my ego conscious. Him warning me not to kill a scorpion and flinging one on me is my ego trying to bully me again. However, I did not listen. I killed all three. This is telling me to conquer my ego. Killing the scorpions is also telling me that good things will come to me, everything is going to work out, and that I will have success with what I do as long as I follow the right path, live from my unconscious guidance, and conquer my past ways of thinking, living, and behaving. The end of the dream is reminding me that my ego will only hinder my path.

I was coming home late like I was a little tipsy. I said oh well, I will sleep in tomorrow. Then I went to bed. Someone woke me up at 7:30 and said an old friend is here to see you. You were supposed to train him to be a sniper. I got pissed and said, 'What the hell is he doing here so early? Screw him, I'm sleeping in." I went back to sleep and got up a couple hours later. He was still here waiting for me. So, I decided to go talk to him. I told him I was not going to train him or do that anymore. I told him I was tired, my back hurt, etc. He said I should have at least called him and told him. He then was telling everyone how good I was at training him before and how smart I was. He then decided to leave. I watched him. He went to the garage and got on this tiny red bicycle and his calves were huge from riding it. I thought, "Wow, he has to ride that all the way back to where he lives! (It was a long way)" I thought, he wasn't who I thought he was, and I felt bad about how I thought about him before, like he was a jerk when he showed up. Then I went inside. There were a bunch of people and my sister there. I was talking to someone, and my sister was being a loudmouth, mean and kept cutting me off. I got mad and told here to shut up, she never lets me finish talking. I left. Then, I was in another room with a lot of people. There were these two dwarf men, older with beards and big muscles. They were looking for me because of what I said to my sister. They started punching everyone. I tried to hide in the people. They found me and each one punched me in the shoulder. Then it was over. Then I went into another room and there was this genuinely nice woman lying there in a white dress. There also was a baby girl sitting on a bed with a golden sheet and she was wearing a white dress. The baby girl then asks me for a glass of wine, so I pour her a glass of rosé. I give it to her, and she takes a sip and says, "Wow, that's really good." Then, I said to the adult woman, "Wow, I can't believe she knows all that and how smart she is. That's amazing." The woman said, "Yes, it is." Then she smiled.

In the beginning of the dream my conscious, the ways I used to think and behave are repressed, which left me feeling bad. The second part of my dream explains to me that was because I would not listen to my unconscious (my sister) and I was trying to control it all through my ego. Because of that, I was beat up by my unconscious (the two bearded dwarfs) because I did not realize my real treasure, my unconscious. There was a price that had to be paid. The fact that there were two pointy bearded men symbolizes I was only living half a life, only living in my conscious. The last part of the dream represents my unconscious (the beautiful woman in the white dress). She split herself (i.e., the baby girl), which symbolizes that I need to realize and accept my unconscious. The baby girl in a white dress also symbolizes my unconscious, my inferior side (child), but that I am now cooperating with it and it with me. It is pure, or there is a purification happening (white dress) but its's early in the process (i.e., she's a child). The golden sheet she is on represents that if I realize this, cooperate, and purify, there will be a richness of life or spirit and the enhancement of my true self (who I am beyond my conscious ego). It is the development of my psyche. The wine glass represents my center (my true self) as it is round. It contains pink wine in it. Pink represents love, sweetness, happiness, kindness, romance, compassion, softness, affection and the healing powers of love and friendship that I will receive by living from my center in cooperation with my unconscious (me handing her the glass of wine and the baby girl drinking it). The gold sheet also represents the rewards I will receive after taming those aspects of myself that have become wild and aggressive through periods of neglect of my unconscious guidance. Ultimately, I need to integrate my unconscious guidance back into my sense of self and my waking life (i.e., the golden sheet on the bed, and once I am awake, integrating my unconscious dreams from when I slept, into my conscious life).

In the first dream all I remember is that I was at my girlfriend's dad's house, and he got two horses and he was riding one and pulling the other. I was walking behind. We went to this spot and there were a few guys there. My girlfriend's dad tried to sell the one horse to this guy for 5 or 20 dollars, but he said no. They said to me that I was that guy that goes over to the island on a boat to get his food. I said yes, just about everything I eat is natural. I then was standing behind the horse. I wanted to ride it, but my girlfriend's dad was going to let the other guy ride it.

I went back to the place I used to work at. It had changed. There were some military people there and they were having a ceremony. I was wearing a military t-shirt and a hat with a flag on it. They played a song and I saluted. An old man said, "There's a Veteran." I was happy I was acknowledged. Then I was talking to these two women who were in the military standing at this control board. All I remember is that she said something about me having my engineer training. I was telling them I was in the Gulf War. Then all those people were gone. The place was completely changed around. Everyone was going back and forth doing their jobs. I kept trying to find work to do but could not find any. I knew I had to do work but every time I tried to do something it did not work out. Then I ran into a woman I used to work with. I said, "things have really changed around here, what's going on?" She said, "you didn't read the email? No, I never got it." She then said, "Let me go in back and get it." But she never came back. Then there was this round room in the center with a bed. I kept trying to sleep in this bed. I kept getting up because I knew I had to work, people kept walking through a door in and out of the room.

I saw an ocean and my dog (a German Shepard who had passed away) was floating above it in a sitting position barking at me. It was a nice bark, like he was happy.

I was in a house, and I had the sense I lived there. A female I once knew when I was younger was there. She was completely different. She was wearing a nice dress with flowers on it. It was an off white/cream color. Her hair was short. We hugged each other. Then she was busy with all these people trying to set up a big party in the house. I kept running into her and we would hug. One time she was naked, and her nipples were covered with circles that were pink colored. We then hugged affectionately, and I held her chest against mine. Then there were a lot of people there and noise. All I wanted was peace and quiet. I said something about it, and someone asked me if I was scared or something. I said no and something about wanting some peace and quiet in my own home. I just wanted to relax or something like that.

The first dream is telling me that the powerful ambitions of my conscious (represented by my girlfriend's dad and the two horses), which are difficult to control, need to be harnessed and that will help drive me to success and prosperity. I need to stay enthusiastic about the future in front of me (That is where the horses were). The horses being controlled by my girlfriend's dad (my conscious) symbolizes my true self being repressed by the ambitions mentioned above that come from my ego conscious. I need to break free from that. In other words, break free from all the things that society has taught me to do. I need to break free of that so that my slate is clean from those distractions, and I can complete this individuation process, so I can live my life as my whole, complete self.

5: *Important life changes are upon you, and they will bring about many positive opportunities for you. Look upon these changes with an optimistic attitude and be positive. These changes are designed to bring you many long-term benefits. Be grateful for these wonderful opportunities. You are being helped to make positive, healthy lifestyle choices that will enhance and benefit you in many ways. Such as, physically, mentally, emotionally, and spiritually. You are loved and supported and if you have any fears just ask for help.*

20: *You are well-blessed in your life. You are being given direction and energy so that you can live your life with love, harmony, compassion, and balance, so that you may serve your life mission with enthusiasm and optimism. Things are happening behind the scenes that will be of great benefit to you in the near future. You may not be experiencing these opportunities just yet, believe that they are on their way to you. Have faith and trust. Trust that due to your positive affirmations and optimistic attitude towards your life and mission your desires are manifesting into your life.*

The second dream is corollary to the first in that it is showing me my past, how all of my ambitions from my conscious controlled me and how every time I went out to do a "job" or "work" it just never worked out. I have been through a lot in my past. It is over now. If I were to continue living from my past ways things will not work out. I have changed. I need to be on a new path now. I need to stay in my center (the round room) and listen to my unconscious guidance (me being in the bed sleeping, my dreams) without the interruptions of my conscious (my ambitions, i.e., trying to get up and work).

The third dream is also a continuation. It is telling me that I am protected (my dog). It is not necessary to be nervous and lose control. But I also need to be attentive to this situation, (i.e., my unconscious: The large body of water/ocean).

The fourth dream is also corollary. At first, the female in the off-white dress represents a blemish on what I once believed, or expected to be perfect (my ambitions, going in Marines, going to college, a career, etc.). Her then being naked (removing the dress) means I need to shed that way of life, those blemishes, and ways of thinking. I need to embrace my unconscious and accept it (hugging her). If I do, I will have love, happiness, kindness, compassion, affection and the healing powers of love and friendship (the pink circles on her nipples) from this union with my unconscious. That is where the true form of those things resides.

I was bringing some food to some little girl I apparently knew named Kimmie. She lived in the old neighbor's house behind me from when I was a little kid. When I got there, there were a whole bunch of Asian kids out front. I talked to one of the girls and asked if I could give the food to Kimmie. She said she was busy and asked if I would be back tomorrow. I said no, and this is for her first day of school. I asked if I could give it to her anyway. They ate some of the food and then suddenly, I was inside the house. I was talking to the old neighbor kid who lived in that house behind me. He was on my left and his mom was on my right. His left lower leg was in a cast. It was black. I asked him what happened, and he said it was a skiing accident. Then I told him about all the bones I broke and told him he would be ok.

This dream affected my mood. It really struck me, and I was confused by it. It seemed out of the blue to me from the pattern of dreams I had been having lately. This dream confused me, and I was unable to interpret it. So, I read some more out of Jung's book, "Man and his Symbols." Usually, when I would do that, whatever I read the day after a dream seemed to help explain it and give me insight into that dream from the night before.

What I read on p.66 about a dream, quoted by Artemidorus of Daldis, floored me (He was a professional diviner, 2nd Century CE, Greece. He is known for a five-volume Greek work, the Oneiro Critica, which means the interpretation of dreams). It was a dream of precognition of a man's impending doom. My dream did not provide a context efficient enough to explain it and it came right out of the blue leaving me to wonder what could have prompted it.

So, I decided to sit there that day and meditate upon the dream and wait until it and its meaning are sufficiently understood in hopes of circumventing some external event from occurring that would explain the dream. Especially since I did not have a good feeling about what this external event may be.

Therefore, I sat there by my window in my bedroom, where I sit every morning and I began to think about my life, all its events and everything in it in terms of the inherent symbolism. I began to think about all the people in my life with an alcohol and/or drug problem. There are a lot of them. It is everywhere in my life. Then I began to recall all of the things that have happened between these people and me. There were a lot of bad things. Then I thought about the bad things that happened to a lot of them and how several of them have died from it at an early age as a sort of culmination of all these things happening and the behavior not being corrected.

I then thought about history and my three war dreams and how alcohol and drugs were so prevalent in all those wars and how many men were affected by that and even died because of it. I then thought about the war I was in and how I used alcohol to deal with things and how I also was on all the medications when dealing with my PTSD. I thought about how I ended up in the wheelchair unable to walk like my old friend in my dream with a cast on his leg. I remembered how all of this is causing an epidemic of Veteran suicides at 22 a day.

Suddenly, the dream began to make sense to me, and I began to see it with some clarity. The dream, and I simplify it here for the sake of explanation, is telling me that if I keep doing what I am doing, and not listening to my unconscious guidance, something will befall me, something dreadful yet again as it did in my past. I thought first I was going to have an accident and break something, but that explanation is too easy and literal.

So, I thought about it a bit. It soon hit me that I would again lose my ability to walk. Not only that but my, shoulders, neck, lower back, and big toe have been bothering me as in arthritic pain, which runs rampant in my dad's family. Especially in the lower back which eventually caused them to lose their ability to walk. The cast on the leg of my old neighbor friend in my dream made sense as well. Back when I was in the Marines, I developed arthritis in my ankle and they told me (it was my left ankle the same leg as my neighbor in the dream) If I really had it, I would be crippled by the time I was 50. At that time, I was contemplating this dream, I was about to turn 48. This puts a time frame on the event that would befall me if I did not start listening to my unconscious guidance to help me complete this individuation process and live my life as my whole self. To simply put it, I have about two years left to get on track, or this event of me losing my way would happen. The dream was telling me I was running out of time. The fact that it affected me so much emotionally, gave me the intuition that right now (within the next two years) is the last chance I have, to get this done.

Furthermore, the dream has other symbolic elements. My neighbor's mom was on my right and my neighbor friend on my left. This shows an imbalance as they should be in opposite places thereby telling me that this thing I keep doing, this ambition, or impulse I keep following is causing an imbalance of my whole self. My neighbor friend also represents me in my physical, conscious life, and I represent my conscious trying to control and trick myself into believing that I will be ok. All of this represents that if I do not quit living my life by the guidance of my ego-conscious, if I continue this behavior, I will lose my way. Now, that dream makes absolute perfect sense to me.

I must draw your attention back to my bedroom window, which I had been compelled to sit by for several weeks and conduct my studies, dream analysis and writing what I had learned. This has me wondering why I had been sitting there every day and doing this work and not doing any of the other chores I should be doing until this part of my work is complete? So, in my typical fashion, I meditated about it.

I have been drawn to, or focused on, two things outside my window. The first is the sun which shines in my window everyday this time of year. I just feel like I need to be in its light and see it while I am working. It is almost as if it was providing me guidance. The second thing I have been focused on everyday are all the birds in these two trees across the street from me and how they always seem to fly in a figure eight pattern around the two trees, left to right.

To me the two trees symbolize the upper and the lower, the vertical part of the cross, and a growth in depth and height. That is only half of the whole self that is represented by the cross (i.e., quaternity). The other half of the cross is represented by the birds flying from left to right, which symbolizes my unconscious and my conscious life. The figure eight pattern they fly in is the universal symbol for infinity and it represents perfection, cosmic Christ, immutable eternity, or the self-destruction and the final point of the manifestation.

Now, I take all of this to symbolize that I have interpreted this dream I just mentioned properly. This is symbolized in a few ways. First, the birds fly from left to right, which is the proper way to read a book, hence reading the dream the right way. Secondly, by the fact that after coming to this conclusion and interpretation of all of this, the birds began to fly in a big circle around my house. The circle pattern represents wholeness, perfection, the self, eternity, God, the sun, and the planets journey around it. It also indicates the end of a process or phase, of striving towards a psychic wholeness and self-realization. Now, my alertness to the sun makes sense. It is my wholeness and my guidance, what my life should revolve around (my center) as the planets do to the sun.

In summation, I conclude that my interpretation is therefore correct, and I must stop living my life according to my ego-conscious ambitions. I need to listen to my unconscious guidance to complete the individuation process, so I can live my life as my whole self and become an example to others of what they can have and be by doing the same thing. It has been a long, arduous journey for me that had to be done in just such a manner. Since this day, all those birds have disappeared, and a big storm came through one day and blew down one of the 50ft tall trees they were flying too. Thus, suggesting to me that my interpretation of my dream and these symbols was correct, and that phase has now ended. It will be time to move on to the next phase.

I was with family members, both male and female. We went on a journey. It was a long, slow journey. It was filled with obstacles, problems, and things we had to overcome and go through. We followed the path as it unfolded to us. In the end, we made it. At the end of the dream, my dog was sitting there waiting for me and his fur was tinged green.

I was inside my house looking outside to the backyard. My ex-girlfriend was sitting there. I waived at her and invited her inside. We were talking and getting along. Then her mother showed up acting all crazy and she wanted to go on this strict vegetarian diet to lose weight and she asked me if I would help her. I said yes, but I knew she would not do it or finish it because it was too strict. Then all I remember is that we were outside at night and her mother was backing up the square cab of a semi-truck down this curvy road. This guy came out and was telling her what to do. She did not listen and backed it into somewhere dark. Then she came out driving it with the square cab off of it and my ex was with her and they drove away.

The first dream relates to my summation from earlier that day of how all of this is a long, slow journey full of things to overcome and go through. My dog with green fur symbolizes that nature guards the way and I am protected. Therefore, there is no need to worry, or for me to let my ego-consciousness try and control, or force, the outcome of anything. It will all happen on its own, in its proper place and time. Recall the old fable where the farmer brings in a cat to eat the rats who are causing him trouble. Then, he must bring in a wolf to eat the cats. Then a bear to eat the wolf, etc. The meaning here is that the more the farmer and his ego try to control this situation, the worse it gets.

The second dream refers to how people think that those in society today who follow their unconscious guidance (their dreams) are crazy. Something I worried a bit about last night as this way of living is so much different than what, or how, society has taught me to live. This was represented by my ex and her mother who I think both live completely from their ego-consciousness. In the dream they also symbolize my unconscious as they are both females and I also know both of them. The man telling them what to do represents my ego-consciousness. The dream foretells the loss of my unconscious guidance, safe spot (the square cab of the truck) and my wholeness, if I only listen to, or live in, ego-consciousness (the truck with my ex and her mother driving away). It was as if the dream was re-assuring me to continue following my unconscious guidance and trusting it, and not to listen to those individuals who criticize those who do. For their loss is the greatest of all. The loss of the whole self. A bifurcation that surely leads to total darkness.

A woman who I knew, was standing and I was laying down in a circular fashion (coiled like a snake) around her. *I was extremely comfortable, relaxed, and sleeping. In fact, I remembered that in the dream, all I wanted to do was sleep, to be completely relaxed and at peace.*

In this dream vertical (the woman) and horizontal (me, man) are present. This establishes four, upper-lower, left and right (i.e., the quaternary), the whole self. The woman is my unconscious and me the man, is my ego conscious. Me being wrapped around her who is vertical, tells me that my unconscious grows, or works, while I am dormant, asleep, and relaxed. This is taken a bit further in that I am laying in a circle, thus representing my whole self, which requires the growth (i.e., assimilation of my unconscious). By doing that, I will complete the individuation process. I will be my whole-self and concomitantly find rest, relaxation, and peace (i.e., total happiness in being complete). It also symbolizes that my unconscious stems, or emanates, from my center, and that I must go within to my center to find it and grow with its guidance.

I was on this four-story ship. The bottom floor was halfway under water. I had to jump down to the bottom floor, swim through this clear water to get to another ship, or the front of the one I was on, and climb up to the top. I went into this area and there were a bunch of Arabic women dressed in black robes eating these dark brown nuts. They looked rotten. They asked me if I wanted some and I said, "no." I went into this room and there was a big fat guy and a lady there smiling at me. The guy gave me his dog to pet, and I had to wait for this lady, so I could tell her I was not re-enlisting. I had finished my tour of duty and I was done. I was petting the dog who was sitting in front of me and had his back to me. It had no hair where its spine was. It was a light brown color and fluffy. The lady came in and I told her I was not re-enlisting and then I jumped back into the water and swam away.

This dream is telling me that after going through the individuation process, why would I be loyal to these man-made ambitions of achieving, or accomplishing things, things of back breaking work. This is all represented by (the four stories of the ship) and diving into my inner self (jumping into the clear water and swimming) and bringing my unconscious into my conscious life (the man and the woman), also refusing my shadow (the black the women were wearing). That would be backwards. That is symbolized by the dog sitting in front of me, not facing me, that I am petting with his spine exposed. I need to refuse it (do not re-enlist, do not do it again) and follow my unconscious and leave this process behind me (jumping back in the water and swimming away after not re-enlisting).

I had a hold of the reins to a horse who was acting up. I was trying to control it. It stepped on my foot, and it hurt really bad. Someone, some guy I think, asked me if I was scared or something. I said, "no." He told me to get control of the horses.

This dream follows the last one and is telling me to get control of my ego (trying to control the horse). If not, they will cause me pain, grief, and suffering (the horse stepping on my foot). My conscious asked me if I was scared (the guy asking me). I said, no. So, I need to get that subdued and I do that by listening to my unconscious guidance. Then what is in front of me in my life (the horse), will be great.

I had to jump in this river with three other people. I think they all were kids. I grabbed the little girl and we had to float down this moving river. It was a little murky, but you could see big boulders in the water. We would crash into them along our way amongst other obstacles. It was a long curvy river. Then we got out at the end of it and ended up in this square room with doors. I got separated from the other three. I kept walking around the square looking for a way to go. This guy comes out and tells me to go through this door and I did. I was in this hallway and an old female co-worker was there. She walked with me and was saying she wished things had worked out for us, but she saw me out with my sister doing things and she was glad. I walked into another area by myself. It was like a cafeteria, and it was square. I got some coffee. I was trying to get stuff to eat and was dropping stuff, there were lots of people there trying to get food. I finally got some coffee and it had vegetables floating in it. A woman had helped me and showed me which way to go. So, I went out a door to the outside with this green grassy area and a bunch of people were sitting around a circular stage area with walls and windows around it that some people were sitting in front of and looking through. Most everyone else was sitting around this area waiting. I saw my old Sergeant from the Marines. So, I sat with him, and he said, "We must sit and wait to see what to do next. All the people were waiting for signs from the cleared area on what to do, but from what he could see it sounded like everything would be ok." So, I then went and sat next to this pretty woman to rest and wait like my Sergeant said. I was sitting there all dirty and soar from my journey. I had no shoes, and my feet were very dirty and so were my clothes. Then, suddenly, I was walking to the right in a circle around this circular thing with a fair, blond guy. We were both in brand new, clean uniforms and feeling good. I said, "The military isn't so bad. I didn't pick my job, it found me." The other guy said, "Yea, it's not bad."

This dream is re-telling my journey to me thus far from the beginning. It made me remember the time when I was writing my first book more than 16 years ago. I remembered when I was in the kitchen of my first house. I had just finished writing my book and I told God that I was now ready to do his work, whatever that may be, and I dumped a martini down the sink that I was drinking. I wrote about it in my first book, ***A Line in the Sand.***

The river represents my life in the purest sense of the form, the Prima Materia, from which life itself is created. It being murky symbolizes my life at that point where my journey began, which was cloudy, not clear and needed cleaning up. The river with its twists and turns also represents the first part of my journey and all the obstacles I had to overcome. The four of us in the river represents my conscious, and my unconscious. The two boys represent my conscious life and the infantile way I was living under the influence of society, dogma, and creeds. They also represent that my life was unbalanced as I was living totally in my conscious ego. What I needed to do was embrace my unconscious, accept it, and take this journey with it (symbolized by me grabbing the girl in the river and floating down it with her).

The fact that there were four of us all together represents the quaternary, the whole self, the four stages of the individuation process that I previously mentioned, which need to be completed so that one can live life as the whole self. The second part of the dream represents my inner self (the square rooms) where I need to be getting my guidance from (i.e., where my intuition comes from). The third part of this dream is telling me that ego is not helping me. I need to get my guidance from my unconscious to help me through my journey.

The fourth part of the dream is telling me my unconscious will provide me with the things I need in life. So, there is no need to worry. I just need to trust it and follow its guidance (symbolized by me in a square room, trying to get food, healthy food, and listening to the lady telling me where to go).

The fifth part of the dream is symbolizing that it is a time for rest and contemplation after my long arduous journey thus far. I have gone through physical, man-made trials, obstacles, battles, and events. I have completed a phase. Now, I need to rest and wait for further instructions (symbolized by me sitting with my Sergeant and the pretty lady, resting, healing, and waiting for further instructions).

The last part of the dream is my future. It represents me cleaned up, healed, rested, bright and happy. It represents success, happiness, growth, and living a complete life as my whole self from my center and living the right way. In other words, everything will be ok. I will be rewarded for taking this journey and doing my proper work (symbolized by me and the guy in the bright new clothes walking around in a circle to the right).

It was at this point that I was waiting for further instructions on just what that next step would be. Over the course of the next couple of weeks leading up to my 48th birthday, I spent numerous hours each day in deep meditation contemplating everything I have been through and learned. I was trying to figure out what to do next with my life.

Before I discuss that, I want to discuss the stages of human life in relation to my development and the individuation process as I understand them to be. This is something I developed based on the events of my life and when those events occurred. I also compared all of that with the events and when they occurred of other people's lives that I knew. That's how I developed this general time frame. There are approximate age ranges where certain parts of the individuation process must occur during relative stages of our development from childhood to young adulthood, to adulthood. The first three stages of my development correlate with the first three stages of the individuation process. Completion of this then prepared me for middle aged adulthood, which is where my real life began, as my whole self. Of course, these age ranges are not set in stone. They are only an approximation, so the reader understands the proper course of things as I perceive them to be.

Infancy: Birth-12 years old (Stage 1 of the Individuation process: Blackening-mind overcoming body)

- Living completely guided by one's unconscious. Never questioning any thought or desire, just acting upon it.

Teenage years: 12-18 (initiation into young adult hood. Stage 2 of the Individuation process: Whitening-transforming of spirit into body)

- Separation of ego-consciousness from unconsciousness and living from ego.
- One learns what he/she needs to be a young man/young woman.
- Then a transcendence into young adulthood.

(The Initiation is where one learns what they must, the overcoming of obstacles. The Transcendence is the stripping of things that would bind you to the current stage you are in. That way one can enter the new stage.)

Young Adulthood: 19-40 (Stage 3: Reddening-purifying of all instinctual impulses into higher, socially more acceptable activities.)

- Still living in ego-consciousness.
- Where one learns what they need for what lies ahead (the real work [completing the individuation process] in middle age) and one learns the limits of one's will (ego) and begins to desire to reconnect with the unconscious and its guidance, trust and follow it, to achieve wholeness in preparation for living life from one's center as an inspiration to others, where one reaps the rewards for completing this process (i.e., living in paradise).
- Then, a transcendence into middle aged adulthood

Middle Aged Adulthood: 40 to around 65 give or take. (Stage 4: Where an individual lives life as a whole self).

- Where life is lived as a whole, complete self with the unconscious and conscious in perfect balance with the understanding of the power and limitations of both, and that they are both necessary for a proper life as a human being.
- Where an individual realizes their potential and how one has been prepared for living life as a complete, whole self.
- Then a transcendence into old age.

Old Aged Adulthood: 65-? (Preparation for the transcendence into death of the physical body)

- Rest, relaxation, recuperation, and reflection.
- This stage begins the preparation for the death of the physical body.
- Then a transcendence of the spirit from the physical body into something new, a new level of existence, whatever that may be, or reincarnation to attain more experience, further development and/or to "try" again depending on one's stubbornness.

I have come to this point in my journey where it appears just about everything has been stripped from me. However, it seems like it all happened on purpose. It seems to have all happened in stages as well. First, about 10 years ago, I was stripped of my career and both of my houses. I was completely stripped of who I thought I was, of my ego. Then I was left to deal with my shadow, my dark side, my mental work. I succumbed to PTSD, which was a compilation of things from my childhood, being in the Marines, the war, and all the things' people did to me as a young adult. During the next four years a mental cleansing occurred where I healed my PTSD in healthy, natural ways and began to study my unconscious and interpret my dreams to help myself.

When that was completed, I was ready to start a new phase of development. I cannot help but recall when I was sitting in a chair in my first house, before all these things happened to me, and God spoke to me. It was as real as anything in my life. If you recall he told me that I would lose everything, my family, my friends, my house, everything. But it will all be ok. It needs to happen, it is necessary. It was so powerful that I became overcome with emotion and began to cry wondering what that all meant and was that all really going to happen? Well, it did, and here I am.

I began a journey of self-realization and spiritual development. After I wrote about everything I went through, everything I healed from, how I did it and what I learned from it, I published it all in a series of books. Three to be exact. Then, I moved into a new house where the next stage of my developmental journey began.

Over the course of a year, I was stripped of everything that I was doing regarding PTSD and helping people with it. I was stripped of all kinds of luxuries in my home. I was stripped of all the activities I was doing to beautify the house in the sense that every time I did that work my back, hips and shoulders would be in so much pain that I would be practically in tears and ready to vomit. So, I had to quit doing that.

Then the issue of paying bills came to a head. I could not make the payments on two of my three credit cards. It was also wintertime, and the heat was not working properly, and I could not afford to fix it. So, I had to turn it off entirely. There was only a little money left over after paying for necessary bills, like the mortgage, electricity, water, insurance, groceries, and gas for the vehicle. There was no money to do anything or go anywhere. I became truly angry and depressed.

I was mad that after everything I have been through and done, I had nothing. I could not enjoy life. I had no friends, no family. Here I was about to turn 48 and I felt completely useless, like a loser, like I was wasting space, time, and my life. I clearly was not done with my development yet and I was having ego conscious reactions to it all.

So, I did the only thing I could do anymore, I sat down in my rocking chair, read, studied, meditated, and wrote. I thought this all must be happening for a reason. It must be. Then it hit me like a bag full of bricks right in the face. Everything in my life that was keeping me distracted was now gone. I had no ties to anything and nothing to do, so it seemed. I then realized that was because I had to concentrate on what I am supposed to be doing, the development I was put here to complete. Which was my individuation process, becoming my whole self, integrating my unconscious guidance into my conscious life, and making all this concrete by giving it permanence in the world to inspire others. In other words, I had to put it in some fixed form like writing. I had been brought into life, developed through a series of events and trials, stripped of all the material stuff associated with that phase of development, conducted a mental cleansing, and was left with a clean slate in order to complete my spiritual development, which is what I had been training for my whole life.

I am to concentrate solely on completing my individuation process and putting it into form by writing about it all. The signs are everywhere and quite obvious. It is time for me to pay strict attention to it and give myself over to it. And, to reaffirm this, I had noticed that over the several days before I came to this realization, my dreams had slowed down and stopped as if I were being given time to process all of this and incorporate it into my conscious life. This is another sign that a new phase was about to begin and the last one was ending.

It all seems to make sense to me now. I had been stripped of everything yet again. It is a theme that has occurred several times in my life. Sort of like a snake when they molt and shed their external skin to get to the new skin that has been developed and perfected underneath. I am stripped of every materialistic, ego created, external form. Whereby, I am then given a chance to find my center, my true self that lies underneath (i.e., within). Once I was stripped of all thing's ego, I needed to turn within and await my instructions and wait for the right thing to happen to lead me in the way I was supposed to go. My dreams (my unconscious guidance) will also corroborate this as Jung describes in his theory of synchronicity.

As one can see, I have had many dreams lately about my past ways. In other words, my dreams were suggesting that I quit trying to live life the way I did in the past. It will not work out. These dreams I had were symbolic of me going through an elimination of the impurities of my life. It was as if my soul/spirit was being beaten or modified by my unconscious through the repetitiveness of these dreams. Just as a drill instructor would do during boot camp to recruits in conscious life. This brings up the idea of balance. What occurs with the conscious must also occur with the unconscious. My life up to this point has been about the development of my conscious, and next my unconscious. This created a proper balance. Once this is complete, the two must be joined in preparation for the next phase. In the conscious side of my life, I must physically do the work. In my unconscious side, my soul/spirit has to do the work (i.e., in the environment of my dreams). My only job here is to learn how to understand it and bring what I have achieved spiritually into my ego conscious life.

I was a servant on this cooking show like Hell's Kitchen. I met this bisexual woman who told me that I could be her partner (as in marriage) and that I was like her little holocaust survivor. After she said that, she passionately kissed me. She then drew stuff on my face and put marks on my glasses. I looked in a mirror, and my face was all white, with black lines on it, like scars. Then they offered me a spot on the cooking show because someone went home. I said, "I would give it a shot, but that I am only a servant." Then before I even started cooking my sister won the show. Her and her boyfriend were sitting at a table getting praised like royalty. Next thing I know, I was looking through all kinds of shelves, boxes, etc., of cowboy boots and cowboy work boots. They were all dirty and worn out and I never could find "my pair."

The bisexual woman in this dream symbolized the great man according to Dr. M.-L. von Franz in the book, *Man and His Symbols*, edited by Carl Jung. This resonated with me resoundingly well. She symbolizes the uniting of the female and male sides of our ourselves. Thus, symbolizing the perfectly balanced whole self.

I have met my unconscious, and the desire for further individuation has come to the forefront for me. I now realize that the real goal of life is to complete this process. The bisexual woman saying that I can be her partner symbolizes me now uniting myself with my female side (my unconscious) and becoming a more complete self. The fact that she passionately kisses me symbolizes that I am united with my unconscious guidance. It seals the deal so to speak. Just like when people get married and at the end of the ceremony the priest says that you may now kiss the bride. The lines like scars on my face, and when she said I am her holocaust survivor, symbolizes my life thus far. It represents all the trials and tribulations I have been through. Indeed, to me, it has been quite like being in prison, tortured and beaten into submission. This was a perfect symbol used in my dream for me by my unconscious. If you have read any of my previous books, you will know what I mean about my life.

In the part of the dream where my sister is with her boyfriend and being treated like royalty is also a symbol of the whole self. Me not finishing cooking in the cooking show and looking through pairs of cowboy boots symbolizes the end of my past way of life. I am moving on with a new way of life as a whole self, guided by my unconscious. I am now looking forward to this next phase of my life and what it will bring me next.

My 48th birthday, as it turned out, had been quite profound. So, as I stated earlier, I was waiting for further instructions from my unconscious.

I dreamt I was back in the military again as I have many, many times before. Only this time, everything worked out. In the dream I had my gun. It worked properly, and I was shooting down airplanes with it. In previous dreams of this nature, my gun never worked right, jammed, broke, or shot terribly slow. I asked for more bullets, and they gave me a box of bullets of different sizes and shapes and a guy told me that is what I needed. I said, "No, I don't." I then told him exactly what I needed, and I got the right bullets. Then we were marching along to our next battle, the Sergeant was yelling orders. We were running. I got my gun reloaded (which in the past dreams I could never do) and the extra bullets placed in my left breast pocket. We got to our location and there were these other people dressed in red (red is symbolic of feeling or passion) and they were attacking this place and the people we were supposed to attack. The Sergeant told us to attack, and I said, "No, they might be carrying out a coup (a sudden, violent, and illegal seizure of power from a government). Let us wait and see what happens." I was thinking they may do our work for us.

In the beginning of this dream where my gun is working right, and I am in the military is where my "instructions" are imbedded. To me, it is suggesting it is time to get back to life. In other words, once again become a productive, responsible part of society and live my life with my new, more acceptable way of behaving. I need to reintegrate into life again now that I have obtained this maturity of my unconscious.

The next part of the dream reveals a man to me, who is trying to convince me of what type of bullets I need. However, after seeing them, I knew what I needed, and I told him so. To me, this symbolizes that I should not let my ego conscious side tell me, or convince me, what to do. I know better and I need to stick to what I know internally. If I do that, everything will be fine.

The last part of the dream with the people in red performing a coup is a reminder to me to not let my sudden or violent impulses of trying to take power, or to control things, rule me (i.e., living from ego consciousness). Do not act on them. I need to stop and wait to see what happens. In other words, wait for my instructions and reflect upon them before deciding. This is something, that once learned, can be applied to all aspects of one's life. It becomes an enormously powerful and potent philosophy from which to live life by.

I am very compelled to finish this. I need to incorporate what I have learned from it into my life and practice it. I also have a feeling that by doing this, what I am supposed to do with my life next, or how I am supposed to live it, will be revealed to me. I am guessing that it will be revealed to me through a dream, or a symbol/sign in my conscious daily life. At this point, numbers started revealing themselves to me throughout my day. It was as if I had now graduated to a new, more advanced level of obtaining my unconscious guidance.

48 (my age at this point): *A cycle or phase will soon be coming to an end, with rewards coming from hard work well done. Do not fear lack of loss as these endings will lead to great new beginnings and opportunities, and your success will bring blessings and rewards of many kinds into your life. The angels of abundance surround you and are with you as you experience these positive changes. Release any fears about your finances and trust that your needs will be met. The hard work and determination that you have put towards your personal truths has fully aligned you with your Divine purpose and soul mission, and because of this you will receive abundance and plenty to maintain and sustain you as you continue down your path. Trust that you are supported, encouraged, and guided.*

42: *Maintain faith and know that your prayers have been heard and are being answered. You are being assisted to help you achieve your success. Set your intentions and make sure they are clear and concise. Release your expectations and allow signs and synchronicities to reveal themselves to you so you can take notice of them and follow their guidance. You are encouraged to pursue your ideal career and/or profession. If you are prompted to begin or expand a spiritually based career, practice or profession or heart-based service or venture, you will be assisted with establishing the foundations that will lead you to your desired results. Working to serve others will manifest all that you want and need in your life.*

47: *Congratulations for the hard work and effort you have put into achieving your goals and aspirations. Keep up the great work. You are on the right life path and are successfully fulfilling your development.*

You are being supported and encouraged through intuitive means. You will need to put in some hard work and effort, but you will find long-term rewards and benefits for yourself and for those you serve. Ask for guidance when you need it.

3: *Follow your intuition and inner wisdom so that you are able to take appropriate action at this time. Use your creative skills and abilities to manifest your desires and enhance your life and that of others. Follow your life path and soul mission with optimism and enthusiasm. The more you do, the calmer, more positive you will be. Your prayers and positive affirmations have been heard and are being responded to. Have faith that your goals and desires will manifest in your life at the right time. Trust your personal skills and talents. Be communicative and social with others and live your life with joy, optimism, and spontaneity.*

43: *Energies are surrounding you, helping you with their calming presence. They are helping you to find peace, clarity, and love within yourself. All is good in your world, and with your natural abilities you will manifest everything you desire. Connect and communicate with these energies and know that they will help you when you ask. Trust that you are completely supported and protected. Your prayers and positive affirmations have been heard and are being responded to. Your manifesting abilities have guaranteed that all of your needs will always be met. Look at your current home and lifestyle and think of ways to better and elevate your environments in order to attract more positive energies.*

15: *Your ideas and thoughts are helping you to make several much-needed changes in your life. You are being pushed and guided into making positive choices. You are being assisted with these transitions. Do not be scared about making these major life changes. In the long term, they will be of great benefit to you and others. You will be cutting loose old restraints. There will be room for new to enter your life. Keep focused on your goals so that you can manifest your ideals. Use positive affirmations and visualizations so that you keep your outlook bright and receptive. Use your natural talents when making choices that concern your own wellbeing and life. Only you know what your heart's true desires are. You have the inner wisdom, talents, and abilities to complete all that you wish to.*

At this point, I was given time by my unconscious guidance to let everything I learned sink in and incorporate it all into my life. About five months passed before I had any more meaningful dreams from my unconscious guidance.

PART 3:

The Reddening

Uniting conscious life with unconscious guidance.

CHAPTER 4

The binding of the soul to either Good or Evil.

At this point the next phase of my development was about to begin. I also acquired a higher level in regard to interpreting my messages and my development. My dreams became more pronounced, detailed, specific, and intricate. They also took the form of a conversation, as if someone in my dreams was sitting there, specifically talking to me, and giving me my personal guidance. Also, a lot more numbers were revealed to me, several times a day, and in my dreams on a more regular basis. It seemed like every time I had thought or a question, I was given an answer almost immediately in the form of a number. I now felt I was at a higher spiritual level. I physically started doing things in my life that my unconscious guidance was suggesting I do.

Have patience. You can achieve your goal, but only after you have put in some long, hard work. Your work is acting as an intermediary between God and men through your writing, knowledge, and art. Do not worry. Your internal guidance is helping you, and will continue to help you to, make the choices you must in order to get what you need in life. This is a new insight for you. A transformation is coming. This is the end of your spiritual journey and the finding of the truth of your soul. You now have a hidden understanding and wisdom in life. New beginnings are approaching. You need to just be yourself.

Your unconscious is in control of your life, and you need to have a passive approach to life. Your ego needs to take a back seat in your life and/or in specific situations. You will become a prominent philosopher and writer and make many contributions to literature through your writings on themes of social change.

I understand this is a harder and longer challenge than you expected. But your unconscious guidance is guiding you through it. It is a difficult challenge. However, there is only one way to reach the top. I know you did not expect this to be quite as hard to tackle and that you sometimes wonder why you went this route. But, through the guidance of your unconscious, you will make it to the top if you listen. You understand more in life now. Watch out so your efforts in life are not compromised because of other life events.

You are beginning something new by accepting your unconscious into your life. This rebirth, understanding the power of life and the powers of the soul, this maturation, are all a part of a transitional time. I know you feel overwhelmed and engulfed. You need to go deeper into your soul. Things are going to change. Your old self, patterns, and what you are focused on, will fall away. I see that you are diving deep into issues that are important to you and you are thinking about it from all angles. I know you are trying your best to understand your views on this subject that you have been educated in, but never really thought about until recently.

Your life is incredibly pure, but also fraught with a lot of different thoughts. While your life may have many issues, and while you are busy with new thoughts every day, you will work through them because of your endless and relentless ability to adapt to what goes on around you and to new lines of thought that challenge you and make you feel a lot more used to what is going on around you. This may seem a lot harder to work with. Your life is always full of new things, and you cannot see exactly what is coming ahead, but your level-headed attitude and ability to stay in touch with your true emotions, will carry you through the roughest of these times. Congratulations for mastering yourself! It is something that most people cannot do.

I had been feeling drained. Like I just needed to rest for a while. At the end of December of 2018, Frida and I drove my son back home to Oregon. It was a long week's drive. He came to visit us for a week for Christmas. It was the first Christmas I spent with him in eight years. We arrived back from driving him home a day after New Year's Day. It had been a busy few months from the end of October through the end of December.

It took a few days for me to feel somewhat rested enough to continue my regular activities, chores, etc. It was at that time, January of 2019, that I had the strong urge to finish writing this book. I also had a lot of very vivid dreams during that time period urging me to do so and that I needed to in order to signify the completion of my personal individuation process and to cement it all in my mind.

So, I set out on that process. It was also time to get caught up on all my chores and projects that I wanted to complete. I was also having all kinds of different thoughts on what to do with my life now that I am attaining a whole, complete self. I just could not seem to focus on one thing and do it. All these thoughts, ideas and life's activities kept delaying me from figuring that out and drained me of my energy.

A day before my 49th birthday, I had a dream. There were a lot of different things going on in the dream. I was in a house full of people and was trying to complete all these chores, but never got anything completed and I was getting frustrated. Then, in the dream, I focused on a yellow, sickly bird outside. I ran outside to get him out of my garden, and he attacked me. So, in the morning upon waking up, I wrote down the dream and began to analyze it to see what my unconscious guidance was telling me.

There is a positive outlook in your professional life. However, you are being pulled in too many directions. Because of that you are experiencing conflict with your spirituality. You are not following your desired path in life. Others, or other things, are meddling in your life and interfering with your life path.

Upon getting this message, I decided I was going to spend the week thinking about exactly what my life path is and stick to that one thing. I also had to try and figure out how to get all my chores done around the house. There are so many things to take care of like cleaning, laundry, cooking, my garden, fruit trees and chickens. I figured if I took the time to meditate upon all of this, the answer would be revealed to me in a dream, symbol, etc., once I got these things cleared out of my mind.

During this time, I had been working on taking a much more passive approach to life. I was working on understanding and practicing that which I needed to be successful. I figured by doing that, what I needed to survive would be presented to me in some form or another. So, there was no need to worry, no need for that emotional distress.

I began to practice what I had previously learned. I was using the numerical system that had been revealed to me through my life's analysis in my stock investing. I was working on totally trusting it and not paying attention to all the nonsense and news. I believe that was revealed to me in order to get me to focus. That would be how I would learn about the stock market, how it works, and how to invest in it properly. I believed that this was to be part of my financial foundation, and one way I would be creating my wealth in the future.

I see that you are bringing your unconscious into your conscious life. I also see that you have been exploring the issues that cause you emotional stress. You now have wisdom and a clear outlook. You are now aware that peace and harmony come from within. You are experiencing inner calm and comfort.

I see that you have decided on which direction to go in your life. You will encounter new opportunities. You are now moving into a new chapter of your life, and to a higher level of consciousness. I see that you have a desire to help others more.

I see that you understand your past, your family, society, etc., are not what you were taught to believe and that you are breaking away from that and are going down your own path. You have justice, purity, and a protective energy about you.

You have a hidden spirituality and divine qualities. With your awareness there are new beginnings. You are experiencing a re-awakening and have a fresh outlook on life. You now have intellect, energy, agility, happiness, harmony, and wisdom.

You have great strength. Work diligently, yet harmoniously, to achieve your goals. Put your ideas into a practical form. You are being guided and supported in your endeavors. So, trust that your hard work and efforts will bring you well-earned rewards. By using hard work, will, and personal effort you will achieve your long-term goals and aspirations. Everything is as it should be. The projects you have been working on will be successful, and you will be pleased with the long-term results. Just have faith and trust in your abilities and guidance.

You will be of service to others. You have achieved a completion and ending. You will display leadership, inspiration, closure, and live as a positive example for others to follow. With your spiritual awakening, your understanding of universal spiritual laws, and the "light" guiding you, get on with your life purpose. A phase of your life is coming to an ending and there is new to come. Everything will work out for you, so do not worry. You simply must prepare yourself and your life accordingly.

You are spiritually advanced. Follow your life path and soul purpose. I know you yearn to see improvement in the world and wish to participate per your life purpose. It is time to put your natural skills, talents, and abilities to good use in serving humanity. Follow your intuitive guidance regarding your life path. Set a positive example and be a torchbearer, lighting and illuminating the way for others to follow. Fully embark without any further delay or hesitation and shine your light brightly for the benefit of yourself and others. You are being asked to live up to your full potential.

 Frida and I were out in the backyard sitting around the fire I had built in our fire pit. I discussed with her all the things I wanted to do and accomplish. How I wanted to have a small farm with animals and a big garden. I talked about buying property. I even talked about how I wanted to buy a huge parcel of land and build casitas on it to rent out. I would have a restaurant on it and have a garden with a small vineyard that would supply the restaurant.

It would be a nice place for people to go and relax and get good, healthy food.

Then I talked about if I could even get any of that done, let alone one of those things. I mentioned how that all would cost a lot of money that we did not have. How would I even go about getting that kind of money and what about all the time that would take if it was even possible, especially at my age. Then, I told her maybe I am supposed to just pick one of those things, like the restaurant, and focus on just that. Or maybe I am just supposed to do nothing but writing. However, if that was the case, then why did I have those desires to do those things and want to accomplish them so much?

We also discussed all the other things that I do, and must do, during the day. There are all the chores that need to be done. We talked about me writing every day and maybe something will take off with one, or all of my books. Then, of course, I started thinking how in the world would I get all these things done? It seems impossible.

Do not worry. You will easily defeat the obstacles you are now facing. With your confidence, your goals, and intentions, you can withstand your layered past. You have a bold personality. Do not care what anyone thinks. You are doing something and taking chances that most people would not.

Your old issues are now finding resolution. So, allow yourself to feel and find rebirth in the present moment. Remember, there is always a period of rebirth after a period of suffering. Your old issues will be brought to a resolution by you reclaiming the power you lost during the time of your wounding. You have many resources available to you, physical, mental, psychic, emotional and spiritual. Use them. You have the power and strength to accomplish everything you dream of. You simply must believe, have faith, and find the right path. Persistence is the key word.

However, there are obstacles in your path. Self-limitation due to your reliance on old ways of thinking and old patterns, are blocking your progress. Something about yourself needs to be respected. You need a clearer understanding of what kind of behavior is appropriate for the attainment of your goals. You need a clearer understanding of what you are not supposed to do. Once you remove the barrier, there are endless possibilities in front of you. In front of you are purity, peace, innocence, dignity, cleanliness, awareness, and new beginnings. You are experiencing a reawaking and you have a fresh outlook on life. I am aware of all the bad things that you went through in your life. However, do not worry. You will feel better in a little while once you remove the barrier from your life.

In the morning, I began to contemplate and meditate on what my unconscious guidance had told me in this dream. I get it. I have what it takes, I have everything I need to succeed and accomplish all my goals. I do not have to limit myself to just one. I need to regain my power and energy I used to have before all the bad things I went through over the years. I do this by eliminating the old ways, habits, and ways of thinking from my past. I then began to identify what those were. I needed to quit worrying about what others think, about what they are doing. I should not be spending time on things that are not aligned with my goals. I realized I have no time constraints. This is a blessing for me because I realized I have the entire day to get things done that I need to. I do not have, or need, a set schedule. I need to make sure I eat healthy and have healthy habits so that I may have the energy to do what I need to do every day, all day. All these things are the "barrier" that is holding me back and sucking my energy dry. This is the last hurdle I must overcome so that I can venture into the wide-open future that awaits me. Goodbye past and welcome to the "new" that awaits me.

Acting as you did in your past and continuing your old ways of thinking and acting are wasting your time and energy. The way to leave your past completely behind you, feel good and have the energy you need is to be healthy, eat healthy and only put good, organic, natural, healthy things into your body. This requires devotion and utilization of your abilities. It will result in wealth and dignity. It will give you the raw energy, vigor, intense passion, and power to thrive. Use this awareness to achieve a purity, a perfection, and a clarity of mind so that you may enter your new beginnings. Listen to your spiritual guidance, be loyal to it. Use all the truth and wisdom I give you. Be devoted.

No matter how old you are, it is not too late to follow your dreams. Understanding this dream may be the most important step you can take that you need to work towards advancement and finish what you have started. It is time to think about the type of life you wish to obtain right now, and it is time to succeed. You must look more deeply into areas of your life.

To clarify and overcome your difficult problems and situation, you must look beyond your own mind and thinking. You must care for your own mind. No matter how many difficult situations or problems you are currently facing, they can be rectified. By looking beyond, you will see problems more clearly. Your problems will remain until you decide to gather enough courage to deal with them. If you ignore your problems, they will develop into something bigger and will block you completely from ever succeeding.

I see that you are trying to look at situations from a different perspective. But I also see that you are struggling with motivation. At the moment, I see you are looking within yourself and searching for your life path. I know you are having a hard time completing your projects. But you should persevere in order to not miss some important opportunities which may turn up.

By continuing old ways, old habits, and old ways of thinking, you will encounter misery, hard living, and poverty in all respects. You will have sorrow, pain and suffering for both your body and your soul. Just look at all those around you who continue past behaviors, ways of thinking and refuse to change. See all the misery, pain and suffering they encounter. Both physically and mentally. Let this be a sign to you that evolution and change

of every individual in life is necessary. If you leave this all behind you, health, order, and good things will come your way. Act and be triumphant in this situation. This will require strength, determination, and over-coming adversity in order to achieve success.
If you can achieve this, you will have good regarding your finances. You will receive gain. There will be good business for you. Remember, you are a cultivated person. You will experience joy and pleasant days. Your wealth will grow. Wealth, richness, gain, and good harvest are within your future. You will have great joy and find spiritual and personal peace.
I see that you are having new and inspiring thoughts. Understand that there is something significant that can grow or develop over time for you. You are making an emotional transition. With this you will receive liberation from the bad in your life and experience a cleansing of your soul.

After this message, I began to contemplate all the things in my life that I need to get rid of. Old activities, ways of thinking and acting must be purged. I need to spend my time focused on completing all my projects. I can accomplish all the things I want that I previously mentioned. I just need to work hard on them all and focus. Through these projects and chores, I will learn how to achieve my desires. It is as if I am being taught how. I am starting from the ground level and will work my way up to making my dreams a reality. I am going to spend each day working toward those goals. I am not going to waste time and energy on anything else. It is time for a new way of life.

You now have an openness to new possibilities. You see the issues clearly. Things are transparent. You can see through your problems. Belief in yourself is your first line of defense. You may have taken some foolish actions in the recent past, but I see that you are currently trying to change that. Your emotions are now calm and collected. I see you are looking within yourself now, that you are looking within and searching for your life path. Follow your intuition and listen to your inner self. A new start is coming. You were refusing to accept this inner guidance due to your ignorance. Now, I am aware you are ready to accept the truth about it all. You now understand the limitlessness of the unconscious and spirit. You have made a change and it is like you are in a different world.

Your emotions are clear. You are exploring deep into your unconscious mind and attempting to understand it. Have more faith in your ability and manage the events in your life. Great things are seen on the way for you. It is particularly important that you look after yourself and your health now. You need to understand the bigger picture, and you need to have more confidence in your ability moving forward. I see that you are now trying to release yourself from the limitations which have recently affected your life.

You will be the possessor of fortune and favor. I see that you have made peace with your path right now and you are on the right track in your life. Walk forward with confidence. You will be able to make things happen. Just do not get stuck in childish situations.

I see that you are trying to remove yourself from your complex situation in life. You have abilities but the way to approach things must change. In other words, quit trying to force things. Your world is too busy. You are taking on too much. You will have help and relief. You will experience a financial increase in your income. You feel alive. You may want to expand your horizons and investigate new interests now that you have reawaken and have a fresh outlook on life.

I see you are integrating your true self. Partnerships and creative collaboration are ahead. You are achieving self-harmony and meeting responsibilities. You will have love, abundance, domestic harmony, and good will.

Stability is needed in all areas of your life. Your monetary and material needs will be met. Be grateful for your blessings to encourage further abundance. Find a balance between your goals and ideals, and your inner spiritual self. Your thoughts are out of balance, and you are placing too much focus on the material side of life. Look to serving humanity and fostering your spiritual growth and expansion. Focus on spirit and service and your material and emotional needs will be automatically met as a result.

Changes are coming up in your life that may alter your course. This is a premonition of important discoveries, adventure, and actions to be taken in waking life. You are learning your life lessons through your experiences. You have become more in tune with your five senses, and you need to pursue your personal truths and freedom. You have a desire to break free from the old constraints and restraints that have been holding you back. You need to begin living your life with passion and purpose.

The changes ahead of you will bring about favorable opportunities and feelings of personal satisfaction. Positive changes are heading your way. Better things are coming into your life. These changes may come about with unexpected speed or urgency and in unusual ways. But they will bring positive energies and opportunities that will propel you in the right direction along your life path. Stay away from overindulgence, the pursuit of pleasure, addictive, and compulsive behaviors that need to be addressed.

You have a balance of male and female energies (i.e., conscious, and unconscious), the yin and the yang energies of the Universe, self-surrender and putting others before yourself. Have faith and trust in the Universe as your prayers are manifesting in your waking life. You may need to be patient, but trust that all will turn out for your highest good.

Partnerships and/or commitments will be appearing. Find your balance and learn moral responsibility. New opportunities will be manifesting. Stay strong in your personal truths to manifest positive outcomes. New ideas and concepts are beginning to take shape and grow into reality. Maintain a positive attitude and outlook and continue your good work in order to manifest your desires. The time to reap your reward is just ahead of you.

Watch your thoughts and focus on your true heart's desires, so that they can manifest in your life. An energetic gateway has opened for you and your thoughts and focus will manifest rapidly in your life. Therefore, choose your thoughts wisely, ensuring that they are a true representation of your heart's desires. Do not focus on any negatives as these can manifest just as quickly as positives.

You are on a winning streak in your oneness, individuality, self-development, progress, and creativity. Develop your individuality and creativity. Develop your clairvoyant abilities and grow spiritually. Pay attention to repetitive ideas and thoughts as they hold the solutions and answers to your prayers.

A new level or skill will soon be achieved, or reached, or success in business is eminent. This is the beginning of a journey, something that can be exciting and exhilarating. Your journey so far brought you the challenge of isolation and loneliness that you had to overcome and learn from. Now you are experiencing a feeling of wholeness and completeness.

Your ideas and visions are coming to fruition in your life. Be committed, keep improving yourself and your meditation. All things are possible. Take notice of your true goals and aspirations and know they are attainable. Your consideration of new directions, your wishes, will come to fruition and the changes will be successful. Help, guidance, and assistance are always available to you, always. All you need to do is ask.

You have potential and possibilities. You now have a clean, blank slate. Do not refuse to acknowledge the thing that is hidden about you (i.e., your spirituality/clairvoyance [the ability to gain information about an object, person, location, or physical event through extrasensory perception]/internal guidance).

Someone you know will soon pay you a visit/contact you for the purpose of reconnecting with you and making up for lost years. The meeting could even turn out beneficial for both of you as you might consider going into a business venture together.

When I went to bed that night, I said my prayers. In my prayers I asked who this old friend was that I was going to encounter and what was this business venture we may do. I then proceeded to ask what was meant specifically by me developing my spiritual abilities. I asked in what capacity. I also asked what exactly is it that I am supposed to be doing, what my soul purpose, or divine purpose was, what was my path.

You are embarking on a task which involves analytical work. There is a new project on going and I see that you are wondering how you will work on this project. You have a desire to lead. Understand that even though ambition is important, it is necessary that you remain wise and not let your plans for the future turn negatively.

I see that you regret parts of how you have acted in life. Soon after this dream you will receive news about this friend. I see that you are freely expressing your unconscious guidance in your writing. You are getting over serious problems and learning to accept a difficult change. I am telling you to pace yourself in your creativity. You are embarking upon new beginnings and a reawakening giving you a fresh outlook on things. You are experiencing peace, purity, and awareness. You will be experiencing freedom and openness.

You are worrying too much about a certain person, thing, or event in your life presently or in the future. Worrying or thinking about this will likely cause you to become displeased with the results and then because of that, suffer from severe emotional and financial losses. Your relationship with spirit will get stronger with time. Your body and mind are healing, and you are connecting to your spirituality and emotions. Have faith and trust. Amazing luck will be coming to your household. This message is an omen for public recognition of your merits. I also see that you have big respect for your spirit guide and intuition.

I see you understand the different directions of your personality. New opportunities and a new life are coming your way. You have an ability to develop new relationships with other people. You will be encountering a new friendship with me in the future.

Happy times and calmness are entering your waking life. Now is time for peace and change. You are trying to accomplish something which is proving to be difficult for you. You have a great need for independence, and it is important to recognize that you need to understand what ties you down in life. You will victoriously overcome some difficult obstacles which are seemingly overwhelming you. Great things are seen on their way to you. It is important you look after yourself and health now.

You are starting to move toward some clear goals. You will experience a spiritual elevation and activation of emotions. You will enjoy success. You have made efforts at your work and now you do not depend on anyone anymore.

You will be rewarded for your efforts and patience needed to achieve this goal. You are connected to the Divine and are receiving spiritual support and guidance. You will have success and financial gain in your projects and activities that you are about to undertake. Good fortune and nice surprises are in your near future. You will have a revelation about your spirit guide. You are now in situations that are out of your control associated with your collective unconscious.

You need to control your aggressiveness and impulsiveness. You will be able to get rid of an exceedingly difficult situation. You will be able to uncover what other people need. Positive changes are coming, and I see your desire to get things done in life. You will have wealth. Specifically, you will have stability in wealth.

You have great potential. You will be very wealthy, and prosperity is yours. Your life is on the right course and your finances will certainly increase. An area of your life is changing, and things are going to be content in the future.

Some unexpected and unusual changes are occurring in a good way in your life. You will be breaking out of financial troubles soon. However, you are too concerned with planning an outcome. Do not worry about it. Everything will be revealed to you. Accept yourself for who you are. You have the ability to act with integrity in all situations in your life. But sometimes you doubt yourself. This is a reminder to recognize your own potential to help you succeed.

We are all connected through our collective unconscious. Focus on your true hearts desires so they can manifest in your life. An energetic gateway has opened for you. Your thoughts and focus will manifest rapidly in your life. I sense some restriction. Look outside the box. Work diligently, yet harmoniously to achieve your goals. Put your ideas into practical form. You are being guided. Your hard work and efforts will bring well-earned rewards. You will have comfort, stability, achievement, and success.

There is a union of mind, body and soul occurring. This is a time of growth, expansion, and manifesting abundance. You need to have self-discipline in your service to others. Commit to improving yourself and your meditation. You are going in a new direction towards achieving wholeness and returning to source. Take note of feelings of holding yourself back or inflexibility. They will not allow you to attain your goals, aspirations, or personal potential.

Stability is needed in all areas of your life. Monetary and material needs will be met. Be grateful for your blessings to encourage further abundance. Your new friendship with me and achieving your desires will be coming full circle. Find balance between your goals and ideals and your inner, spiritual self. Your thoughts are out of balance, and you are placing too much focus on the material side of life. Look to serving humanity and fostering your spiritual growth and expansion. Focus on spirit and service and your material and emotional needs will be automatically met as a result.

You are having a spiritual growth spurt and attuning to the spiritual realms. Pay attention to your inner-growth and intuition and that you continue growing spiritually towards enlightenment. You need to meditate and go within in order to find a greater spiritual awareness and enlightenment. Meditation can take the form of contemplation and deep thought, prayer, faith, intuitive and inner searching, questioning and the like. I am telling you of a beneficial time to come, obstacles overcome, and your success realized. You are on the Divine path that is right for you. Keep up the great work that you are doing, and positive things will continue to flow into your life that will help and assist you along in your journey. You may find that positive things naturally flow towards you in your life. You will overcome any hinderances and concerns in the extremely near future. Listen to your intuition for guidance and solutions. You are on the right path and are doing very well. Your positive efforts and hard work will bring you well-earned rewards, and your wishes and true desires are coming to fruition. You will have self-satisfaction, inner joy, and blessings. Isolate yourself and get this work done.

Your inner-spirit and you are going through some challenging times. You are going through a rebirth and renewal spiritually. You will be enlightened by some event. You can think clearly and make the right choice in the worst situations. Do not block your intuition. You are going to be intelligent going forward. You will have wisdom, awareness, and new insight. Use your intuition to solve some of your inner issues. You will soon experience personal growth and increased awareness. Do whatever it takes to make you stronger, better. The best is yet to come for you. Stop running away from your dreams.

You will soon be planning new things in your life, and it is important you also consider other possibilities. With great strength, you will be able to discover new ways of approaching people with fresh and new ideas. Waves of new opportunities should materialize during this time. You may encounter a period of strangeness, but you must make sure the situations that you find yourself in are stimulating your spiritual being. Do not do reckless things that could hurt others, or even yourself. You *are gaining spiritual knowledge and power in life. You are going to encounter a spiritual journey in the future. Things that are hidden will come to the surface shortly. You will be able to challenge yourself better and ensure other people will not harm you.*

After this message, I knew exactly what to do. I had to work more on developing myself physically, mentally, and spiritually. This would be the foundation for all things to come in the future. This is what I am supposed to be doing for now. I now know that whatever it is that I will be doing in the future, it is going to have something to do with this development. At that moment I realized that I must train myself to work on this development just as an athlete trains for an event. I then realized that I have been perfectly prepared to do just that. I played sports my whole life. I trained for that. I was in the Marines. I had to train endlessly for that. I was in college and an archaeologist. I had to train for that. It all makes perfect sense now. I need to start this period of training and I know exactly how to do that.

I see that you have joined with your unconscious and are acting as one now. Regarding your inner hopes, fears, and questions about your abilities, you must train to use them and develop them to the point where you have them perfected and can perform to the best of your abilities.

You are starting new beginnings and you will receive goodness. You are learning new things and going through a phase of growth and development. I can see that you feel like you are trying to learn how to walk all over again. Remember, we must learn to walk before we run. When we can run, we can learn to fly. Practice developing your abilities.

On the previous day, I sent a message to my publisher asking him to set up a phone meeting so we could discuss business. A few days later, on Monday, he asked me what days worked for me. We worked out a day and a time to have a phone meeting on Thursday. So, on Monday night, when I went to bed, I asked God what I should say to my publisher about publishing my book and/or possibly becoming my own publisher and doing it all myself. I was also wondering what would happen with my royalty account when he ever decided to retire.

There is balance in your partnership. Remember your service to others, have faith and trust. This is your Divine life purpose and soul mission. There will be unions, partnerships, and new commitments. New opportunities are coming. New ideas and concepts are beginning to take shape and grow into reality. Maintain a positive attitude, outlook, and continue your good work in order to manifest your desires. The time to reap your reward is just ahead of you. Work diligently, yet harmoniously with me, to achieve your goals. Put your ideas into a practical form that is adapted or designed for actual use. Know that you are being guided and supported in your endeavors. The projects that you have been working on will be successful, and you will be pleased with the long-term results. Have faith and trust in your abilities.

There are new beginnings, potential and possibilities ahead. So, go ahead with your book. Use your self-expression and stay connected to your personal goals. I see that you are contemplating how strong our relationship is. You are connected to your unconscious, intuition, and your conscious creativeness. There has been a "marriage" between us, so to speak, and you are connected to your unconscious/guidance in your waking life. Keep developing your intuition, your abilities. If you do not develop them, you will be stuck in a destiny that is constantly leading you on the wrong path. You will repeat the same mistakes and encounter the same problems.

There are new beginnings, positive changes, and luck in your life. Great things are in store for your life. You want to be sure that you are taking advantage of all opportunities in your life currently. You are a strong person. There is a lot to gain in your life right now and you are under favorable stars. Your life has fallen into place. You are in a good place, and everything is where it should be. You are experiencing a spiritual entirety. You have emotional stability and fluidity. You are finding replenishment and balance through your relationship with me. You are going through a religious conversion so to speak. Positive changes and new adventures in life are ahead.

You are being secretive about using your abilities. They need to come out for you to progress in life. You need to find someone whom you feel you can trust and share it because it is standing between you and your prosperity.

A friend is having private issues which result in a possible stagnation in their development. All you need to do is make sure that you offer advice and teach them how to forgive and forget.

You need to meditate and think about what you want from life. You are embarking on a new path and trying to find a resolution. You are about to make a transformation. Your subconscious needs work to formulate questions or issues in your daily life. You need to make choices regarding decisions on an important event in your life career. You are experiencing a combination of new phases in your life. You will encounter a new spiritual path soon. You will enjoy openness if you engage on this spiritual path. You have a fresh start. Take the initiative. I also see that you are feeling emotionally insecure, or helpless, in this part of your life. There is a more suitable direction or way of doing things in this aspect of your life.

You must review your own inner thoughts. You can hear and see things that are hidden. You are being required to try to understand what is in front of you. You have wisdom, hidden visions, control, power, and the ability to see clearly. Look beyond various directions in your life and try to gain the wisdom that you need. You are approaching cross-roads in your life. People are taking too much from you. You need to understand the responsibilities of caring for others, but also the time to care for yourself. You have a hidden sense of intuition, and this is the rational and logical way that you are going to make decisions in the future. You will rise in the light of the day from the depths of destruction. I see that you are trying to gain the wisdom that you need in order to progress in life. Develop your abilities, your sense of intuition.

This is the doorway that needs to be open which leads to your prosperous future.

After going through this sort of transitional phase that the last dream was talking about, I was feeling incredibly drained. I had been having several dreams a night at a fast pace one after another. Each time I would wake up, I would have to write them down because I knew another one was coming, and I was worried I could not remember them all in the morning. I did not want to miss any of my important messages. Also, my neighbor had been partying for two weeks straight until 3am or longer every night. He would be in his backyard drinking, doing drugs, screaming, yelling, and laughing with all of his friends he would invite over from the bar he was hanging out at all evening. They would chop wood in the middle of the night and have gigantic fires in the back yard. This also kept me awake and very tired every day. I finally got frustrated and did not do anything for three days except rest and try and get some nap time in. I had to step away from my messages as well. I told God to leave me alone for a few days. I needed rest. I felt absolutely drained physically and mentally.

There will be a coming together of your power and intelligence. I see that you are affected by negative energies caused by a difficult person and the situation. You have access to the particular characteristics which make you unique. It is important to take any energy released over the next couple months and use it to your advantage. There may be some conflict between your conscious and unconscious attributes, maintain some kind of balance between the two.

Stop worrying as things will sort themselves out. I see there is someone in your circle of friends or acquaintances is not acting in a correct manner. You will recognize that this person is an enemy, and he seeks to trick you into thinking that you are a friend. You are going to discover many attributes about yourself on a psychic level. You are going to try and move beyond your comfort zone. Somebody is going to be rather deceitful. I see you have been having some worrying times lately.

You are looking to solve a problem in life, you yearn for the freedom of expression, you have the strength to challenge anything and the power for success. You have the ability to work towards something that will become a success-materially. You will gain satisfaction in life. You must fight in order to win. You have the emotions and energy to succeed in life. You have the opportunity to manage a deceitful person in waking life. You have the inner ability to overcome any obstacles. It is important to try to use your unconscious mind to understand the real problems in waking life.

Your goals will be achieved. This is a specific call to action in your waking life. You are receiving this message because you are reaching higher levels of consciousness. You are trying to move away from someone who is dishonest. You have a difficult task with someone who is deceitful. This person gives you displeasure. It is a minor problem in life that you can overcome. You have the feeling of being suited or adapted in spirit, feeling, temper, etc.

You have encountered a rocky time. You are going to save something important going forward. You need clear emotions and preparedness for bigger changes. You have invested your creativity and you need to focus on your "family" precious times. Your worried about someone acting irresponsibly. You should not let your emotions overwhelm you. Your inability to manage your emotions is leaving you feeling overwhelmed by your feelings. You need to focus better on your emotions in life.

Yesterday I decided to really work on controlling my impulses, urges and emotions in an effort to improve and develop myself even further. I knew I needed to remove these "barriers" from my life. When I went to bed, I meditated. I told God I was working on these things, that I will get there. I started telling him about my neighbor who was partying again. I was complaining about it and telling God this behavior was ridiculous and something needed to be done about it, please. While I was complaining I remembered that my previous dreams had told me to focus on the positive, the good things and my true desires in order to manifest those things in life. I realized I was complaining, hence focusing on the negative. My dream also told me to be careful of that because that will also manifest itself in my life, if that is what I focus on. So, I quickly changed my thoughts to the positive and I also thanked God for the abundance in my life in order to manifest more of that. Then I fell asleep and had a dream. In the dream I was actually spoken to. This happened two other times in my life, many years apart. I talk about them in my book, *A line in the Sand: The true story of a Marine on the front lines of the first Gulf War*. When I woke up in the morning, I wrote it all down.

I see you are achieving self-mastery and understanding the knowledge that "all things are possible." Have faith and trust that in the Universe your prayers are manifesting in your waking life. Be patient. All will work out for your highest good. Stay strong in your personal truths, forming the foundation of your life, living by this code/standard, establishing respect for yourself and others by acting certain ways in certain circumstances.

Keep working diligently and harmoniously to achieve your goals. Keep putting your ideas into practical form for use. You are giving off vibrations of illumination and initiation. You are being guided in your endeavors. You will have comfort and stability in your life. Build a strong foundation and work to achieve your goals and dreams. The projects you are working on will be successful and you will be pleased with the long-term results. Have faith and trust in your abilities. However, take note of feelings of holding yourself back, limiting yourself, and allow yourself to attain your goals and personal potential.

You will have abundance in whatever your true heart desires. You will reap the rewards, attract your desires, and achieve personal improvement if you follow your guidance. Trust your intuition and instincts to manifest your desires and take appropriate action. Success, wealth, and abundance is on its way into your life. Your goals are coming to fruition and a state of completeness. A favorable offer or windfall is coming your way. Trust that all your wants and needs will be met. You will be rewarded for work well done. Keep your finances in check to ensure a solid foundation for yourself and your loved ones. Although the Universal energies always ensure that you are supported, it is your personal responsibility to make sure that you are living up to your full potential. We all must integrate our true selves. You must obtain self-harmony, meet your responsibilities. Once you do, you will have love, abundance, domestic harmony, and good will. Stability is needed in all areas of your life. Your monetary and material needs will be met. So, be grateful for your blessings to encourage further abundance in your life. Family matters will come full circle. You will achieve your desires in regard to home, family, and social life. Find balance between your goals and ideals and your inner, spiritual self. Look to serving humanity by fostering your spiritual growth and expansion. Go within. Your material and emotional needs will automatically be met as a result of that.

By integrating both parts of your true-self, your conscious and unconscious, comes the whole you, the whole-self. Deny your impulses and urges. Stick to your work. You need to focus on the things you like to do in life. Obtain a new mindset. Everything you worry about will resolve itself, and you will feel free and easy again. Your being overwhelmed by your own emotions, and soon you will experience a break-through. You are undergoing a period of transformation, and this is a sign of good luck.

Positive things are about to happen in your life. You have spent a lot of time and money on some things in your life (i.e., my books, stocks, and my development) to enable it all to succeed, and now it just happened that it is successful. This will make you extremely happy. You need to enjoy yourself as well as utilize this period by using this opportunity to improve any area of your life. You need to work hard in the future.

When I went to bed, I meditated as usual. I started talking to God about how good of a job I did during the day working on eliminating barriers from my life and the progress I am making. I said to God, "See, I am making progress. I will get there. I promise."

Then I started thinking about this particular person. I have been thinking about this person quite a bit the last several months and even dreaming about this person. Then I remembered about not focusing on negative thoughts. So, I quickly changed my thoughts. I started thanking God for all the blessings and abundance in my life and how much I appreciated them all. I was doing this to attract more of these positive things in my life. Then I just started meditating to cleanse my mind of all the days thoughts and activities, so my mind was clear. Then, I fell asleep. I had several more dreams and one of them was about this person and it really affected me. Thoughts of this occupied me all day the next day. I did not know what to think or if I interpreted the dream correctly. However, I remembered in a previous dream God told me to pay attention to repetitive thoughts and ideas. The answers to my prayers lie within them. Then I remembered these same themes have been appearing in my dream analysis, but I kept ignoring them. I did not even write those interpretations down because I thought, "No, that's not going to happen!" Well, this time I wrote them down. We will see what happens in the near future. I could be completely wrong here, but we will see what happens. Here is what my unconscious guidance told me about the things that have been repeated in my messages that I left out.

You have great ambitions in life, and you are likely to succeed. Maintain a deep focus on yourself, stay grounded in life, and continue to be in touch with yourself. You will receive good news in a form of femininity (my unconscious guidance [my feminine side]) and sweetness. There is good news coming, joy, harmony, peace, and love. You will be experiencing a happy period, an inner awakening, a new love is coming (i.e., a new love of life).

I see you have been preoccupied with someone who was absent from your life for some time. There will be a new beginning happening in some area of your life soon, like someone returning to your life after a period of separation, making you incredibly happy.

Watch your thoughts and focus on your true heart's desires, so that they can manifest in your life. Develop your intuitive and clairvoyant abilities and grow spiritually.

Pay attention to your repetitive ideas and thoughts as they hold the solutions and answers to your prayers. A new level or skill will soon be achieved. It will be the beginning of a journey, something exhilarating.

The changes ahead of you will bring about favorable opportunities and feelings of personal satisfaction. Positive changes are heading your way. Better things are coming into your life. These changes may come about with unexpected haste and in unusual ways, but they will bring positive energies and opportunities that will propel you in the right direction along your life path. A new friendship will enter your life soon and you will be achieving your desires regarding home, family, and social life. Take a more relaxed approach to this situation.

I spent some time last night mediating about this last dream and the person in it. This person caused a lot of problems in my life in the past. While I was mediating, the thought popped into my head that this person is a metaphor. Because of how upset this person makes me, I realized that it was all designed to really make me remember the dream and to really think about the actual message. I then realized that what the message was really saying is that this new beginning, good news, all these good things coming are my "new love" coming. In other words, I will have a new love of life, new love of myself. The someone returning to my life after a period of separation is the "real me", my "real self". In other words, through all of this I am going to get back in touch with, and be one with, my real self once again. Obviously, with everything I have been through on this journey I have been separated from the real me. It had to happen that way in order for me to develop properly. Now that that is over, my body and soul will be reunited. This is why my unconscious was telling me at the end of the dream to take a more relaxed approach to this situation. I was worrying over nothing.

Last night I had a dream. I was meditating on what I had just mentioned briefly. Then I began thinking again about my neighbor who had all his friends from the bar over again last night partying and getting drunk all night. This has been going on for almost three weeks straight now. It has really been annoying me and I want this behavior to stop. I have been thinking about this a lot since it has been happening every day and I just want it all to go away. My neighborhood is really nice and peaceful except for the guy next door who disrupts it all and is constantly about noise and chaos. He only cares about himself and getting drunk and stoned. I have been wishing he would just disappear, be gone from here so we could get a normal, nice neighbor.

I see that you have a big concern and are in a state of turmoil, and you have a tribulation that grinds you. You are being deceived by a neighbor. This person exhibits traitorous behavior. You have enemies. This person is not to be trusted in your waking life which makes it harder to deal with. You will overcome this deceit by having a spiritual perspective, or point of view.

I see you desire rules, recognition of obligations or rules in your life. I see you are trying to manage others. Steer clear of reckless behavior. Both on your part and theirs. Someone is lying to you so do not be weak and gullible. You need to make sure you are tolerant and understand what is happening in your life. I see how much this person annoys others. Remember, friends close to you are your secret enemies.

I see you have intense feelings of dishonesty. You are going to win over your enemies. You will get help from an unexpected source. You are in contact with people who are not true, and they pretend to be a certain person to get your attention. Trust your gut. This is a warning about others.

I see you have an outlook on this situation as being self-involved. You are noticing something about it all the time. You need to pay attention to how you are noticing everything you are doing revolving around this specific problem. You need to use your mind. You need to notice yourself thinking in a certain way. You need to be aware of negative thinking patterns that you are aware of in yourself. You are going through negative experiences that you cannot stop. This problem has taken on a life of its own, become exceptionally large, or hard to control. I see you are compelled to feel or act in certain ways. Your desire to please others is at the risk of sacrificing your own needs and happiness. You have a fear or inability to act.

You are being overly concerned with other people and with their directions in life. You are worrying too much about a certain person, thing, or event in your waking life. Although this attitude can seem appropriate and worth the trouble at this time, it is highly likely you would eventually become displeased with the results and possibly suffer from severe emotional and financial losses.

When I went to bed, I said my prayers and meditated as usual. I told God that I was thankful for all the abundance and blessings in my life. I then told him I have noticed changes in my life since I embarked on this journey of personal development. I also told him that I noticed my dreams got a bit more complex and a little more challenging to interpret and that I surmised that this was part of my training and development for the future. I told him that I hoped he saw the changes in me and that I hoped I was doing a good job and interpreting my dreams correctly and living up to his aspirations. I then meditated to cleanse my mind and I began to see a bright light and I began to see faces, but they were hard to make out. I also kept seeing an eye or a pair of eyes and I kept hearing this sort of high-pitched hum. I soon fell asleep and had a couple dreams. This is what my message was.

There are changes coming up in your life that may alter your course. You are learning your life lessons through your experiences. Become more in tune to your five senses, hearing, sight, smell, taste, and touch. You need to pursue your personal truths, the way you live your life, the code you live by, which helps to form the foundation of your life.

You have an internal desire to break free from old constraints and restraints, ways of living, that have been holding you back. Therefore, you need to begin living your life with passion. Passion is contagious and the only way to be truly fulfilled is to inspire others. Your passion gives your life purpose and meaning. It would be a shame to keep what you know and what you experience to yourself. Telling your life story or showcasing your creativity to the world is a way to pass on your passion.

The personal freedom and major life changes ahead of you will bring about favorable opportunities and a feeling of personal satisfaction. Positive changes are headed your way.

There is a need for change, variety, and new growth. Better things are coming into your life. These changes may come about with unexpected haste and in unusual ways, but they will bring positive energies and opportunities that will propel you in the right direction along your life path.

Stay away from over-indulgence, the pursuit of pleasure; sensual self-indulgence, unreasonable thoughts and fears that lead you to do repetitive behaviors. These interfere with daily activities and cause big distress.

It is time for something to end, so that a new phase can appear in life. You will need to try to improve the way that you are doing something, be better at what you do and be creative because now is the time to begin a new thing which could improve your life.

New beginnings are predicted this year. This year it is important that you do not ignore opportunities. Success is likely to present itself. This may come through your own initiative.

You have come to terms with past events in your life. You have moved on in life to something more challenging. There are many different aspects of yourself that need to be covered. I see you are trying to deal with a stressful situation in life, calm times await you. You are looking to expand your curious mind; you are constantly looking for new knowledge. You can have many different options in life. Good times are ahead. Take good care of yourself and your health as a priority. You have a passion for the future even though you have been frustrated or discouraged in the past. A new situation will present itself.

A new idea or project is coming to fruition. Some new project is in the works. Fake friends will be with you for their self-interests. You will get rid of fake friends easily as soon as possible. You need to review a relationship that is especially important to you, or of deep interest to you, that is to make sure you pick the right person to engage together with in the same activity from the start. You will have unusual and unexpected changes in your waking life. You will have a new start. You have the ability to intelligently overcome obstacles. So, do not give up. You will have prosperity and good times in your life even though there is something difficult in your life. So, think about your diet. You are going to have a reunion, or rebirth, in your life. You will meet someone you have lost touch with some years ago. When you reunite, it is going to make you be filled with much joy and happiness, which will create unforgettable memories. This someone is your real self. You are ready to be reintegrated and become whole. I see that you are welcoming your real self into your life.

However, I see that you have a fear of getting lost in this experience that is challenging to the extreme. But you will overcome negativity. You will have financial luck and wealth. You are now ready for a new phase in your life. However, you have a difficult issue that requires your focus to overcome. You will get an opportunity to make some extra cash. So, seize that opportunity but be careful. An unexpected benefit is coming your way due to someone else's neglect. This could involve a large amount of money. So, it is important for you to be strong in order to re-gain your own inner strength because at the moment you cannot move on in life because of your barriers. You must recognize what those barriers are and then you will be able to pave the way to your own success. I see you are having feelings of opening yourself up to higher levels of spiritual connection. Therefore, you need to clean yourself.

Then for about a week, I did not have any dreams that I remembered when I woke up. Almost as if I were being given a break to let this all sink in before moving on again. I remembered that in past dreams, I was told several times to remember that there will be periods of death and rebirth. Well, I just now realized that is exactly what has been happening. I had another series of dreams, and the death and re-birth cycle began again.

A hopeful situation and happiness will be yours in the future. You will have great success at your work, and through forthcoming events, which are going to be significant to you and others. I see that you wish to change. You need to remove barriers. I see that you are under a lot of stress and pressure from your deepest feelings and inner issues. But underneath all of that are peace and happiness. You need to connect with your spirit, your spirit guide. You are embarking on a guidance system from within.

If you want to get to that next level and experience that raw energy, force, vigor, intense passion, power, and courage then you must obtain purity, perfection, peace, dignity, cleanliness, and awareness of what you are doing and what is going on in your life and your new beginnings. You are experiencing an awakening and a fresh outlook on life.

I see that you are working on your self-development and that is why you are having this dream. New opportunities are coming your way. Something is ending. There are different phases in life. You are opening up to new events and people. You need to grow in life. Try to let go of the past. Your health is particularly important and there is no need to jeopardize it because of useless worries and anxieties. It is time to start seeing and doing things differently. There is no need to keep on doing something that has no return on it. A treasured and valued past time must end because you are too busy.

A change is required for you to feel more content. You need to conduct some work on something in your waking world. You are feeling bad due to a part of your area of life having reduced function. You are currently ready to move forward in your future life and there is nothing you feel can obstruct you. Everything that happened in your life in the past and everyone who is no longer in your present life no longer matter to you and you must let go of all the negativity that you hold. At the moment you need to tidy up. You are currently experiencing emotional and psychological challenges, which are making you feel worried or depressed. Rid yourself of these feelings in order to be able to regain control of your current situation before it goes out of control.

Something new is about to happen. A change is around the corner. Apply your knowledge and experiences that you have learned so far in your life so that you can deal with any problems in the future. There are numerous possibilities in life that have yet to come to the surface for you. You will engage in profitable speculation. Many plans need to be put into place to fulfill your true destiny in this world. You have returned from spiritual crisis, and you have been fulfilling your objectives.

You are now ready to continue your life's goals and plans. You are ready to start something that you have long put off. You have all the resources you need to achieve your goals. You just must look deeper and figure out what you do have. You will have a gain from an unexpected rise in staple food products. A lavish lifestyle is coming your way. God will be bringing forth gifts related to your vision/revelation and to an increase in spiritual authority and the healing of past wounds.

You will be getting rid of some unpleasant problems and a desire of yours will be fulfilled. You have full creativity in what you are currently working on. A passion has surfaced, and you are ready to get working to make this happen. I see you are trying to replenish and end anything bad happening in your life. Good moments are coming your way.

A transformation is predicted. This is the end of your spiritual journey and finding the truth of the soul. You have a hidden understanding and wisdom in life. There is something amazing that is about to happen to you, starting next month. This could be quite a remarkable new start. There is energy being moved to an area of your life, as well as uncovering your destiny. Important luck is

coming your way, which will help you be self-sufficient for some time. You need to keep your balance in life.
You will have moments of enlightenment. You may want to learn something new and exciting. You want to approach a new task in life. You have spiritual growth. You will have new beginnings and a brainstorm of creative ideas. You will find your source of your inspiration in an unexpected place. Great things are coming your way. Are you ready to handle the pressure that comes with success? Are you ready to accomplish your wildest dreams?

You have had difficulties in your waking life from lack of financial security and a general lack of belief in your own abilities. You need to understand the bigger picture, and you need to have more confidence in your ability moving forward. You have lacked money and you are trying to escape from that situation. You have some untapped creative talent in your job which you have not been able to use. Allow events to occur at the right pace.

You will get lucky. You ought to try something risky, such as playing the lottery. You will be extremely lucky. In the coming days you are going to be successful. You are strong and have overcome big difficulties. You have been working too hard on everything and you feel that you are not representing your ideas in the best way. You have a desperation to go back to your carefree days. Stop worrying about minor issues. You need to look at people's actions and try to understand what they are thinking. You are going to have an unhindered vision of how people are acting in the future. This will be your strength.

Your unconscious mind demands attention. You are trying to search for answers to a certain difficulty or problem in your waking life. You are searching for the answers to improve your life. You may not notice right now, but answers will come with time. You have a bright future. You are going to start new beginnings. Pay attention to your mind. Accomplish your important decisions. Success is coming your way only if you go your own way in life. You will receive help from me to help you along your path to success. Expand your horizons and investigate new interests.

It is time for something to end so that a new phase can appear in life. You need to up your game and be creative because now is the time to begin a new thing which could improve your life. Success is likely to present itself. This will come through your own initiative. Success will be yours. You will escape your old life and experience freedom. New opportunities are opening before you and you need these to make sure that you get the most from life.

Working hard is the key message of this dream. Hard work, persistence, diligence, and productivity come to mind. Hard work is needed in life. This is a reminder of how you used to be working towards something but never actually achieve what you set out to do. Do not do that with your new opportunity and life.

The usual course of your life will be changed. Be careful in making important decisions. Happiness and satisfaction will dominate your affairs in the future. God is on your side. You will have intelligence, light, and generosity ahead. You will have energy and fullness of life and a rich harvest. Other people will be envious of you because of your special skills and properties.

There is an opening of new possibilities and challenges in the future. There are hope, opportunities, new beginnings, and transformation. You are experiencing the separation of two paths, leaving your old and following your new. You are embarking on a new path. The catalyst for your transformation is about to be crossed. There is so much more that is beyond your path. A way to a path in life is opening. There may be opportunities going forward. Choices will be made in regard to a decision about an important event in your life's career. You are experiencing a combination of new phases in life.

You will discover a secret. You will have positive energy in life. You are going to have the power cleaning your life, a fresh start. This is the gateway to your childhood dreams. You will finally find your inner peace. You will finally come to your senses and show the world what you can do. There are new opportunities which will be created by yourself.

Do not forget the importance of your mind, your own internal sight. No matter how old you are, it is not too late to follow your dreams. It is time to think about the type of life you wish to lead right now, and it is time to succeed. You must care for your own mind. With this, all your problems can be rectified. This is a spiritually important time right now. You see obstacles more clearly.

You are changing for the best, no matter the situation. You are being open to new possibilities and changing your view on things. You have made a discovery about a certain skill you hold. Other people will turn to you for help. This is God reminding you to listen to your intuition. You are being proactive over this situation in your life.

You will need to make decisions about important things, and you need to do that by searching for answers in order to reach those decisions. This is the start of new beginnings. It is time to give you peace and ability. It is important to let go of things, i.e., your old ways of living. The reason being is that they have become too stressful. Move on so you can seek more happiness. You need to move forward and try to challenge yourself in the future.

Remember your service to others, as well as your faith, trust, your divine life purpose, and your soul mission. Maintain a balance of the energies of the Universe, self-surrender and putting others before yourself. Have faith and trust in the Universe as your prayers are manifesting in your waking life. Be patient but trust that all will turn out for your highest good. You have a new commitment and partnership with me. Find balance with your time, work, chores, etc. Miracles and new opportunities are ahead. Stay strong in your personal truths to manifest positive outcomes. New ideas and concepts are beginning to take shape and grow into reality. Maintain a positive attitude and outlook and continue your good work in order to manifest your desires. The time to reap your rewards is just ahead of you.

You have self-mastery and the knowledge that all things are possible. You have knowledge, intelligence, and mental capacity. Work diligently, yet harmoniously, with me to achieve your goals. Put your new ideas into practical form. You have been illuminated and initiated. You are being guided and supported in your endeavors. Trust that your hard work and efforts will bring well-earned rewards. You will have comfort and stability in your life. Use hard work, will, and personal effort to achieve long-term goals and aspirations. All is as it should be. The projects you are working on will be successful, and you will be pleased with the long-term results. Have faith and trust in your abilities.

You have achieved a union of your mind, body and soul and the holy trinity. It resonates with the Ascended Masters. Your ideals and visions are coming to fruition in your life. Maintain your self-discipline through your service to others, manifesting abundance, productivity, and unity with me. The Ascended Masters are working closely with you, guiding, encouraging, and supporting you. Your prayers have been heard and are being responded to and answered. You have vitality, motivation, enthusiasm, creativity, and experience. Be committed, keep improving yourself and your meditation. All things are possible. Take notice of your true goals and aspirations, and know they are attainable. Your wishes will come to fruition and the changes will be successful. Help, guidance, and assistance are available to you, always. All you need to do is ask.

Abundance will manifest in the forms of happiness, money, love, bliss, and whatever your true heart desires. You will reap your rewards, attract your desires, and accomplish your personal improvement. Trust your intuition and instincts to manifest your desires. Success, wealth, and abundance are on their way into your life. So, trust your intuition and instincts and take appropriate action. Your goals and a state of completeness are coming to fruition. A favorable windfall is coming your way. Material and financial abundance are on their way into your life. Trust that all your wants and needs will be met. You will be rewarded for work well done. Keep your finances in check to ensure a solid foundation for yourself and your loved ones. Although the Universal energies always ensure that you are supported, it is your personal responsibility to make sure that you are living up to your full potential.

You have spiritual enlightenment, mastery, intuition, personal creativity, self-illumination, and insight. You have a new partnership with me, equality, and balance. You have a thirst for spiritual awakening and advancement. You will have new occurrences, opportunities, and progress.

Everything in your life will go well and you will have prosperity and health. You will have balance and harmony. Things will grow. Your problems will work out in the future. You will have good health, growth, great luck, and money. You will overcome your worries. You will have happy times in the future and victory over others. You will have happiness and health in your family for many years. Things are going as planned and you have nothing to worry about. You will have wealth, relaxation, happiness, and growth both spiritually and mentally. You are experiencing personal growth, soul awakening and a positive outcome. No matter what you will overcome anything. You are attaining growth of your soul and mind. You are digging for a deeper meaning of everything you see, touch, feel, do, and accomplish. You wish to accomplish meaningful things. You have a natural protection from evil forces. Keep your faith so it stays protective. You are being given an opportunity to create something better from scratch to make your current world better than it has been. Your about to enjoy a peaceful, happy life very soon. It will be a gift for your patience and faith. Your efforts will pay off. Be patient.

You are experiencing unusual and unexpected changes in your waking life and a new start. Reflect on elements of your life. Always think about your personal feelings first i.e., your intuition and instincts. You have the ability to intelligently overcome obstacles. Do not give up. You will have prosperity and good times in life. I see friendship is important to you. You have great people around you. You have a deep sense of wanting freedom in life. You will have financial wealth and prosperity. You will have prosperity as long as you work well with me. Your current projects are going to be successful and will make your life more interesting than it already is. You will have both financial and emotional stability. Those around you will notice the improvements that will happen in your life. Everything is well. You are embarking on an unplanned trip with me so to speak. You are being taught a lot of things that will enable you to view life differently. You have experienced a re-birth and are re-uniting with me who you lost touch with long ago. This is filling you with much joy and happiness, and this will create unforgettable memories. You are welcoming me into your life.

You are connected to the world around you, and you have the ability to grow and develop spiritually. You will be building something small into a beautiful and one-of-a-kind situation. Things are going to go well in life. Do not fall back into your old bad habits. Stay away from people you think will bring bad influences into your life. Remember the hard times you have been through. You are the strongest person you know and refrain from listening to anyone who tells you the opposite. Remember to take a break and rehabilitate your mind and body when your exhausted, grab a beer.

There is a deep unconscious desire to progress in life. You are trying to get in touch with your unconscious guidance, your anima. Maintain your health and nourishment. This is a call to lead a real change in your life. Do not worry, things will work out fine. Be sure to physically nourish yourself in order to thrive and live a happy life. You have comfort, desire, contentment, and a sense of responsibility. Connect with nature and be one with the world. You will have riches and prosperity, a new life, a renewal.

 My neighbor was partying all night again and being loud and noisy with all his friends all night. It was making me angry, and I was begging God to do something about him and this situation. I kept concentrating on it, repeatedly. I finally realized I was having negative thoughts and I then changed what I was thinking about. I started concentrating on having abundance in my life and the things I desire.

This person you perceive as worthless and this activity you see as contemptible, the emotions you are stuck on will only suck the life right out of you. It will consume you and your tranquility. I see you are tired of feeling constricted by the demands of others, your emotions, and opinions towards what's going on in your environment and those who have power over you. There are questionable, dishonest, or illegal activities and manners of conduct for people that you know in real life.

Stay on top of things by being alert and making careful observations. Be alert to small changes around you. It is not up to you to decide what is right or wrong for others. Everyone finds their balance of moral integrity, and in doing so must walk their path. The only way you can lead them through is by setting the example. Make sure that you are clear with what your principals are first.

Something difficult to control is happening. You are having emotions that are difficult to manage, such as anger. This difficult situation in your life that you are experiencing needs to be dealt with by rising above it. Do not let yourself be controlled by this bad and harmful thing. Become better than that. Keep going with the courage of a lion.

I am uncovering your intuition, your spiritual insights, and the spiritual steps you need to take in the forthcoming future. There is someone who would cross you, or deceit you. Do not trust this person. You also need to improve, or encourage, your financial security. Money just seems difficult to obtain. It is not really. It just seems that way. There is a coming together of power and intelligence. You are having this dream because you are affected by negative energies caused by difficult people and situations. You have the capability to survive in difficult situations. Keep trying to work towards your goals.

Stop worrying as things will sort themselves out. Someone that is in your circle of friends is not acting in a correct manner. You will recognize this person is an enemy and they seek to trick you into thinking that you are a friend. This is a warning that dark power is associated with this situation you are struggling to come to terms with. You will encounter great luck beyond your dreams. You are trying to work towards gaining wealth. All your looking at is clinging to projects that you know will be a success. You have the ability to look beyond people's personalities. Store your own power and energy.

Hard work, patience, and efforts are required to achieve your goals in waking life. Power is at risk, and you need to hold onto your own power. Quit wasting it on issues you have at home. Relax because there is a dragon in your life, and he protects you. You do not have to worry about anything in your life. There are many good things that will happen to you in the next period. You will gain strength, luck, and good fortune. Be aware that your emotions come from your unconscious mind. This is a part of your unconscious self which needs to undergo a transformation in response to an enemy or somebody in your waking life. You are at an advanced level of spiritual awareness that connects your fears, enemies, and unconscious power. We can have power over others even though this power could be somewhat destructive. In other words, at this advanced level of spiritual awareness your emotions and activities are connected to others and can influence them even if it is destructive. So be careful or mindful of that.

Through anger and aggression, you will see the light and understand this difficult situation in your life. Whatever happens in your life will work out quite well for you after having this dream. These are small, minor problems. You can break this person and situation like a twig at any time you want by becoming aware of what you are doing and thinking and redirect your attention. You are ready to let your true self shine through for the world to see.

On Sunday, I decided to not do anything that day but hang out. I needed a break from all of this spiritual work, and I was also tired from spending all day the day before completing chores around the house. While sitting out front and trying to relax, I was talking with Frida. One of the neighbor's friends came over. He parked his truck, opened the door, and turned his stereo as high as it would go. It was so loud I could not hear what Frida was saying to me even though she was right next to me. I finally got upset and went over there and told the guy to turn it down. He was leaving. My neighbor was not there. So, he turned it down and took off. This set me into a foul mood for the rest of the day. As the day progressed, I became more and more mad. By the evening I just started venting about everything that makes me angry. I was going off on everything. Frida got fed up and went to bed.

You need a level of control over your emotions. You need to look at your ability to deal with negative emotions and situations. Look at the way you are confronting your problems, problems you cannot easily solve, or simply abandon.

A calming, peaceful period of your life is coming regarding your home life and your work and romantic relationships in the near future. You will have financial gains. You will make some good decisions or even investments and get some profit out. You are getting more power and influence. Make sure to attract favorable energies in the future. The only way to do this is to think more positively about what has been given to you on this earth. Your mind is sharp, and you have a great capacity for understanding. You will have financial improvement in the near future. You are going to make some profitable decisions which will make you become wealthier. You are going to be a more influential and powerful person that people will look upon to help them meet their goals and aspirations. You are going to have an easy time while searching for prosperity and success. New, steady, and slow beginnings are occurring. Your plans are going to succeed and at the same time a new endeavor is likely to happen soon. It will be slow and then gradually grow, expand, develop, improve, and evolve.

You will have prosperity, profit, and an increase of wealth. You will be rewarded for your efforts. You are receiving spiritual support and guidance. You will have success in projects and activities you have begun to undertake. You will have good fortune and nice surprises in the near future. You will have comfort and the ability to understand and share the feelings of another.

You are on the right path to achieving success. However, you need to stop or give up on areas of your life that are not going to succeed i.e., dead end job, bad dealings with money, or needing to restructure your life to get your priorities in order. Things will change over time but are likely to get better going forward.

Currently you are in the right place. There will be profit. You are about to get lucky with your finances. Take the changes you are making and use them to take what you need in order to find nourishment and self-worth. You have a sophisticated, intelligent, mature approach to the experience you are having. You have a made a change in direction that will help you provide for yourself. You have a powerful focus on expanding your own spiritual life. A spiritual awakening is occurring. You have had a revelation about denying the sinful nature and living by the Spirit through wholehearted submission to God, by devoting your life to God. Rely on God every day for your direction.

Important fascinating times are ahead. You will have luck in business, but especially your economic and financial aspects, which will be doing really well in the next period. Be careful not to believe everything you are told and do not exaggerate to others either. I see your anxiety about a male person in your life. I see you would like to be more comfortable in your own home. I see there is a situation you feel is too difficult to confront. However, you may finally have gotten the courage to do something.

You have a strong desire to be the best at what you can in life. You have hidden emotions of being critical of others. There is a need for logical action. It is important you seek knowledge and always learn what is important in life. You should not over think things in life. You are living on the positive side in life. You have truth, wisdom, heaven, eternity, devotion, tranquility, loyalty, and openness. You have an optimism about the future and a clarity of mind.

You will have wealth, prosperity, health and happiness for you and your family in the times to come. You are improving your finances and sources of income. Your problems are going to work out in the future. You will have victory over others. Goodness will be yours. A unique situation will occur. Your about to enjoy a peaceful, happy life very soon. It will be a gift for your patience and faith. Your efforts will finally pay off. Be patient. There is an essential opportunity that has been presented to you. You have the ability to protect yourself against any wrong doings.

You need to stay away from rude and envious people. You are wasting time with the wrong set of people. Someone will try to block your potential. You should reconsider some recent decisions like worrying too much about a certain person, thing, or event in your waking life. There will be an upcoming, new chapter in your waking life. You are currently the supporting pillar in the life of someone very dear to your heart. They depend upon you.

Eliminate depression inside of you to make room for positive things in your life. This can be done by spreading joy and exempting the darker side of you. To lead a balanced life, you must watch out for your weaknesses, and you must overcome them with the joys in your life. A blend of these two opposites creates life. The balance must be created by you.

Listen to your inner-self and control your speaking ability. It gives you patience to enlighten yourself as well as others. You have the power to control your voice, feelings, and emotions. It guides you to the manifestation of healing yourself, in order to breathe the air to have a new start in life freely, without any hindrance.

You will have a great life, full of happiness, wealth, and good relationships. You will have happiness and harmony in your life. You may receive some unexpected happiness as well. You are communicating your own special viewpoint to others. You have intellect, energy, agility, happiness, harmony, and wisdom. You will have a positive change, good health, growth, healing, hope, vigor, vitality, peace, and serenity.

You will undergo changes that are going to be major. They are going to be personal, but also related to work. Along with this great opportunity, a big change in your personal life is going to happen. Even though changes are not always easy, it is especially important for you to embrace this change and go along with it. Many beautiful things are waiting for you, only if you accept the change.

You could fall back into your old habits. You are doing things that are bad for you and spending time with people who bring nothing but bad habits into your life. If you want your life to stay the way it is now, without many incidents and problems, then stay away from negative influences and concentrate on important things in your life. This is the only way you can save yourself from these bad habits.

You are refusing to confront issues and instead trying to live with the negativity in your life. You know certain bad actors or energy are apparent in your life, yet you are opting to ignore those obvious issues. Unexpected guests will soon visit your house. Such guests are typically uninvited and will invade your comfort zone.

Things will go good in your life. Love, goodness, and prosperity are coming your way. There will be a renewal and curing. You need to move through into a territory of higher spiritual development. You need to have a deep devotion to religion. You will experience new beginnings, sudden changes, cleansing and determination.

You will experience healing, spiritual knowledge, and intuition. You are going through a spiritual growth spurt. Pay attention to your inner-growth and intuition and that you continue growing spiritually towards enlightenment. Meditate and go within to find a greater spiritual awareness and enlightenment. There is a beneficial time to come, obstacles overcome, and success realized. You are on the Divine path that is right for you. Keep up the great work you are doing, and positive things will continue to flow into your life that will help you along your journey. You will overcome any hinderances and concerns in the extremely near future. Listen to your intuition for guidance and solutions. You are on the right path and doing very well. Your positive efforts will bring you well-earned rewards, and your wishes and true desires are coming to fruition. You are experiencing a feeling of wholeness and completeness. You are returning to source.

Pay attention to the practical ways you have been moving towards your goals and how well you are progressing, and you are heading in the right direction. You just started a new project and moved off in some new direction. You have had new inspiring thoughts or ideas. This is a little hint or spark of something significant that can grow and develop over time for you.

Make the best of your situation right now. Look at this situation as a gift and find all the spiritual, and emotional growth you can find in it. Trust your instincts. You are being asked to discard what no longer serves you so that you can embrace something new. Look for new things on the horizon that will be of the most benefit to you. This is an opportunity for growth, emotional balance, and prosperity. You are now entering a period of emotional learning and self-discovery. You are being asked to keep an open mind so that you can accept the lesson or lessons as they come. The objective is for you to grow emotionally. Only then can you live from a place of unconditional love and acceptance. You need to develop your clairsentient skills. You have a gift for sensing and understanding emotional energies.

You are an excellent communicator. You have an affinity for the written and spoken word. You know how to *make the best of any situation. You know how to seize the opportunity that presents itself. You know how to sift through the emotional waters to keep yourself balanced and grounded. You have a natural gift for prosperity in life.*

Also, someone in your waking life is not what they appear to be. For some reason, they are hiding their true self from you as well as their true nature. Their real intentions may not be immediately apparent.

Last night I talked to Frida about how I now understand my feelings, things that happened to me in the past, and why that all happened. I now understand the ability I have, and I now need to work on developing it as my last dream told me.

There has been a union and a cutting of negative elements from your life. Something new has happened in your life which has made you review life. You have changed the way you view the world around you. You have experienced and grown into something deeper and meaningful which has made you feel like a new person.

You have unpleasant feelings about a situation and problem in your life that you feel is an unbearable waste of time to deal with. It is easier to let it go than confront it or speak up about it. I see you have a concern about exhausting yourself with needless recurring arguments over the long term.

You have a new start. This is positive but you must learn how to control it. You must learn how to show your authority, your right, your power, and your ruling strength. You must behave morally and honestly.

You will have power and prosperity. Something is powering up your life. Look at how you focus your own energies in life. There has been a death of old, a connection, growth, rebirth, and life. You have competence, virility, happiness, and power. I see you are feeling capable of doing this thing in your life. You are feeling more powerful and successful than those around you.

Look at how you help people in life. Success will be yours. You are extremely likely to achieve your goals. You are exploring life in your own way. You have made a completely new move in life. You are feeling a sense of personal gain and enjoyment in life.

Real spiritual growth is taking place. You will have happiness and contentment. Your goals need to be met. Emotional pleasure will enter your life soon. I see you are trying to understand your own personality. You will have good times in life and spiritual happiness.

You have a complex relationship with yourself, others, and the world around you. I see you have accepted a major life change. So, do not give in to old habits. Your respect for a male is decreasing. This is growth. A male around you is having issues with finances.

You will be prosperous and influential beyond your highest hopes. Boundless love and affection will be heaped upon you. Your family life will be very peaceful. Your emotions are clear, and you have feelings of inner peace.

There is a possible new job. A situation is coming to a standstill. A new start is coming washing away the past. It is a new beginning. So, try not to fear things in your mind because deep down you will realize that anything is possible. Review what you are doing and have hope for a brighter tomorrow.

After interpreting this dream, I was overcome with a sense that sitting here every day writing these dreams and their meanings down is coming to a standstill. I accomplished this part of my development and now it is time for something new. I also got the impression It is time to review everything I have wrote up until this point as the answers on what to do next and how to proceed lie therein. The thought also popped into my head that a few dreams ago, I was told I have an affinity for the written and spoken word and that perhaps this all means it is time to get back to writing my book.

After reviewing everything I have written and done up to this point, I came up with a lot of answers to my life, its stages, their meaning, clues, and directions towards what would happen next, what to do, etc. It all came from the repeating themes and ideas that were showing up in my dreams. And, in fact, a previous dream had told me to pay attention to those repeating themes and ideas. Here is what I came up with:

- Work on your meditation
- Trust your intuition.
- New opportunities and new life
- You will make profitable investments.
- Keep finances in check to ensure a solid foundation.
- Let go of past and old ways of doing things and thinking.
- You will have an abundance of health and wealth.
- Foster your spiritual growth and expansion of your abilities.
- An old friend will come back into your life and bring good news/opportunities.
- Something amazing is going to happen starting next month (It's March).

You will have profit, new chance, and daily bread. Prepare your path towards inner knowledge. You are planting a seed for good results in the future. You need raw, powerful energy and passion. So, stop and think about your actions that can cause you to have a lack of energy, be lethargic or to feel tired.

You are strong and you will have success at work. You have a lot possible in life. A tumultuous period has come to an end in your life. You will have further revelations on how you can succeed in life. You will have the drive to succeed in life.

Stop being so complicated. If you want a simple life do not complicate it yourself. Remove drama and unnecessary worries. Just enjoy the walk. New opportunities are coming in a natural way in your life. Self-realization, adventure, life journey and directions you must follow to succeed are the directions your life is taking right now. A sudden change is coming your way. So, be prepared. This is an omen of good things to come. Follow your instinct and your gut. Someone from your past will be coming into your life. Spontaneous events will put a smile on your face. Follow your intuition!

You are ready to build a new life for yourself. You will use current assets to get what you want. You are going through a transformation. Your past is something you no longer wish to think about. You are ready to create the "new" you!

You will discover your own spiritual growth and happiness within yourself. Relax and be natural. This comes from your higher self. It is the equality and integration between feminine and masculine principles, your individuation. You have the ability to develop new relationships with other people. There will be an opportunity of many new friendships. This will involve masculine energies. A new life and new opportunities are coming your way.

You grow from the past into the current time by using positive energy, and by allowing new people to enter your life and help you. You have tremendous charisma and longevity. I promise that fulfilment of your dreams is about to happen because of your work.

You have a complex relationship between yourself, others, and the world around you. The bad times are over. So, let go of them to make room. The good times are coming. Perhaps it is time for a small reunion or get together of friends.

You will have access to new opportunities and changes and an available option. You will have a chance to do something different. You are transitioning from one stage of your life to another. There will be a choice you need to make or there will be initiative that you will need to take in order to start an opportunity.

Remember the process of the circle of life. There always is life, death, and a re-birth. You will have a new start. Someone will come to you for advice. You will have future plans and good times. Positive business relationships will occur. You will have gains and unexpected luck.

I see the difficult times you are encountering in your life with someone. You are very protected in life. I also see you are content and enjoy life. Expand your horizons and investigate new interests. You have liveliness, sociability, and an outgoing nature.

All of your wishes to be healthy and vibrant are going to come true. You will have health in all fashion. You are letting go of negativity, frustration, as well as the feeling of not being content in much of your life experience.

Do not be alarmed in life. But have caution, especially in relation to others. A period of retreat is coming to an end. The winter of your soul is becoming warmed by the sunlight of new hope and personal growth, and it is time to re-emerge back into the world. You are experiencing a period of spiritual cleansing that is profoundly uplifting. You are experiencing a time of deep emotional peace, a relief from grieving, and or a sense of psychologically clearing things that have been distracting, superfluous in life.

You have been working properly. You have been letting go of some projects and ideas. You are being receptive to new information about spiritual knowledge, healing, and refreshment. You are in tune with your spirituality. You will have serenity, peace of mind and rejuvenation.

You are trying to overcome problems in an effective way. You have the potential for a successful life. Things will begin to improve over the next few months. Things are going to be calm in the future. You have incredibly positive times ahead. People are going to come to you for advice. Things will change over time but are likely to get better going forward. You need to seek assistance from others to reach your goals regarding finances, work, and lifestyle. It is time to start something new. You will have good fortune in finances.

Great times are planned for the future. You will eventually get what you want from life. You will encounter better communication in life. You are waiting to hear some important news from work. There is an actual plan at work.

You will meet somebody who has a great sense of humor, a great laugh and is kind in general and generally optimistic in spirit.

You will have material gain. You will gain something in life. It will hit you unexpectedly and you will be incredibly surprised. Do not let your excitement take away your focus of what is most important in your life and from your commitments. You are a person who cannot be fooled by anyone anymore. Your overall health is positive. I see you are suddenly feeling that things will work out well for you.

Your moral will increase, you have courage, self-confidence, and positive energy. You will have a positive change, good health, growth, healing, peace, and serenity. You are moving forward, and you will have peaceful space in your life. You will have adventure and progress moving forward and you will be taking people, things and even emotions along with you for the ride on a future path. There will be productivity and potential opportunities in the future.

You will have well-being and wealth. You have an ability to overcome your ordinary way of living and demonstrate to others how to do that. You have been standing up to a problem in a way that leaves you feeling confident that the problem is noticeably impossible to become a problem again. You have a desire for peace and quiet existence.

You are looking for happy moments and good friends in your life. Good times are ahead. A charming friend will arrive in your life soon. It might be possible that he or she will support you greatly in the times ahead.

You need to slow down and take time from your daily activities. With your determination and confidence, you will be able to make things happen. You will have progress towards your goals. You will get rid of some unpleasant problems, and a desire of yours will be fulfilled. You have full creativity in what you are currently working on. A passion has surfaced, and you are ready to get working to make it happen. You have been chosen by a spirit in order to carry out an important task. Things will become clear in the near future.

There is an exchange of power and influence taking place in your life now. It is important that you act upon this power in order to execute responsibilities. Luck is coming your way.

You have a need for peace and peace of mind. Something new will happen in your life soon. There has been a renewal of something, and you have restored something from the beginning. An experience will be available if you are obligated to your tasks.

A phase of your life is now over. Time to focus more on life. You are changing for the best. Be open to new possibilities. There will be a discovery about a certain skill you hold. Other people will turn to you for help.

You have infinite possibility and the ability to accomplish your goals. You have an infinite number of ways that you could possibly get to the place you want to be in life. You have only to pick the one that looks most attractive or effective. You are about to meet with unexpected good fortune. Be prepared to take the opportunity when it presents itself because it will lead you to great prosperity and potential.

You have the ability to go easily throughout natural obstacles in waking life. You are in the company to the heavenly powers. You are in complete harmony with your surroundings and there is not any anger or other bad emotions. You have a higher level of consciousness. A special gift has been awarded to you. You will have uncomplicated growth of your financial and professional capital. You are doing very well in reaching your goals without rush and infliction of damage to others.

I see that it has been a struggle to achieve your goals. I see your attempts to work against obstacles and your feeling of the difficulty of the situation. You toughed it out. Your patience and dedication will benefit you. You have overcome your challenge. You are noticing that your struggle is over with. You are now feeling that you are moving away from a problem. Life feels like it is getting easier.

There is a part of yourself that you can always rely on. You will have certain wealth, health, and prosperity. Things are going to start happening soon. Your life will soon be filled with a new and exciting beginning. You are now in the preparation or organization stage that will achieve certain satisfactions. Wealth has presented itself through your challenges. You will be able to claim your land and little hill of prosperity.

You have made a journey from within. It was a journey where you headed for enlightenment. You are currently feeling comfort and safety. You will have enlightenment, peace of mind, goodwill, tranquility, insight, and fortune. Develop and improve your potential which in turn will help you when it comes to achieving greater heights in your life endeavors. Nothing is impossible in life.

Focus on paying more attention to your friends and family. You will soon hear good news and you will overcome any difficulties that you may be having during your waking time. You will earn money thanks to your opinions. You will get the things done that you want. You will write a book.

You will succeed in life. There is always a solution to every problem, and you can work towards getting the right info to get yours solved. You must trust your instincts. You are being watched in a positive way.

Problems in your waking life are starting to melt away. You are beginning to let go of a feeling you have been holding back and are getting ready to face obstacles that may be coming toward you. A stage of your life is over and there is a new beginning coming. Something in life will take shape and be more concrete going forward. You are entering a new phase of life.

You are going to experience peace, contentment, and happiness in your life. Your desires and pleasures are going to come true because you do not lust for gaining widespread fame. You are easy to please, and your wishes are modest. Your life is simple, and thus, you live easy.

This is the end of a long season of misfortunes and bad luck that have been present in your life. After a period of misery and suffering, you are about to enter a season of plenty and empowerment. You will enjoy the warmth and togetherness of being in the company of people who are on the same wavelength as you.

You are getting in touch with something that is foreign to you. Your desire to please others is at the risk of sacrificing your own needs and happiness. As a result, you are experiencing many setbacks. Someone is trying to mask their true feelings, thoughts, and intentions. You are distrustful of other's activities.

Develop yourself in the future. Express your intellect in terms of logic and spirit. There is a male in your waking life who is quite cold hearted. You can overcome anything in life. Start being more focused on your own goals in life.

There is someone protecting you and the person is especially important in your life and the community at large. You will have happiness, vitality, youth, and good health. You will have new ideas and good news. You feel cared for and incredibly happy and all your needs are being met. Your life is a blessing. Your new ventures are going to be successful. You are taking the right steps in your life to make sure that you get a favorable future.

Be careful planning and in selecting your targets in life. You are at a point in your life where you are pinpointing your goals in life. You have a clear goal in mind. You are confident about a task. You carry a strong belief in your performance in a task in waking life. Positive changes are going to happen.

There are negative people around you. No one is listening to you about a particular event. You are also feeling that your protests are not having any impact on those around you. Other people's behavior will impact you. Try *to look at different ways that you are approaching problems. You will have health, positive change, growth, and peace and serenity. Good news is coming your way.*

You will have successful ideas. You are using your energy to help achieve work related endeavors. Self-expression and creativeness are flowing freely in a well-balanced manner. Feelings are being handled well and your wishes are being met. A new style or image is required.

You have had a rebirth, a transformation. This occurred in your dreams because you are undertaking an important task in life. You want to improve yourself so you can live life better. You understand life is much more than just working and you would like to explore other aspects of life. You have made a personal transformation. Undertaking self-awareness through a journey that involves nurturing others is an important step in life.

You will be coming into money or a financial windfall. Much luck and positive changes are coming in your life. There is a desirable choice or experience that you are considering. You will have money; financial gain and you will save money. You will take a financially valuable gift. Fake friends will be with you for their self-interests. You will get rid of these fake friends easily as soon as possible. Pleasant moments are about to enchant your life. You will get some good news. Your wishes are coming true. You will have luck and good fortune in the immediate future.

A few months went by where I just lived my life. I put the book away for a while. I felt like I needed a mental break from all of my dreams and spiritual work. I needed a period of rest so to speak, so that I could let all of this set in. Sort of like how the dirt settles after a dust storm. I did not really have any dreams that I remembered. After this pause I started having dreams again. It felt like at the moment, a new phase was in its infancy.

There has been a re-birth, the overcoming of conflict and a transformation. You will be coming into money or a financial windfall. A huge amount of luck and positive changes are coming into your life. This is all associated with gaining money or prestige. Emotional pleasure is soon to enter your life. I see you are trying to understand your own personality. Good news is ahead. This is the end; something has finished in real life for you. You will have health, wellness, and care for yourself. Pay attention to how you treat others or meet their needs. You will be rewarded in your waking world in the form of money and/or prestige for doing a job well done.

You are trying to take a more rounded view of your life and consider other people and other things around you, rather than just from your perspective. Something has happened recently to bring things into focus for you and opened your eyes to the wider picture and those who are in it.

You have wholeness, perfection. We are all connected. An energetic gateway has opened for you. Your thoughts and focus will manifest rapidly in your life. Choose thoughts wisely, ensuring that they are a true representation of your heart's desires. Negative thoughts can manifest just as quickly! So, do not focus on those! You are on a winning streak, self-development, progress, and creativity. You need to develop individuality and creativity. Develop your intuitive and clairvoyant abilities and grow spiritually. Pay attention to repetitive ideas and thoughts as they hold the solutions and answers to your prayers. A new level or skill will soon be achieved, success in business is imminent. This is the beginning of a journey that's exciting and exhilarating. You are returning to source, wholeness. You are experiencing a feeling of wholeness and completeness.

Remember your service to others, completions and endings, inspiration, closure, living as a positive example for others to follow. You are having a spiritual awakening. This is a prompt to get on with your divine life purpose. All things must come to an end for new beginnings to occur. A phase or cycle of your life is ending or coming to completion and there is a promise of new to come. All will work out for your highest good. You simply must prepare yourself and your life accordingly. You are spiritually advanced. Follow your life path and soul purpose. You yearn to see improvement in the world and wish to participate as per your divine life purpose and soul mission. Time to put your natural skills, talents, and abilities to good use in serving humanity. Follow your intuitive promptings with regard to your life path and soul purpose. Set a positive example and be a torch bearer, lighting and illuminating the way for others to follow. Fully embark upon your sacred soul mission without further delay or hesitation and shine your light brightly for the benefit of yourself and others. You are being asked to live up to your full potential.

You will experience activity, energy, changes, resourcefulness, adventure, and life changes. Changes are coming up in your life or life path that may alter your course. Important discoveries, adventure, and actions to be taken in waking life. You are learning your life lessons through your experiences. Become more in tune with your five senses and you need to pursue your personal truths and freedom. Break free from old constraints that have been holding you back. Begin living your life with passion and purpose. Personal freedom and major life changes are coming. The changes ahead of you will bring about auspicious opportunities and feelings of personal satisfaction. Positive changes are heading your way. You will be experiencing change, variety, and new growth. Better things are coming into your life. These changes may come about with un-expected haste and in unusual ways, but they will bring positive energies and opportunities that will propel you in the right direction along your life path. You will experience cooperation, union, love, home, family, domesticity, ownership, and monetary aspects of your life. There is a union of opposites within you and the integration of your true self. There will be partnerships, responsibilities, and creative collaboration. You will experience self-harmony, meeting responsibilities, love and abundance, domestic harmony, and goodwill. Stability is needed in all areas of your life. Your monetary and material needs will be met. Be grateful for your blessings to encourage further abundance.

New love will enter your life soon. Family matters will be coming full circle, there will be a new addition to the home, a new friendship, and the achieving of desires in regard to the home, family, and social life. Find a balance between your goals and ideals and your inner, spiritual self. Your thoughts are out of balance, and you are placing to much focus on the material side of life. Look to serving humanity and fostering your spiritual growth and expansion. Focus on spirit and service and your material and emotional needs will be automatically met as a result.

Remember service to others as well as faith and trust. This part of the message reflects your divine life purpose and soul mission. Balance of male and female energies, self-surrender and put others before yourself. Have faith and trust in the universe as your prayers are manifesting in your waking life. You may need to be patient, but trust that all will turn out for your highest good. Things will be appearing in two's, such as unions and partnerships. This can include new relationships, commitments, engagements, and marriages. Find a balance and stand on your own two feet. There will be manifesting miracles and new opportunities. Stay strong in your personal truths to manifest positive outcomes. New ideas and concepts are beginning to take shape and grow into reality. Maintain a positive attitude and outlook and continue your good work in order to manifest your desires. The time to reap your reward is just ahead of you.

There will be growth, expansion, and manifestation of abundance. This is a message that your ideals and visions are coming to fruition in your life. Maintain self-discipline through service to others, manifesting abundance, productivity, and unity. It is implied that the ascended masters are working closely with you, guiding, encouraging, and supporting you. It suggests that your prayers have been heard and are being responded to and answered. You will experience vitality, motivation, enthusiasm, creativity, and experience. Remember commitment, improving yourself, and meditation. All things are possible. Take notice of your true goals and aspirations *and know they are attainable. If you are considering a new direction, your wishes will come to fruition and the changes will be successful. Help, guidance, and assistance are available to you always. All you need to do is ask. Remember, the third time is the charm!*

Solidity and great strength. Look outside the box! Work diligently yet harmoniously to achieve your goals. Put ideas into practical form. There is a vibration of illumination and initiation. You are being guided and supported in your endeavors. Trust that your hard work and efforts will bring well-earned rewards. You will have comfort and stability in your life. Using hard work, will, and personal effort to achieve long term goals and aspirations. Build strong foundations and work to achieve goals and dreams. All is as it should be. Projects you have been working on will be successful, and you will be pleased with the long-term results. Have faith and trust in your abilities.

After this dream I took another break to spend time with my son who came to visit from 6/19/19 to 7/16/19. After that, the dreams started again, and I got back to work.

Everything in your life will go well. You will have means, prosperity, and health. There is something in your life that will grow. Problems are going to work out in the future. You will have victory over others, satisfaction, and organization. Happiness and health will be in your family for many years. At the moment, everything is going to plan. You have nothing to worry about. Goodness will be yours as well as wealth, relaxation, being happy and growth, both spiritually and mentally. Your about to experience personal growth, soul awakening, and a positive outcome. You wish to accomplish meaningful things. Maybe undertake a new hobby. This will boost your awareness. You have natural protection from evil forces.

You will gain wealth and prestige soon. All your worries, especially those related to financial issues will finally come to an end. You will enjoy a stress free, content life. Do not forget to thank others for their efforts, patience, and determination.

Good things are on your way. You are about to enjoy a peaceful, happy life very soon. It will be a gift for your patience and faith. Your efforts will finally pay off. Be patient. Happiness is just around the corner. There is an essential opportunity that will present itself shortly. You will also have the ability to protect yourself against any wrongdoings.

Continue to follow your intuition but work on your attitude and expand your horizons. You must consider giving up bad habits and set up a healthier lifestyle. Your body is your own temple, and it is your steady job to take good care of it.

You will have the opportunity to appreciate and understand yourself better. You must know how to tap into your inner world of feelings, your imagination, and other inner resources. There will be quiet times ahead. A good future and happy acquaintances, as well as some peace and quiet, are ahead. You are content and happy. Great changes are on the horizon.

You need to recognize the process of life, death and rebirth, the circle of life. Your subconscious mind is trying to heal. I see you are unsure of your direction in life. Good luck, gains and unexpected luck are headed your way.

You need to take a new path in your life. You are grounded and approach life in a welcoming but down to earth way. Great times are on the horizon. You will find happiness, peace, and contentment. Others will turn to you for advice. Be ready to change your life in some way.

Focus on your inner-self, rebirth, spiritual awakening, enlightenment, and solitude. You are going through a spiritual growth spurt and attuning to the spiritual realms. Pay attention to inner growth and intuition and that you continue growing spiritually towards enlightenment. Meditate and go within to find greater spiritual awareness and enlightenment. There is a beneficial time to come, obstacles will be overcome, and success realized.

You are on the divine path that is right for you. Keep up the great work that you have been doing, and positive things will continue to flow into your life that will help and assist you along your journey. Continue on your current path as you have been manifesting positive energies. Positive things naturally flow towards you.

Your ambitions will be realized, and obstacles overcome in the extremely near future. Listen to your intuition for guidance and solutions. You are on the right path and doing very well. Your positive efforts and hard work will bring you well-earned rewards, your wishes and true desires are coming to fruition. Self-satisfaction, inner joy, and blessings are on their way.

Remember your service to others, completions and endings, leadership, inspiration, closure, and living as a positive example for others to follow. Get on with your divine life purpose. All things must come to an end for new beginnings to occur. A phase or cycle of your life is ending or coming to completion and there is the promise of "new" to come. All will work out for your highest good. You simply must prepare yourself and your life accordingly. A situation that is no longer positively serving you is drawing to an end.

You are spiritually advanced. Follow your life path and soul purpose. It is time to put your natural skills, talents, and abilities to good use in serving humanity. Follow your intuitive promptings regarding your life path and soul purpose. Set a positive example and be a torchbearer lighting and illuminating the way for others to follow. Fully embark on your sacred soul mission without further delay or hesitation and shine your light brightly for the benefit of yourself and others. You are being asked to live up to your full potential.

There will be a union of opposites and the integration of your true self. You will experience self-harmony, meeting responsibilities, love, and abundance. However, stability is needed in all areas of your life. Your monetary and material needs will be met. Be grateful for your blessings to encourage further abundance. Family matters are

Chapter 4 | 181

coming full circle. There will be a new addition to the home or a new friendship. You will be achieving your desires regarding the home, family, and social life.

You need to find a balance between your goals and ideals, and your inner, spiritual self. Your thoughts are out of balance, and you are placing too much focus on the material side of life. Look to serving humanity and fostering your spiritual growth and expansion. Focus on spirit and service and your material needs will be automatically met as a result. You need to go within to find the "God spark."

Changes are coming up in your life or path that may alter your course. A premonition of important discoveries, adventures, and actions to be taken in waking life will be realized. You are learning your life lessons through your experiences. Become more in-tune to your five senses and pursue your personal truths and freedom.

You have an internal desire to break-free from the old constraints that have been holding you back. You need to begin living your life with passion and purpose. Personal freedom and major life changes are coming. The changes ahead of you will bring about auspicious opportunities and feelings of personal satisfaction. Positive changes are heading your way.

Change, variety, and new growth are needed. Better things are coming into your life. These changes will come about with unexpected haste and in unusual ways, but they will bring positive energies and opportunities that will propel you in the right direction along your life path. Be sure to correct your lack of focus and materialistic outlook on life, your over-indulgence, hedonism, addictive, and impulsive behaviors which all need to be addressed.

You have a lack of energy and are feeling tired or lethargic. Out of this will come positive change, good health, growth, healing, hope, vigor, vitality, peace, and serenity. So, go ahead with your strive to gain recognition and establish your independence. Abundance will manifest for you in the forms of happiness, money, love, bliss, personal improvement and whatever your true heart desires.

Trust your intuition and instincts to manifest your desires. Success, wealth, and abundance are on their way into your life. Trust your intuition and instincts and take appropriate action. Goals are coming and a state of completeness are coming to fruition. An auspicious offer or windfall is coming your way.

Material and financial abundance are on their way into your life. Trust that all your wants and needs will be met. You will be rewarded for work well done. Keep your finances in check to ensure a solid foundation for yourself and your loved ones. Although the Universal Energies always ensure that you are supported, it is your personal responsibility to make sure that you are living up to your full potential. Trust your intuition and instincts and take appropriate action.

This is a message that your ideals and visions are coming to fruition in your life. Maintain self-discipline through service to others, manifesting abundance, productivity, and unity. The Ascended Masters are working closely with you, guiding, encouraging, and supporting you. Your prayers have been heard and are being responded to and answered. You will experience vitality, motivation, enthusiasm, creativity, and experience.

All things are possible. Take notice of your true goals and aspirations and know that they are attainable. Going in your new direction will result in your wishes coming to fruition and the changes will be successful. Help, guidance, and assistance are available to you, always! All you need to do is ask. Remember, the third time is the charm.

Think about your inner-knowledge and how you connect with others. You must accept changes in your life and become more caring. You are entering a new era. There is a part of your life which is seen to change. You will be coming into money or a financial windfall.

Make plans, adapt to life's strategies, and have the patience to see your plans through to completion. I am warning you to be conscious, to extend love, respect and consideration towards friends, family, and associates. This must be done with effort as you are comfortable in your solitude. You will soon need to teach others your own valuable life lessons.

You need to keep a certain distance from certain people in your life. You need time by yourself to reflect and gather strength. You will be in the public eye for a while. Things have been exhausting you and it is time for a respite regarding the last few weeks. There will be more opportunities or an offer that will enrich your life. You were stuck in a rut and the recent challenges will invigorate you. Focus on your spirituality. You must step back from the bustle of modern living. Look inside yourself and reconsider your past feelings. Delve into your deepest thoughts. Remember your secret dreams, your real passions and it is important to show others your true characteristics.

I am your spirit guide as you share the same fortitude as me. I, like you, am philosophical and we organize our lives intellectually, seldom receiving emotional support from anyone. We are protective of ourselves and at times we feel isolated. I aide you in your spiritual maturity. I have helped you with your emotional growth, intellectual development, and much needed flexibility that you have needed in your life. I have shown up now and in the past when you needed clear vision and you were, and are, seeking to know about mystical mysteries.

Pay close attention to your family, home, and prosperity. I see you have been confused lately and are waiting for a sign to tell you to start moving things around again. I am the sign you have been waiting for. I am a symbol of God's care of people who worship him.

Relax, your problems will not grow into bigger issues. You are protected spiritually. I have appeared because you have encountered hard times recently. I am here to restore your faith in humanity. You will overcome your enemies.

You are too focused on your family life and less focused on what you really want from your life right now. It is all in your hands, your future, your family, everything. You will have hard work and happiness in life. You are going thru a transition. You are digging for something important in life. Periodically, life will seem stressful for a while. You will focus on meaty projects going forward.

Money is in your cards. People will think highly of you. People will talk about you. You have met a woman who has a good soul. You need balance and regeneration and to balance opposing forces. A bright future is ahead of you in the distant future, so do not worry.

Things are going to be relaxed in your life. Things in life are complicated, but they will sort out soon. You will learn a new skill to pass the time. This is a positive phase of your life. You are going to experience something wonderful anytime soon. You must have the will and strength to do what must be done.

You are being distracted in your waking world from the real issue. You know what is going on, but for some reason you want to pretend that it is not really happening. You will be starting a new gateway in your life.

You have come to terms with the past events of your life. You will eventually get what you want from life. You are looking for a change. Take charge of your life and focus on the direction. You are looking for adventure, happiness, and joy. There is an actual plan at work. You desire to achieve something "real" in waking life. You need nurturing and care. You will fulfill what you wish to do in life, with happiness.

Others will provide you with confidence. You have a challenge in your life, and it is time to be creative and determined. Look at how you can be more positive in the future. You have a fear of facing a tough decision you need to make soon, and you will have to live with the consequences that this may bring you.

Positive changes are afoot. There will be great energy like a fire. You are getting a new start in life. Safeguard *yourself. You have the ability to intelligently overcome obstacles. Do not give up is your key message here! You can win and attack your enemies without ever needing to face them directly in person.*

You will have prosperity and good times in your life. You are facing something difficult, and you need to think about what you are putting into your body more. You have great people around you. You need to focus on yourself for a while.

Your time has been spent wasteful. Your future holds financial wealth and prosperity. But you must be free of things that hold you back and you are well cared for. You will encounter a re-birth in life. You are welcoming me into your life.

You will experience growth. There has been a lot of upheaval and problems in life recently. You will have good health, growth, great luck, and money. You can have happy times in the future, but you need to surrender to issues that are holding you back. You are about to experience personal growth, soul awakening, and a positive outcome.

Start digging for a deeper meaning of everything you see, touch, feel, do, accomplish. You wish to accomplish meaningful things. You have a natural protection from evil forces. Good things are on your way. Your about to enjoy a peaceful, happy life very soon. It will be a gift for your patience and faith. Your efforts will finally pay off. Be patient. It is time to put all the things and people that worry you in the past.

Pay attention to your lack of motivation for control over your life and your daily habits that affect your mind in a negative way. You are going to grow as an individual. There will be an emergence of a new phase in life. Growth is the key message of this dream.

    A couple weeks went by before I had another dream. It was as if I was being allowed to process all the info from the past several dreams, allow it to sink in, and apply it as I have previously done. Then I began having dreams again. I believe these dreams were related to the next step in this new phase of my life. It took about a month to unfold. On 9/11/19 I had this dream:

I see that you have some feelings of anxiety and uneasiness about your new situation that you're entering involving your new way of living and your spirituality. I also see what you are feeling about old social situations returning that you have not been involved with for a long time. I see your anxiety and displeasure at these old arguments returning and old ways of living being repeated. I see that you have been immersed in your past and your former habits lately.

You need to continue moving through this with your strength. You must get away from these problems and achieve personal growth. Focus on your goal in life. You need to understand your goals and your personal focus on life. Your personal focus is what leads you. How quickly and efficiently you can change your behavior pattern is an indication of your personal power and focus. Desire is a key factor to your focus, and you automatically create desire when you challenge yourself. This you need to understand.

You cannot find your way in life. You are feeling completely alone and like you always must fight hard to get what you want. Nothing seems to come easy for you. But this is not a bad thing. In fact, it is great you are not getting anything the easy way. This way you learn to appreciate things more and will not take them for granted. You are going to take on new challenges that will need your mental fortitude.

You need a new approach to life's problems. Stay away from the old habits you have been using to get through these things. That is your old way. Everything seems to be happening so fast for you. In fact, you are the one rushing to accomplish it all at once. That too is an old way of doing things for you. Take a small break. Remember, accomplish one thing at a time.

You are headed toward something in life. But you have become so obsessed with achieving your goals that you forgot how it is to enjoy the moment. Relax, just go with the flow for a while. You need a re-charge. Your creativity needs renewal.

I understand your dependence on someone in your waking life for companionship but learn to love solitude. Focus on your transformation. Apply the changes in your life that you wanted to for so long. Right now, you are trying to put the cart before the horse. New developments will reveal a part or aspect of yourself you did not know existed.

I see you are ready to embrace the challenges of the future without having to look back into your past, into people who were in your past life who are no longer in your life. That negativity will definitely remain in your past.

Your old life and your old way of thinking are all in the past now. Some of the things you have been currently doing could make you lapse back into these old ways and habits. These current things you have been doing are bad habits you were involved in in the past. Be strong and resist these habits from re-entering your life.

There will be changes in the way you think and in the circumstances of your life as you progress to the next stage. I see that you are waiting for something else to happen after having completed this last phase. You will experience a process of change and improvement.

I also see you have bad feelings of having re-transitioned back to an old way of living after having made significant efforts to transition to a new way of living. You must understand that you are embarking on a new path now. I see you are trying to find a resolution. Remember habits you need to stop when you have these feelings of being blocked. Those are barriers that limit your growth in this world. Stopping these things is the catalyst for transformation that you are about to cross. Know that there is so much more beyond your path. I see that you are trying to deal with this inadequate problem.

You will discover a secret. You will encounter a new spiritual path sometime soon. You will enjoy openness, a lack of restriction, if you engage on this spiritual path. You are going to have the power to clean your life and even a fresh start. The gateway to your deepest emotions, childhood dreams, and the purest part of your soul remains untouched. You will finally find your inner peace. You will finally come to your senses and show the world what you can do. You have been living with self-doubt and low confidence for too long. The time has come for this to end. There will be new opportunities, which may be created by yourself.

Breaking down or through your past and your difficulties is the remedy. Your outdated ways of living are the obstacles you need to overcome in order to succeed. You need to find your own way in life and not follow someone else's path. No matter how old you are, it is not too late to follow your dreams.

Reading this dream meaning may be the most important step you can take that you need to work towards advancement and finish what you have started. It is now time to think about the life you wish to lead, and it is time to succeed. There will be a discovery about a certain skill you hold, and other people will turn to you for help.

You have been in the dark about these problems you have had in your life. But you are now in a position to solve it all. Your personal problems have troubled you for an exceptionally long time and it will all be resolved soon. Once you solve this, you can then focus on bigger things in your life.

I understand you are feeling despair and loneliness in your life now. I am reminding you to listen to your intuition. I see that you are being proactive over this situation in your life. I see that you are looking within yourself and searching for your life path. Just follow your intuition and listen to your inner self.

I see that you are on high alert to the things that are not right in your world. Follow your instincts, use your courage and wisdom to get to the truth. You are fully supported no matter what you decide to do. So, you do not need to lose control or become nervous.

You are not alone. Those that you do care about support you no matter what path you choose. They are always there when you feel alone or unsupported. I see you are missing people and things in your life. Just relax and take it easy. I also see your having feelings of being held back in your life and that you hold internal doubts.

Recently there has been someone who is angry, and these feelings are being portrayed to you. You are also angry with someone who you feel has an "alpha male mentality." Your life is about to fall right into place. You are in a good place in your life, and everything is where it should be. Your natural life cycle is right on track. I am reminding you to be strong about your beliefs and enjoy life as it is. You are experiencing a spiritual entirety or completeness.

You are going to plan about a matter you had failed at. This time you will achieve success. You will also change some of your traits you do not like, and you will improve yourself. You need to get back to your roots, your values, principles, and core spirituality that make you who you are. You need to understand your spiritual side, the inner workings of what makes you who you are in order to find inner peace.

This is a warning and a caution from your unconscious guidance, your intuition, your spirit, to use your strength and your belief in God to keep your past failures, ways of living and habits, from coming back to the surface. If you do, you will be victorious. Then, and only then, will you achieve your success.

Focus on your true heart's desires. Watch your thoughts, so they can manifest in your life. An energetic gateway has opened for you. Your thoughts and focus will manifest rapidly in your life. So, choose them wisely. Do not focus on negatives.

Develop your individuality and creativity. Develop your intuitive and clairvoyant abilities and grow spiritually. Pay attention to repetitive ideas and thoughts as they hold the solutions and answers to your prayers. A new level or skill will be achieved. Success is imminent. This is the beginning of a journey, something that can be exciting. But it may bring the challenge of isolation and loneliness that you must overcome and learn from.

Work diligently to achieve your goals, putting ideas into practical form. You are being guided and supported. Trust all will work out with well-earned rewards. You will have comfort and stability in your life. Use hard work, will, and personal effort to achieve your long-term goals. Build strong foundations. All is as it should be. Projects you are working on will be successful, and you will be pleased with the long-term results. Trust your abilities. Do not hold yourself back with old ways and habits.

There are changes coming up in your life that may alter your course. Important discoveries are ahead and action to be taken in waking life. You are learning your life lessons from your experiences. Become more in-tune to your five senses. Pursue your personal truths and freedom. Break free from old constraints that have been holding you back. Begin living your life with purpose and passion.

You will have freedom and major life changes. The changes ahead of you will bring about auspicious opportunities and feelings of personal satisfaction. Positive changes are headed your way. New things are headed into your life. These changes may come about with unexpected haste and in unusual ways, but they will bring positive energies and opportunities that will propel you in the right direction along your life path. Your over-indulgence, addictive and compulsive behaviors need to be addressed.

Stability is needed in all areas of your life. Your monetary and material needs will be met. Be grateful for your blessings to encourage further abundance. You will achieve your desires regarding the home, family, and social life. Find a balance between your goals and your inner spiritual self. Serve humanity, foster your spiritual growth and expansion. Focus on spirit and service and your material and emotional needs will be met as a result. Go within to find your God spark.

Trust your intuition and instincts to manifest your desires. Success, wealth, and abundance are on their way into your life. Trust your intuition and instincts and take appropriate action. Goals are coming to fruition/completeness. An auspicious offer or windfall is coming your way. Material and financial abundance are on their way into your life. Trust that all your wants and needs will be met. You will be rewarded for work well done. Keep your finances in check to ensure a solid foundation for yourself and your loved ones. It is your personal responsibility to make sure that you are living up to your full potential.

You are having a spiritual growth spurt and attuning to the spiritual realms. Pay attention to your inner-growth and intuition and continue growing spiritually towards enlightenment. Meditate and go within in order to find a greater spiritual awareness and enlightenment. A beneficial time to come, obstacles overcome, and success realized. You are on the divine path that is right for you. Keep up the great work and positive things will continue to flow into your life that will help and assist you in your journey. Continue your current path as you are manifesting positive energies. Positive things naturally flow to you in your life.

Ambitions will be realized, and obstacles will be overcome with enough strength of purpose. You will overcome any hinderances soon. Listen to your intuition for guidance and solutions. You are on the right path and doing very well. Your positive efforts and hard work will bring you well-earned rewards, and your wishes and desires are coming to fruition.

You are working hard, overcoming obstacles, and rising above petty, everyday quarrels. It has taken great effort to climb your mountain and you have encountered many obstacles in your path. When you get to the top you will have a great sense of achievement at the new skills learned getting there.

There are new adventures on the horizon. It is time for trying new things. You have recently overcome some challenging situations and past obstacles. Everything in your life will go well. You will have good health, growth, great luck, and money. You will have happy times in the future. Surrender to deep issues that are holding you back. You will have victory over others, happiness, and health in your family for many years. You have a fresh start in life, and you will have growth spiritually and mentally. You are about to experience personal growth, soul awakening, and a positive outcome. You will enjoy happy moments with your family or friends. You wish for a simple but happy life, and soon, your wishes will come true thanks to your positivity. You will have enjoyment in life and there are new opportunities that will arise shortly. Things are going to start happening soon and your life will be filled with new and exciting beginnings. You have the green light to go ahead with your current plans. You are entering a new stage in life.

Unexpected events will continue to occur in this stage of your life. You will reach your goal and be emotional about it. You will have a good future and happy acquaintances, as well as some peace and quiet ahead. Great changes are on your horizon.

You will make new friends. You have a fresh start in life. There is a re-birth of old ideas and pleasures. Try re-visiting some of your past hobbies and you will be surprised to find that they still have much more to offer you.

The obstacles you have been experiencing will be overcome by using your creative mind. You are at the end of an era in life. I see you are searching for your goal and knowledge. Learn what you must to achieve your goals. You will have profit, wealth, inner-peace, and tranquility. Something positive is about to happen and you are defining your goals. Prosperous and great times are to come for you. You will achieve your goal. You will gain in life. Luck will be on your side. You have the freedom to catch your goals. Learn new things to acquire more spiritual knowledge and focus on your spirituality. You will have easy times ahead.

You are conscious of spiritual development. You need to make your own judgement about your abilities. You have a positive attitude towards life. It is time to start an important project and act. You can expect success in the near future. You must believe more in yourself and your own abilities.

An idea will be born. There will be a disruption in a situation which is associated with a new career move, but a bright future is ahead of you in the not-too-distant future so do not be worried. You will have huge financial gains. You are simply confused and waiting for a sign to tell you to start moving things around again. This dream is the sign you have been waiting for.

Things in life are complicated and they will sort out soon. You will learn a new skill to pass the time. A positive phase in life. You are going to experience something wonderful anytime soon. There will be unusual and unexpected changes in life. A new start in life. You have a fear of leaving your comfort zone. Your feeling anxiety about a new development or transition in your life. Your finances may be at risk. If you were thinking of investing your time and money into something risky, you may want to rethink it.

You have great people around you. You are welcoming someone into your life. Rely more on your inner senses and gut feelings. There are small obstacles you need to overcome in order to achieve success. There is the need to change something in your life to achieve a desired outcome.

You will overcome some obstacles in your life. You will probably successfully finish some goal you have been working on for some time, even though you might have some obstacles in the way. Good things related to your business. You may experience a great job-related success in the near future.

Get back to the basics. Money is coming your way from a business deal or decision. Focus and keep your eye on your current work. You need focus and resolve to complete the task at hand. You need to act. It is time to start earning the things we want instead of waiting for rewards to fall into our laps. You will have power and status laid before you in the near future. You are acting, or can act, in an over-the-top manner. It is time to tone your behavior down. You are a leader. You can lead with compassion and kindness and bring balance to everything around you. You show there are better ways than violence and hurtful words.

You will have victory over the difficulties in your waking life. Prosperity and abundance are in the near future, as a result of your hard work and effort. Pay attention to the people who are getting close to you. You may find yourself in trouble due to some actions of an inconsiderate friend of yours. Do not irrationally spend your money jeopardizing your financial stability.

You need to look at people's actions and try to understand what they are thinking. You are going to have an unhindered vision of how people are acting in the future. This will be your strength. You are confused about the next phase in your life. Try to engage change.

You feel you are letting yourself down in some way. Instead of making the most of your unique talents, you are relying on approval from other people to boost your confidence. Reaffirm your faith in your own abilities and to make decisions based on your own judgement, rather than by being too influenced by other people around you. It is time to leave behind past feelings and characteristics that are hindering your growth. Let go of your old attitudes.

Abundance coming after poverty, peace coming after fight, order coming after disturbance. You will rise in the world. You achieve to keep yourself away from the community which has disorder. An extremely exciting journey for you. You are about to go on a new adventure, travelling to an exotic place.

You will have a problem with your neighbor, but you will come up with a solution as soon as possible. You will contribute to a good work by drawing two people together. Peace increasing within your family life. Unity within *your family will enhance. Soon joyful events will happen. Now, a new and happy stage in your life begins. It is not a time for sorrows and bad mood.*

You will start a journey which will leave only pleasant impressions in your memory. You will be accompanied with a true friend or a partner and will share positive emotions together. There will be money in the future, future success. Many new opportunities will soon cross your path. Be opened to changing your life. Future wealth, future happiness will be coming to you. Your hard work is rewarded.

You are trying to make sense of the world around you. In daily life you have absorbed a lot of information. You are aware of the new opportunities and possibilities. There is a lot about yourself which you need to learn. Embrace your own confidence and the fact that you are taking on challenges for growth.

Through a period of hard work, you will understand more about yourself. You are completely aware of your skills and the possibilities in life. You have learned an important lesson in life. You need to approach things in a different way. You are grounded and connected to mother nature.

You are supported. You will have a desirable experience you have never had before. It is time to finish what you have started and have not ended. You are trying to overcome problems in an effective way. There is the potential for a successful life. There will be good business ahead.

I am a spiritual messenger sent to you about your life. This is a call to lead a real change in your life. Do not worry, things will work out fine. This is a new phase of life. You are connected to others and transformation. There will be abundance and fruitfulness within your family and a lot of money which will come soon.

Build areas of your life and grow. You have intellectual abilities and the option to study and progress in life. You are experiencing the need of talking to people, even if they are far away in terms of a geographical distance.

You will experience a happy event or endeavor, luck, and good profit.

You are going through a spiritual development, and you have excessive energy in your life. Think about what you have and what you want and then focus on stripping back to the basics and celebrate living life. Do not worry about the material side of life. You have a deep understanding of the future.

Your life needs to become better structured than it has been until now. Opinions of others are important. Think about what others say. You have a desire to bring something new into your life that will bring you an opportunity for better work and bigger earnings. You will be happy because of the upcoming change and new acquaintanceships it will bring you.

This is a sign to go on your adventure. You will have enough time and money to do everything in your life as you imagined it, your house, life, things you want, your adventure/journey of the people in your dreams, etc.

You need to do something you have been postponing for an exceptionally long time. There is a need for new people in your life. You feel the need to connect with someone who you can learn a lot from and who can expand your horizons. It is possible you will want to travel somewhere in order to experience an adventure.

You will invest a lot of effort, money and hard work in an investment that will be profitable. You may be afraid of putting everything at risk, but you are aware that without it you cannot expect good results. Good advice can come from an influential acquaintance who is really experienced in your field of work. Try to take their suggestions the right way because they will be really beneficial.

You will have a challenge in your life that will result in many good times. Your hopes and your future are likely to change. Good times are ahead. It is time to take on new challenges. You will soon get great support from your friends. The bad times of your life are over. A new friend will arrive in your life soon. This person will support you greatly in the times ahead.

Good times are ahead. You will have great support from your friends. Your friend will support you greatly in the times ahead. Good times are on their way. You and someone else are getting along really well, you are a good team. You feel contentment with your life at present.

You will soon be on your way. You are going back in time. Seek knowledge to start on an inner journey. Think about taking time to travel to faraway places to find happiness and joy. You have certainty and a vigorous approach to working. You will hear good news.

Emotional pleasure is soon to enter your life. You are trying to understand your own personality. Real spiritual growth is taking place. Happiness and contentment are on the cards. Goals need to be met. Progression in life and your desire to fortify your standing, to attain popularity and fortune are occurring. People will listen to you.

There will be a new venture, new beginnings. A happy family life is ahead. New financial agreements are coming ahead. Adventure ahead. An exceptionally good new start in life. Become creative and come up with new ideas in the future.

There will be changes in your life, a pleasant surprise for you. Your about to get good news. Now is the perfect time for the development of your personality, education, travelling and penetrating the unknown. Expand your horizons. The time could not be better for it. You will be filled with creative inspiration like never before. Devote yourself to a creative work. You do not have to worry about your financial position because everything in this sphere will be put in good order.

You will feel disciplined and be able to achieve your goals. You will be the best at your job. You will gain a letter which will bring good news. Although you know you may face social rejection for doing something you wanted to do for a long time, you are ready to face everyone

and everything in order to be happy and live your life the way you want it. I am telling you to go for it.
You will get the respect of others for a good deed that you did. There will be good opportunities for your life and activity. You will receive high dignity. You have important friends that can help you to accomplish your wishes, fame, and honor.

I took a break from all of this for several days as I felt a bit overwhelmed. I had to block it all out for a bit to give myself a mental break before I got back to work on all of this. Then on 10/4/19, it all began again.

Something new is developing in your life. A new way of thinking, new ideas, new goals, projects, or a new life situation. Preparations, choices, or consequences are leading towards a new life situation. This is a period of gestation of ideas or plans. You are carrying within you new life that may be in the form of a book, project, or new lifestyle. This is a time of transition. Feelings about a new self are about to emerge. You are contemplating making a big change.
Something will be born such as a new approach to matters or a project. A major shift is being predicted. There will be sudden dramatic changes, so make sure you prepare for a new idea or a sudden movement in life.
This is a period of preparation to achieve a goal or a project. You are harboring an idea which is currently growing inside you. Think about your hidden talents or interests which you are good at and start nurturing them. It is time to renew your passion which could enrich your life for sure. Set some goals. A new start is on the horizon, and you are not yet ready to express it to the world, which is the reason for this particular dream. There is a particular aspect of your personality which is trying to grow and enter into a new phase. An aspect of you Is trying to grow at the moment and it is undergoing a lot of changes. A new project is about to be born. You are going to encounter some luck and fortune in the coming days.

There is a murkiness of character and a desire to change. This dream is associated with changing your life for the better, meditation or seeking internal tranquility and having balance and clarity. Remember the rewards of hard work. It is time to put things into place and create something beautiful and orderly out of chaos.

You will find out the things you want to know. You will have an inheritance of a lawfully earned money, or money from a business partnership, or profits in general. You have knowledge which you want people to hear about or to learn.

You will have a wonderful life, prosperity, prestige, and wealth in your life because of your hard work. You must work a lot in order to make a good and happy life. You will have happiness in life, the fullness and satisfaction of your own life. It is the period in your life when you are able to enjoy your hard work and everything that you deserve.

You need to buckle down and get the work done, be more disciplined. Make sure you put in all your effort. Although you know you may face rejection for doing something you wanted to do for a long time, you are ready to face everyone and everything in order to be happy and live your life the way you want it. I am telling you to go for it. Your about to put something you have been tolerating for a long time where it belongs, in your past. I am encouraging you to do it. You must muster the qualities of discipline, courage, and determination to deal with your internal conflicts.

This is a reminder of your own discipline. You have important friends that can help you to accomplish your wishes and you will get the respect of others for a good deed that you did. There will be good opportunities for your life and activity. You will have fame and honor. You will have authority, challenges, and a good situation with your work.

You are approaching a new departure in your life. Some new idea is taking off or is ready to take off. You may have a gain. Health, order, and good things coming your way. You will have triumph in a situation or action. Real spiritual growth is taking place. You have proficient communication skills. You will have all of the pleasures of life as well as what joy others have to offer. You will be coming into money or a financial windfall. A lot of luck and positive changes are coming in your life. Time to leave behind past feelings and characteristics that are hindering your growth. Let go of old attitudes.

It was around this time that I felt that this last phase of my development was ending and that a new one was about to begin. I had felt the "urge" to go back through all of my dreams from the past couple months and see if I could ascertain the bigger picture. As Jung had intimated, one single dream may not mean as much, but put them together in a series and they tell a story.

At the present moment, you cannot find a solution to a problem, things in life just seem to be spiraling out of control. Everything in your life in the past seems disorganized. Your subconscious mind is not able to understand what you need to do next. There is an inner conflict in your mind.

You are at a loss in your current circumstances. Cleanliness, clarity, and a possible fresh start are ahead. A stage in your life is over and there is a new beginning coming. Something in life will take shape and be more concrete going forward. You are an observer of difficulties and hardships which you are encountering. You have a fear of failure, especially regarding finances.

You are entering a new phase in life. There will be an adventure on a deeper level. Your soul and spirit will be renewed. There are problems that surround you at the moment. You have feelings of unrewarded efforts. You are in the process of seeking answers to questions which are in your subconscious mind. You are taking an interest in an elusive object. You are trying to get to know more about a mysterious phenomenon happening in your life.

This is the end of a long season of misfortunes and bad luck that have been present in your life. After a period of misery and suffering, you are about to enter into a season of plenty and empowerment. You are involved in a project or activity which needs your devoted energy and time.

It is time to review your life. You will eventually get what you want from life. Take charge of your life and focus on the direction. You are looking for adventure, happiness, and joy. There is an actual plan at work. I foresee good times, power, and control. You have passion for the future. In the past you have been frustrated or discouraged.

A stranger that you do not know at all will be offering you help. There will be some disappointing situations and events in the near future. These events may somehow be related to your everyday life and might even cause you to give up on some important goals you have. You will have success, but you are undecided about something.

You are getting overworked by doing so much that is beyond your strength and ability. You have so many responsibilities that are weighing you down, yet you really must fulfill these duties and accomplish the responsibilities. You have heavy responsibilities you are required to carry as an individual and family. You are really working extremely hard so that you are able to take the responsibilities. You must cater for them well and work towards that. You are carrying the load you have by working extra hard.

You are feeling overwhelmed, and you are trying to block out something. There is so much more beyond your path. There are barriers to you moving forward. You may encounter some difficulty in solving issues. There will be a new start or a new approach in life opening the way to a path in life. There may be opportunities or associations going forward. There will be choices regarding a decision about a combination of new phases in life. You may discover a secret. You will encounter a new spiritual path sometime soon. You will enjoy openness if you engage on this spiritual path.

You cannot stop things from happening. You need to transform to a higher state of awareness regarding *spirituality. Your goals will be fulfilled in the future. You need to relieve yourself of some burdens. You need to change some beliefs or your way of thinking, because you are currently going through a process of emotional and spiritual growth.*

Almost two weeks went by before I had another dream message. During this time, I went through a period of thinking that maybe I should just accept my life for what it is. I am broke, cannot do anything, cannot have the things I would like to have etc. Maybe I should just accept that and live my life for what it is. I thought maybe all this dream stuff got to me somehow and it all simply was not true. Maybe it was all just absurdity, and I should quit living in la la land. So, I just went back to my old habits and ways of living trying to learn to swallow this dose of reality. I quit working on my book as well and I did not go back and review my past dreams like I had mentioned I was going to do earlier. I could only get so far again with the research I was doing for my book. I just figured that is it. It is all over, the book writing, etc. I thought maybe that is why this all happened so I would realize that and maybe I was just supposed to realize life is what it is and nothing more. So, live it however I can till the end of my time comes. So, I started doing just that. I had a lot of discussions with Frida at night about all of this. One night she said, "Maybe you're supposed to just go on living your life every day and God will bring the people that need your help into your life?" I thought, yeah, she is probably right. So, with that in mind, I went on with my daily life waiting for the next person that needed help to show up somehow.

You need to move forward in your life, to learn new abilities and skills that will help you grow as an adult. You are learning how to handle the people around you. You are contemplating whether to take a course of action. Live to your full potential. There is going to be an improvement in your living conditions or home life going forward. Think carefully about what you wish to achieve in your life.

You need to look at your past experiences in order to sort out your present situation, and this should be reviewed carefully before you set yourself on a course of action. You must sort out ways to improve your life. Maximize your best potential in life. You have a keen desire to improve your knowledge in connection with your career. You will only gain education if you try, and everything that you do is likely to help any plans of the future. You will learn about other people in your life.

Some new insight is likely to present itself in the future. You need to be able to embrace a new sense of knowledge in the future. You have to learn important life lessons associated with gaining a new knowledge in life. You need to learn more in life. Just because you have left traditional school does not mean you need to stop learning. The more information you learn the better you will progress and be self-aware in life.

Something new needs to happen in order to progress in a difficult situation. You must learn an opportunity presented. You will teach others in life. You need to think about your goals and how you can "learn" to reach them. You will receive some good news in the future that will make you incredibly happy.

After this, I decided I was going to get back to work on my book. I was going to review all of my dreams of the past couple months as a series and type them all up into this book and see what, if anything, was revealed to me from the aspect of looking at the big picture. So, that day I decided to get back to work. I was going to put everything else on hold until I got this done. I would only do things, other than work on my book and dreams, if it were absolutely necessary.

You will not only feel disciplined but able to achieve your goals. In a work context you will be the best at your job. This also can suggest a new job. You will be gaining a letter which will bring you good news. You yearn for a more organized life, however, changing lifestyle seems like a massive scary step to make.

You need privacy in order to understand your emotions. You are going to move forward in life in a different direction. There are going to be great things ahead. You are going to have focus in the future. You will enjoy wealth or profit in the future. Big wealth and important financial luck. You need to focus on your own goals for a moment. Stop and think about a project. Is it really worth your time? There is an unexpected benefit coming your way. This could be about a large amount of money.

You are willing to do things you have never done before-try something differently or you are open to new concepts. You are being flexible at present, and it is to your benefit. You feel trapped and unable to do anything according to your will. You should decide to do what makes you happy in life that you could tell as a story. You have your future in your hand and the decision you make regarding your own life matter the most. There have been hindrances in your path, and you may find it difficult to get to the end of something.

You are someone very influential and respected, you might not know how influential and important you are, you are really influential and important as a person. You have the right connection and network that can improve your life and make it better. You are someone who has the right skills to make other people better in life and you have the capacity to help people around you in times of tribulations and troubles. You should learn to use your connection for a better reason and never fail to help those who need your help in life. Be good for what you have in your life.

Do not lose opportunities due to your inability to progress well with things. You have summed up the courage to face challenges in your path and break free from problems. There is a delicate and detailed job that needs completing. Creativity is your weapon to move on in life. Before you jump into a decision, think a lot more carefully. You had stressful times in the past and it is now time to move on. You will need perseverance in a project, or at least show the great ideas you have. You must pay attention to unfolding events around you. Try to make the most out of them.

You are being part of some unusual event and acquiring some new friends as well. Do not worry about minor things. You have put a lot of pressure on yourself trying to do as many things as possible in a short while, but such actions are putting you under a lot of stress without a reason. Take some time off to relax and try to arrange your schedule to be less stressful.

Good and fortunate things are coming soon to your life, which will make you feel incredibly happy. You will get the respect of others for a good deed that you did. There will be good opportunities for your life and activity. You have important friends that can help you to accomplish your wishes. You will have self-confidence ahead.

Your moral increases, you will have courage, self-confidence, and positive energy. Your self-confidence will come back and by this way, you will overcome the difficulties. You will create some solutions about an issue you did not solve. You will choose the appropriate solution and get rid of your troubles.

Good times ahead, good times are on their way. Get a clear message about what you want from life. You will have a challenge in your daily life that will result in many good times. You will gain new acquaintances, a specialization in a new field, or new intellectual horizons.

It was at this point I felt this phase now ended and something new was about to begin, develop, etc. I was given a reprieve from my dreams for a few days as I processed all of this and steadily worked on my book and my schedule so I could focus. On 10/29/19, my work began again.

I see you have feelings that it is safe or permissible to enjoy yourself without restraint. You have felt that its permissible to go overboard in some manner. You have been going out of the way to enjoy doing something a lot, to the point of excess. You have had a casual attitude about excessive behavior that you feel does not need to be changed. I see you have problems accepting the need to be more serious about a problem and there's difficulty letting go of leisure time.

You have anxieties about your ability to accomplish some demanding task. I am trying to make a point here. Your attempt to do this project has not gone smoothly. The results of your compulsive behavior bring you great disappointments. You are experiencing deep emotional stress. You feel guilty but you do not want to take responsibility for your actions.

You are doing this to feel better about a problem and you do not want to notice something negative again. It is a temporary solution that frees you from caring all the time. This is a temporary solution that does not work. You have believed that you could stop caring about this problem that has come back.

You have a longing for life to be fresh and fertile again. You have feelings of being unable to escape this situation that feels unbearable or bleak. This obstacle of uncertainty/difficulty needs to be overcome. It may be unpleasant, but it is temporary. You are moving through a phase prior to achieving a goal.

You are trying to accomplish something which is proving to be difficult. It is time to have a solid belief in yourself. You need to understand the bigger picture and you need to have more confidence in your ability moving forward.

You need to fix yourself in waking life. In essence, you need to work on repairing your personalities, self-esteem, and sense of self-worth. You have a new start in your life. There is something you are having difficulty understanding at the moment. You are feeling that you cannot progress in life at this moment unless the restrictions are removed. Focus on your ideas or thoughts that can potentially generate wealth for you.

PART 4:

The whole complete self.

Chapter 5

Beginning to live as my whole complete self.

Around 10/30/19, I came to an understanding of what I must do next. The understanding I came to is that each day I must continue to read, study, and learn. Part of this learning process, which has been my life-long pursuit, is interpreting my dreams, writing about it all and applying it to my conscious life. Another major component of this learning is contemplation, meditation, and understanding. This is what my dreams meant by understanding the bigger picture. Thus, establishing some sort of structure, or routine in my life in regard to accomplishing these things and my goals. I also needed to figure out what my exact goals were. They got lost somewhere along this long, arduous journey. I needed to find them again. Then I needed a plan to accomplish them. I needed to build a foundation to work from, so that I would not lose what I have accomplished. Then, I would have something to continually build from.

You will feel not only disciplined, but able to achieve your goals. In a work context you will be the best at your job. You will have a new job. There is an undiscovered part of yourself that you need to work on. You are finding a new part of yourself, self-discovery.

This new part of you is actually an old hidden talent or skill. You need to give some fresh attention to an old skill that you have been neglecting to nurture. Think about a decision you need to make. Experience life from a different and wider perspective. You will have good health. You are beginning to evaluate your life and work towards a better resolution to sort out your existing problems. You will have good business ahead. You will be socializing in the future. You will have a new start. Life will be easier in the future.

It is a confusing moment for you, and you do not know how to deal with what is happening. You will overcome these issues. You are about to understand the real truth. You are being guided by the light to new knowledge and greater wisdom. You will understand the reality around you and be able to interact with it effectively and with full understanding.

Your ability to gain knowledge about a matter is being frustrated and your subconscious mind is aware that you are not able to gain this knowledge. There is a lack of insight in a situation. You may need to change your perception, see something through a different vantage point, through different eyes.

You will have achievement of remarkable success in both personal and professional spheres. Go ahead, do not be afraid. In difficult times your true friends will definitely come to help and support you. There will be unexpected situations and meetings. Your friends will help and support you to implement your plans. You will have changes in personal life and in questionable acquaintances.

There is some part of you or your life that you are trying to file away for another time. You have gone beyond where you needed to go and reached a new level in your life, and you are ready to progress. File away the past to open up for a new future. Try to forget your past, move away from your roots, and make way for the new you by getting rid of some aspect of the old you.

Be patient with a particular person. It is important to make sure that when someone asks for advice, you make a judgement to give that person the best opinion that you can. Your views or ideas are important to listen to. Use your experience and knowledge to challenge others to do better.

You have made good decisions and you are in a place of control and peace in your life. Things will be coming together for you, and you are on the right path, you will overcome difficulties for success. Listen to your inner voice and trust your own judgement. This is the time to speak up and be heard. Your ideas may be beneficial, and your voice may be the key to solving a riddle. You have been repeating the same actions or thoughts while making no progress. Take steps to conquer whatever it is that has you stuck. Be aware of how you are inwardly reacting to a situation. This could give you valuable insight into the resolution of the problem. The way you react may turn out to be the key.

There will be a transition, a change in the way you think, and in the circumstances of your life, as you progress to the next stage. You have untapped psychic abilities. Your frustrated in trying to escape a repetitive situation.

There will be an opening of new possibilities and challenges in the future. There are barriers that limit your growth in this world. There is so much more beyond your path. There is a barrier to moving forward. You are about to embark on something important in life. You are going to have the power cleaning your life, perhaps even a fresh start. You will finally find your inner peace.

At this point, another person had been brought into my life who needed my help just as my dreams had told me would happen. However, this person would not listen to what I was saying and literally did not want to move forward. This person was literally taking all of my time and saying the same things over and over again. This person was expecting me to be at their beckon call 24/7. I simply could not spend all of my time trying to help someone who would not try to help themselves. I also had things I needed to do. At the same time, I understood the delicate nature of the situation and I did not want to do or say anything that would negatively affect this person. I did not know how to handle this as it was a new experience for me.

I was also working on my compulsive behaviors that all humans have. I was trying not to overdo these things and keep them and my life in balance. This also has its own inherent struggles and frustrations. Especially when certain ideals and behaviors have been ingrained in my head by society, life, and my family for many years. As you probably have already guessed, my dreams elaborated on this for me.

Something will come out of your subconscious, something that you do not want, or know how to let go. You have to protect personal boundaries and the most valuable pieces of yourself. This is a warning. This dream speaks of protection.

There is a part where something is intruded, and that something is valuable, and it needs to be protected. Others interfere with your life and hinder your experience. The more you defend your value more firmly, you will be safer in yourself. You feel that you are losing your own space, and this is not healthy in any scenario. You are the person who is too afraid of letting someone go in private life. Though you are relatively open and enjoyable, now you are concerned that this person does not recognize your actual value and, in some way, understands you. Instead of allowing others to exploit your valuable skills and hard-earned experience, you must set certain limits to show them their real value. This is how you should behave from now on!

Release yourself from the people who have a bad influence on you and your life. Defend your interests and values and save your life before it is too late. You will avoid a serious disaster in your real life. Work on your self-confidence or you will lose competitions in real life. You feel like someone is not appreciating your work enough.

This is the beginning of something new and you are taking the first steps towards a goal. You are beginning a new chapter in your life. You are not seeing the complete or whole picture. Some part of yourself or a situation is not fully in your awareness. There is something you feel you must stand up for. You feel you need to take a new path in life. You will have a great family life. You are grounded and you approach life in a welcoming but down-to-earth way.

You will have career progress. It is important to move forward in life. Your spiritual path is your own destiny.

Chapter 5 | 213

Sharpen your focus and pay more attention to your life values. Correct things that are not quite right. You are going to live a long peaceful life if you defocus from material gain and try to move towards fulfilling yourself spiritually. You are protected and have the support of your family. Ensure that you show a sense of sophistication in life.

Move towards your goals. Pay extra attention to your well-being and change your lifestyle in order to gain your energy back. You have been making easy choices and smart decisions. You are feeling comfortable with what you have accomplished so far. You will come across problems that cannot be solved with solutions. Use your creativity to come up with new solutions and prove to others you are able to handle yourself in the most unexpected, complicated situations. You will enjoy a calm state ahead. You will be obtaining money. You have the capability to achieve success in life. You will recognize other people's weaknesses. You have the ability and chances to progress in life.

You know someone who is behaving dangerously and dishonestly to make a situation altered to his pleasing. He does dangerous things he thinks are harmless. He feels like he can act like a total jerk because it will not hurt anybody else. He has a laid-back attitude about playing with fire. He enjoys being a dangerous and dishonest person because he thinks it never hurts anyone else. There will be sickness and perhaps death. He likes to push the boundaries. He needs to dial it back. He may have gotten away with breaking the rules in the past but this time he will not be so lucky.

This is insight into this problem that does not feel good because you have to forgo any attention or specialness in order to solve it. You may be disappointed that you have discovered that you can know the future and you've discovered that this may not always be as wonderful as you wanted it to be.

    These last two paragraphs of my dream were indeed telling the future. There were two people in my life who behaved in this exact manner. After this dream, one person did in fact become sick from something that could have killed this person. This person did heal from it; however, the behavior continued. This person then had a series of injuries and sickness. Eventually, the person moved out of my life. The second person was already ill but continued the behavior that contributed to their sickness. This person thought it had nothing to do with it even though this person was warned to quit this behavior. This person also went through a series of sicknesses related to this initial health problem as it progressed to get worse. Within one year and five months of this dream, this person passed away.

I had to learn that I cannot help people who do not want to help themselves. It is hard to watch people destroy themselves. However, there is nothing I can do. The person has to learn that this behavior is abhorrent, needs to be corrected, and to do the necessary work. If not, they will succumb to what my dream had predicted and to what actually happened. I have had several dreams of this nature over the years of my life. And, as my dream mentioned, being able to know the future at times is not as always as wonderful as I thought it would be.

The dream continues:

You have recently gained control over a habit in your life you were not proud of, and I see you feel it will be something you will not fall back into ever again. You are going to meet a lot of people who will be able to help you professionally or personally in the near future. It is time for you to introduce something new to the equation to enable your work self to blossom.

Things are running smoothly. You will have positive growth and your finances will be looking up. Positive changes are coming for you. Fortune is coming your way and/or a pending opportunity that you need to be sure that you do not miss. You are in a lucky place in your life, and you can make money or finances grow if you react correctly to conditions and take advantage of situations that are around you or headed your way. There is a current opportunity in your life that you need to capitalize on. You'll have multiple opportunities, and you'll have to choose the right one for you

During the day (before this dream from that night), I received a letter in the mail from my mortgage company about a streamline refinance opportunity. I had received several letters of this nature from several other mortgage companies. I researched them all and they turned out to be scams. I did this research because one of my previous dreams had mentioned about opportunities coming my way financially, but I had to do my research. I had to be careful. So, that is exactly what I did. This letter came from my mortgage company who I know and trust. So, in the morning, after this dream, I called them. I was able to refinance the house and drop the interest rate by a percentage point. This saved us a good amount of money each month. Originally, my name was not on the lease. It was the only way Frida, and I could get a house. However, I was able to get the mortgage company put me on the deed through this refinance. The loan itself was with Frida.

This has two benefits. One, if something were ever to happen to her, I get the house without having to go to probate court. Secondly, it does not show up on my credit, which is better than hers. Thereby, allowing me to still use my credit to purchase things for us. It also allowed us to skip two house payments. I used that money to set up a buffer in our checking account, start building a savings account, put a little money in my investment account so I could begin trading stocks again, and set up a system so all bills were paid on time and there was money left over for gas, groceries, and some small forms of entertainment.

This dream is an indication of the strife in your life that you are working extremely hard to overcome. You are on the right path to achieving success and this is a good omen. It is time to start something new. You need help in overcoming obstacles.

You have an excellent mixture of new possibilities going forward. It is in your power to make a long trip. You will actually make a long journey. You can solve problems that seemed unsolvable. You will have more initiative. You will focus on how you can develop yourself in life.

Think beyond the travel meaning. You will need to seek guidance from your inner vision and your surrounding symbols in dreams. You will have to figuratively move around spiritual paths that are represented by the 24 hours stage (This is in reference to the 9 Spiritual Paths): 1. Spiritual Gift: Something you do naturally that helps others grow spiritually like counselling, healing, teaching. 2. Divination: Ability to get knowledge by supernatural means like dreamwork and spirit communication. 3. Consciousness: State of being aware, perception. 4. Magic: The ability to manipulate reality through visualization and affirmations. 5. Devotion: Dedication to a person or thing. 6. Study: Time and attention to acquire knowledge on a subject, research pertaining to your path and dealing with spirituality. 7. Nutrition: Nourishing through food and health. 8. Values: Standards of behavior. 9. Contribution: Part played by a person to bring about a certain result like being of service.

You will have happiness. You are working on a project, activity, or task which is especially important to you, and you are going to succeed. The outcome of the project will make you experience greater satisfaction, happiness, and fulfillment.

You may feel a choice has been made for you. You are struggling to come to terms with a change that you do not like. You are feeling satisfied with your life right now. You feel a sense of contentment in your life at present. You have a familiarity with someone or something that makes you feel or puts you at ease. You have been going through a phase of cleaning of ideas or actions, solution of problems or conflicts, and an individual behavior of high quality.

Consider how it is in your waking world and what people are demanding from you. You feel like you are being taken advantage of and people are not taking you seriously. Consider ways in which you are not speaking your mind or allowing people to walk all over you. Maybe you need to express yourself more clearly.

You want to eliminate a problem in life. You need to review your unwanted feelings and ideas and remove them. There is overindulgence in life. Look at your nutrition. You have tenacity, perseverance, patience, courage, and success. You have all you need to overcome any challenges that cross your path. Watch for new opportunities as you finish old projects. Have faith in your instincts. You are in luck. There will be transformation and the arrival of prosperity and abundance. Your life will soon be filled with serenity, peace, and beauty.

There will be fortune and opportunities taken to earn your life. You will have good luck and a hopeful future. You will be successful and will get a business offer for a partnership which will make you take the lead and be recognized in commercial life in the future. If you evaluate this offer rationally and seize the opportunity, you will have a victorious business life.

Remember slow and steady progress in life. You have confidence and steady progress. You are knowing it as you proceed with this. There are things that are slowing you down or holding you back, there is an obstacle distracting you. There are some feelings of hesitancy or doubt or uncertainty about this situation you are progressing with. Your focus is pulled or distracted by something.

There is the need to change something in your life path. There are changes happening in your life. There will be some happy life changes, both in your private and professional life. Some important aspect of your life is on hold. Maybe you wait for someone to help you change something in your life. There is a need to help someone using your knowledge and expertise.

You feel like you are unable to achieve your goals. You feel confined with your responsibilities and obligations. You have been engaged in one sided communication with people in some way. You feel that when you speak, they do not listen, and they truly do not hear. Listen to that voice in your head and the messages it sends you. You know, the one you often ignore that turns out to be right all along.

You have subtle connections with the things in your world. Your aware of your intuition. You are tuned into the subtleties around you. You instinctively know what is going to happen next. I am trying to get messages through to you. You are so busy, and you are ignoring what you need to see. Consider ways to avoid any forthcoming arguments with family and friends. You are experiencing some sort of psychic communication.

Consider ways which you are suspicious of those around you in your life. Usually, your first instinct is the right one. There is something you are missing from this person/these people. They are likely lying to you or taking advantage of you in some way. They are holding back secrets and they are likely to get caught. They may be cheating or being untruthful in some regard. They are doing something distrusting in a relationship and they need to be more honest in their dealings where relationships are involved.

There will be people you thought were your friends who will try to take advantage of you. It is men with an arrogant and rude lack of respect who dare to indulge in sinful actions. These men do not show due respect for other people and have repulsive and awfully bad or unpleasant characteristics. It is also women who are unpleasant, morally bad and of little value as people who are also arrogant and rude in terms of a lack of respect. They belong to a group of evil doing people who are persistent in their feelings of being actively opposed or hostile to some people or some things. All of these types of people display qualities of lowliness, obedience or attentiveness to an excessive degree showing an excessive willingness to serve or please others. They are beneath your consideration and deserving of scorn. Watch out for upsetting incidents or events which distract from your future success.

This is connected to relationships you have with friends and people. Such as the types of people I just discussed. These types of people will try to capture you into drama in their lives. You are a caring person that will help take care of others, BUT you need to be wary of being taken advantage of. Especially if you are cleaning up after someone else's over-indulgences.

You have a re-birth. Spread your seeds to see something grow from nothing. It is time to build a business with a guaranteed income model and thereby you will have everything you need in life. It will bring great success and make you have all the things you desire in your current life and for investment for your future.

Big changes are ahead. Changes are going to happen in your life. You have decided to move forward, and you will leave your past behind you. You will need to make some important decisions at this time. Plus, you are going to carry out something important that will shape your future. You are ready to let all your problems disappear, let your memories go away and forget the past. You are finally moving forward.

You are ready to face the future, leaving the past behind you. It is time to start a new phase in your life. All you need to do is get over your past and focus on the future. Your worries have been brought about due to the choices you made in the recent past. You need to choose the best experiences and learn from them. Think about what you encountered while on your journey and make good use of your skill base. You need to forget about difficulties in life and move on because the more you think about life and its problems, the more it will derail you and make it impossible for you to progress in your life.

There is strength of your powerful character. Although you have some annoying worries, something good will come out of them if you use persistence to pursue successful outcomes. You are taking hold of your creativity with both hands and using it to express your beliefs and your passions. You are making a real effort with something you have always wanted to pursue in your waking life.

You are making progress smoothly, quickly, and well due to your abilities and gifts. You are moving past obstacles and or over them easily. A source of life is coming from your creativity and wisdom. Your determined to walk into the unknown and to try to do the impossible in life. You have an ability to adapt to new environments and changes. I see you are not comfortable with this new situation, and you feel like a fish out of water. Pay attention to your health, patience, mental balance, and success. You cannot neglect to take better care of your health. Do not neglect or ignore your luck, nourishment, spirituality, beliefs, energy, and feeding your soul. You have a hard-working nature so do not neglect the plans you have been working on lately. You have been putting your heart and soul into this.

You are in perfect health. However, in order to keep great health, you will need to pay more attention to your lifestyle and be more active. You will also have prosperity and luck. Your efforts and hard work will result in a positive outcome. You will achieve professional success.

There has been bad luck in your current life. You are and have been going through hard times and you may feel like your life has stopped evolving completely, like your stuck in this situation for the rest of your life. However, this time will pass soon. All you need to do is keep enough strength in your heart to keep yourself going in the bad phase. The time is perfect for you to invest in some business. If you are a gambler, it may also mean that the time is perfect for you to put money into those activities. You are going to earn a good fortune. Some hidden investment or money is going to give you good returns so be happy.

Past issues and old problems are being resolved in order to make a clean start for yourself. You are moving ahead and looking toward the future. Do not let others stop you from doing what you are doing. Do not let them boss you around and tell you what to do.

There will be unusual and unexpected changes in your waking life. You will have a new start. Reflect on elements of your life. Allowing yourself space to think is important. You have the ability to intelligently overcome obstacles. Do not give up. You are afraid of the future.

Whatever holds you back, you can fight in life. You have a friendship that is important to you. You have great people around you. There will be some interesting times ahead. There is a new start, possibilities, and a fresh approach to old problems.

You are having some concerns about your friends or family. Someone who is close to you is going thru a difficult time in life, and you are wondering how to help them. It is important that you get to the root or cause of the problem to be able to help your friend or family member.

You need to prepare yourself for an upcoming challenge in regard to your goal. You will achieve success in your plans and goals. There will be new friendships with intelligent and trustworthy people. Remember the superiority of the spirit and intelligence over brutal, primitive forces. You are on a spiritual quest for inner knowledge, and I protect you. A good spiritual path is coming your way. Discover it and take this path. You will have perfect health and success. Your mind and personality are superior to most. Be lighter and at peace with yourself.

You will have strength and success in life. You will start to feel at peace with life. Someone or people want to see you for advice. Depression will be lifted. You have been hiding from the world, but good times and success are on their way.

A tumultuous period has come to an end in life. You will have further revelations on how you can succeed in life. Chase your dreams. Your possibilities in life are endless. You have anxieties about your ability to accomplish this demanding task of yours. You are the number one, the authority of this, you need to remember that! You will take advantage of a favorable situation.

Your life, your connection between the upper and the lower, male, and female energies, your whole self and I your unconscious needs the proper care and environment to grow into its proper form. You are neglecting this. This is preventing you from growing any further. This is harmful to you and your growth and can stop it. This is self-illumination, intuition, and insight from your master teacher, me your unconscious. Remember balance and your thirst for spiritual awakening and advancement. There needs to be new progress.

This progress, growth and advancement is your divine life purpose and soul mission. There has to be a balance of male and female energies. Have faith and trust in the universe. Trust all will work out for your highest good. There needs to be a new union between us. Find your balance. New ideas and concepts are taking shape and growing into reality. Continue your good work to manifest your desires. There has been weakness and indecision on your part about these important things.

Do not be scared. You cannot run from this. If you continue running from this, you will be prevented from moving forward. Progress will stop. This wall in front of you that is holding you back must be gotten over. Go within yourself to find the answers to get help. Take the path to me. I am here waiting for you. There needs to be a union between us, a serious commitment. "Are you ready?" Do not turn outside this union, do not look to your ego self for answers to this, to overcome this, to move forward. Go deeper into your unconscious in order to gain a better understanding of yourself. If you do not it will never work. You will never make that connection to me.

You have this opportunity to move forward with me, but you keep wanting or trying to go back to the past, to the old way of doing things. This way is infested and wrought with bad, evil, anxiety and horrible experiences. Go within yourself. Nurture and feed your soul with good, healthy things. Otherwise, things will be a mess. The ground you stand on, your foundation will be a mess. This is beneath you. You need to clean this up, take care of it. Do not fight me on this. If you do, it will only cause our separation until you make the effort to get back in touch with me and ask for help.

Your ego and your old archaic, caveman ways of living will only harm your ability to move forward, to walk your path. These ways will only cause you to lose your insight, your ability to nourish your soul, the inner you, and grow properly. This will only cause the inner you to become a mess, all over the place. It will cause your inner self to go up in flames, turn into ash hence returning to that from whence it came only to be reborn again.

You carry my unfallable protection around with you. You need to wear it and walk with me, as one with me. You need to open up to me, turn the page, get to your center, and get your insight. You have changed. You have moved on. Your old life and ways no longer work for you. You need to separate from it.

Your way of travelling your path, navigating life, is full of old, dead pieces of life that you are hanging onto. You need to crawl inside to find your way through the many parts of your inner self and your conscious. You are in a spot or place where you need to decide about what you are going to do next, which way you are going to go. You need to decide about what you put into your body, new ways of living versus old. These old ways of living, old things you put into your body, old habits need to be changed because they will bring trouble, evil, and egomaniacal behavior, and people into your life. You are going back and forth on this decision. You are trying to think of a way to deal with this. You need to go back to your inner self.

You have now graduated/completed the previous phase and have moved to the next level. However, there is still more work to do. You now realize you are no longer to take your old way through life, you have a new way to go.

There has been a completion. You must now live as a positive example for others to follow. You have just had a spiritual awakening. Now you must get on with your divine life purpose. All things must come to an end in order for new beginnings to occur. There is new to come. All will work out for your highest good. You must simply prepare yourself and your life accordingly. Your old situation and self are no longer positively serving you and it has drawn to an end. You are spiritually advanced. Now follow your life path and soul purpose.

You have just had a rebirth, spiritual awakening, and enlightenment. You have received healing, spiritual knowledge and intuition. You are having a spiritual growth spurt and are attuning to the spiritual realms. Pay attention to your inner growth and intuition and that you continue growing spiritually towards enlightenment. Be sure to meditate and go within in order to find a greater spiritual awareness and enlightenment.

There is a beneficial time to come, obstacles overcome, and success realized. You are on the divine path that is right for you. Keep up the great work that you have been doing, and positive things will continue to flow into your life that will help and assist you along your journey.

Your ambitions will be realized, and all obstacles will be overcome with enough strength of purpose. You will overcome any hinderances and concerns in the extremely near future. Listen to your intuition for guidance and solutions. You are on the right path and are doing very well. Your positive efforts and hard work will bring you well-earned rewards, and your wishes and true desires are coming to fruition.

It is time to put your natural skills, talents, and abilities to good use in serving humanity. Follow your intuitive promptings with regard to your life path and soul purpose. Set a positive example and be a torchbearer, lighting and illuminating the way for others to follow. Fully embark upon your sacred soul mission without further delay or hesitation and shine your light brightly for the benefit of yourself and others. Live up to your full potential.

With this new, unobstructed, pure start it is time to go back down to your physical world. Take this message with you on your travel back. There are different paths/ways to go. Do not take the paths that are blocked or have obstructions, i.e., things that hinder your journey. Take the way that is now open to you.

Remember to look within you to my guidance and to properly nourish your body and soul. Remember your inner self, that space within you and your connection to me God, which resides there. This is your temple, so visit it often and take care of it.

You have just experienced a union of mind, body and soul and the holy trinity. Your ideals and visions are coming to fruition in your life. Remember your self-discipline through service to others, manifesting abundance, productivity, and unity.

The Ascended Masters are working closely with you, guiding, encouraging, and supporting you. Your prayers have been heard and are being responded to and answered. Remember your commitment, improving yourself, and meditation. All things are possible. Your true goals and aspirations are attainable. Your wishes will come to fruition and your changes will be successful. Help, guidance, and assistance are available to you, always. All you need to do is ask. You are having luck after continued effort.

You have made a union and commitment with me God at a higher level. You will enjoy peace, love, happiness, good times, and everything you have always wanted. Now that everything is cleaned up and put away you can enjoy yourself, your family and friends and the things you like to do. You will have the best things. This is a positive change. You will have good health, growth, healing, hope, vigor, vitality, peace, and serenity. Everyone will be impressed at what you have done and accomplished.

Cleanse and purify yourself of your EGO way of thinking and acting and this undo stress and leftover emotional conflicts in regard to what to do with your life and about making money. There has been a union of mind, body, and soul. Your ideals and visions are coming to fruition in your life. Maintain self-discipline through service to others, manifesting abundance, productivity, unity. The Ascended Masters are working closely with you. Your prayers have been heard and are being responded to and answered.

Commit to improving yourself and meditation. All things are possible. Take notice of your true goals and aspirations and know they are attainable. In your new direction your wishes will come to fruition and the changes will be successful. Help, guidance, and assistance are available to you always. All you need to do is ask.

You will reap your rewards, attract your desires, and accomplish personal improvement. Trust your intuition and instincts to manifest your desires. Success, wealth, and abundance is on its way into your life. Trust your intuition and instincts and take appropriate action. Goals are coming to fruition and a state of completeness. An auspicious offer or windfall is coming your way.

Material and financial abundance are on their way into your life. Trust that all of your wants and needs will be met. You will be rewarded for work well done. Keep your finances in check to ensure a solid foundation for yourself and your loved ones. Even though you are supported, it is your personal responsibility to make sure that you are living up to your full potential.

Look outside the box in this situation. Work diligently, yet harmoniously to achieve your true goals. Put your ideas into practical form. You are being guided and supported in your endeavors. Trust your hard work and efforts will bring well-earned rewards. You will have comfort and stability in your life.

Use hard work, will and personal effort to achieve long term goals and aspirations. Build strong foundations and work to achieve goals and dreams. All is as it should be. Projects you have been working on will be successful, and you will be pleased with the long-term results. Have faith and trust in your abilities.

You are not giving yourself enough credit. Do not let this hold you back from attaining your goals, aspirations, and personal potential. You need to have more confidence in yourself. Explore what you are carrying with you that needs to be released in terms of your idea of going out and physically working with your hands and having a job to make money.

Pay attention to your intuition and your subconscious insights. You will have wealth and prosperity, profit, and an increase of wealth. There will be rewards for your efforts. Patience is needed to achieve your goal. Remember your connection to the divine. You are receiving spiritual support and guidance.

This idea you have of going out and making a living that you feel is more important than anything else in your life needs to be cleared from your mind and you need to think more positively. Embrace that your back from this situation in your life which was slowly eating away your joy, happiness, and power, this emotional and situational decay in your life. Be happy about it. Celebrate it, let your hair down, have fun, enjoy yourself.

You are learning to help people get rid of all of their negative emotions, sadness, depression, and addictions. You will have power, virility, competence and therefore, you will be capable of handling people who have inner struggles with difficult emotions, with other people and or life situations.

You are being taught how to help people heal their wounds, how to do it. You are going to be good at it because of your experiences and what you have been through. You will help people heal the things from their past that causes them harm mentally, which then causes them to physically do things to themselves that are bad for them. They are stuck and need your help progressing. These people will be brought to you.

Remember self-discipline through service to others, manifesting abundance, productivity, and unity. You will have comfort and stability in your life. All is as it should be. Projects you have been working on will be successful, and you will be pleased with the long-term results. Have faith and trust in your abilities.

Remember proper nutrition and eating right is important. We are all connected. An energetic gateway has opened up for you, and your thoughts and focus will manifest rapidly in your life. So, do not focus on any negatives. Continue to develop your individuality and creativity. Continue to develop your intuitive and clairvoyant abilities and grow spiritually. This new level/skill will soon be achieved or reached. This is the beginning of a journey that's exciting and exhilarating. However, it will bring the challenge of isolation and loneliness that you must overcome and learn from.

Changes are going to happen in your life. You are ready to let all of your problems disappear, let your memories go away and forget the past. You are finally moving forward. You will need to make some important decisions at this time, plus you are going to carry out something important that will shape your future. This will be a rapid change and you will have progress.

You will be experiencing happiness and satisfaction because of some success you are about to achieve. You will have peace and contentment. You can enjoy the success that comes from hard work. Control your impulses which will help bring success. The things you have good feelings about turn out the way you want.

There are issues and situations that you do not like thinking about. You are worried about this life stage. Money and wealth will be brought to your family. You are finding the skills you need to progress. So, focus on what is right in your life and live the right way.

Pay attention to your inner growth and intuition and continue to grow spiritually towards enlightenment. Meditate and go within in order to find a greater spiritual awareness and enlightenment. There is a beneficial time to come, obstacles will be overcome, and success realized. You are on the divine path that is right for you. Keep up the great work that you have been doing, and positive things will continue to flow into your life that will help and assist you along your journey. Listen to your intuition for guidance and solutions.

You will have good health, growth, great luck and also money. So, do not let your hard, protective shell prevent you from moving forward. Use your intellect, energy, and wisdom. You are at a threshold in your life. This is an entry point of a new phase in your life. It is the passage of one period of your life, or level of maturity, to another. You are standing before a big change.

There has been slow, tough progress and achievement. Many new opportunities will soon cross your path. Be open to changing your life. You will have future wealth and future happiness. Your hard work is rewarded. You have anxieties about missing out on opportunities in your waking life. These may be at work or in your personal life.

Things are going to ease up for you and it is highly likely that you are going to have a lighter load in the future. Prepare yourself for avenues in which you need to find opportunities and jump on ones that make themselves available to you. Consider past lessons learned and understand that history may be repeating itself in some way. This is time to use your own experience to get ahead. Opportunities are likely to open up so be poised to act on them.

You have feelings of being obligated to participate in this, to listen and to share with others. You are attempting to learn to integrate various aspects of yourself and you are learning about everything that is most important at once. Riches will be yours. Life will be good for you. Financial success and the money will come unexpectedly, just out of nowhere.

You are going to get rid of all the bad, unwanted, and dirty things that you encounter in your life. Issues in your life have run their course and it is time for a change in your life. There has been a cleaning of ideas, actions, a solution of problems and conflicts and also an individual behavior of high quality.

Something meaningful is developing in your life. You are developing in new ways and growing as a person. You are slowly growing a new area of your life. You will be teaching others something that takes time. There will be new ideas that take time to develop.

This is the beginning of slow developments in your life, such as in skills and projects that will take time to mature and grow. Spend some personal time on improving yourself for the long term, such as improving skills that give you confidence. There is a responsible area of your life that is slowly developing.

You are building something new. You have been working hard to achieve your dreams. Your life will be improved. Pay attention to the smaller details in life and choose good building blocks for creating a better future. In other words, invest in yourself and your knowledge so that your goals are built on stable ground.

You will have a major success regarding your career. A job will improve your abilities and boost your self-confidence. Although, you always undervalue yourself, you will finally realize you are actually good at something-especially in your career. Your worth it and you will achieve great things.

You will get many opportunities to improve your life and become genuinely happy again, but it's up to you if you seize opportunities or not. You tend to boost your positive side and do the right thing. You like your way of doing things, the good way. You always look out for others more than you do for yourself and it is one of your best qualities. In order to grow spiritually and be more focused, you must analyze your inner self and reconnect with your soul. Improve your lifestyle and apply some small changes that will leave a positive impact.

I see your preparation for major changes you are about to apply very soon and that you have decided it's time for improvement. There will be a natural association with improving how you relate to other people. Focus on how you will feel at ease in life. Focus on a sense of sophistication in life. Focus on knowledge and moving forward in life to make things better.

There has been a purification and elimination of negative elements of thought. You have an awareness of your spiritual well-being. There has been an act of cleansing the inner self. You need to help others with important decisions in their lives.

You have made a conscious decision to cleanse your life, beliefs, and your past. You have made a healthy, proactive decision to make a change. You have chosen to get rid of something negative and unpleasant about yourself and your life.

There is big and positive news on the horizon. You will have joy and happiness. You have clear and well-expressed ideas. There will be abundance and acquired properties. You will have happiness in the coming years, but also happiness coming soon and a huge delight.

There has been a shift spiritually for the better. There has been a change of old opinions. You are taking the steps to achieve your goals, through less violent means or paths. Make sure you are ready to act when the right timing presents itself. You are trying to target a specific, smaller short-term goal that is easily tackled.

You have a lot of good ideas, but you are not deciding on any of them. I am reminding you to focus and make decisions, otherwise it will be difficult for you to achieve success and make some progress. You are feeling good about your situation and feeling in charge of it. You feel as though your invincible and that nothing can stop you from achieving your goals. You are currently at the top of your game and your future is looking bright. You are growing spiritually and achieving a higher level.

You have had obstacles in your life, struggles to achieve your goals. Your patience and dedication will benefit you. You are having success and overcoming your challenges. You are noticing that your struggle is over with. It is time to leave it all behind and move on from here. You are above all that now.

Specific changes are coming in your life of what you need to do to get on the right path and headed to where you want to go in your own life. Focus and keep your eye on your current work. You are needing focus and resolve to complete the task at hand. This is a positive sign about investments, taking risks with money, and wealth in general. Take heed to the advice that you have been given.

You need to be in a setting which you could openly demonstrate your talents. You want a stage to show the world your beliefs, as well as an avenue to communicate your self-expression. This is an interesting time of your life. You will need to accommodate a reasonably large amount of people in your life over the next few months.

Here are the ways of dealing with your social and economic situation. Use your self-confidence and will to succeed in life. You will experience some sort of gain in a financial sense of the word that could come from your investments or business projects. Progress towards a prosperous life will become evident. However, such achievements need to be worked hard for and proper caution regarding the means of attaining such prosperity needs to be considered.

Your thinking style that is focused on purging or getting rid of problems has given you strength, stability, and protection. Concentrate on achieving goals and establishing yourself to become successful in your projects or whatever business you are venturing into. You have an awareness of your ideas coming to life, of seeing your ideas happen for real. Do not let your feelings about how easy it is to be served particular feelings or experiences in waking life get in the way of doing this.

There needs to be different changes in your life. Your wishes are coming true. Remember the circle of life, which is in constant movement, always changing. In your current life situation, something has taken a part of life, especially the part related to your health and personal development. Remember balance, remember the way you are balancing the different parts of your life. You need to bring that back to your own soul and self. You need to distance yourself from a situation in waking life. You have a struggle within to do what you need and what you want. This is a warning from someone with authority and who can be trusted. You need to become more reliant on your own ability to succeed.

This is a sign that you have someone to guide you. Messages are trying to get through to you, but you are ignoring what you need to see. I see you would rather deal with something in a different way. In the near future you will have to make a serious choice. Get on with your divine life purpose. All things must come to an end in order for new beginnings to occur. A phase or cycle of your life is ending and coming to completion and there is *promise of "new" to come. All will work out for your highest good. You simply must prepare yourself and your life accordingly. This situation is no longer positively serving you and it is drawing to an end. You are spiritually advanced. Follow your life path and soul purpose. It is time to put your natural skills, talents, and abilities to good use in serving humanity. Follow your intuitive promptings with regard to your life path and soul purpose. Set a positive example illuminating the way for others to follow. Fully embark upon your sacred soul mission without further delay or hesitation and shine your light brightly for the benefit of yourself and others. You are being asked to live up to your full potential.*

You have a wish to acknowledge a side of yourself that is out of your normal ways. You are hiding your true self. You are being someone you are not. You will be pleased with this situation that needs to be changed for the better. You will have happiness to see this goal achieved. You will enjoy experiencing success and an accomplishment being realized. You will feel grateful to be away from conflict, arguments, and people that are starting to annoy you.

You need to get your obligations in order. You may think they are pointless and unnecessary, which is why you do not feel compelled to fulfill them. However, they will turn out to be especially important and you will find out just how important very soon.

You will have to work hard to overcome all difficulties. But no matter what, do not give up and everything will certainly be positive in the future. Now is the time in your life that you need to take a closer look at the options and opportunities before you. You will realize that there are possibilities for growth and potential in your life regarding work. But you have to make the right decisions.

You want to live a more honorable and highly respected life. An air or professionalism is going to be required in your life as is a managerial approach to life. You are looking to gain business ability to make good judgements and quick decisions. Your life is going to be influenced by a great amount of change especially in matters of predictions of future events. Be more confident and managerial in your endeavors with others, especially in a professional process or system. This is something that is going to be important for you to do.

Things are peaceful and this is a time of harmony and happiness. You have independence and freedom. You are good at expressing yourself. A big change in your awareness is being foretold and an important period for your life is coming your way. Your wishes will be fulfilled, and peace and calm will enter your heart.

You will receive some financial incentive in the future. You are in the process of resolving inner issues and experiencing inner healing. This is a time of transformation and transition. You are moving to a higher level of consciousness and awareness in your waking life.

This is a time of spiritual development and renewal. It is about acceptance, love, encouragement and also forgiveness of all the conscious things running through your mind. It is a focus on regeneration. You have some religious needs that need to be met and you are looking to others to have those needs fulfilled. You have a lot of questions regarding your spiritual beliefs, and you want someone with authority to help you to answer them. You are trying to sort out aspects of your life. You are attempting to learn from your past and take something positive from it. You need to re-use an idea you once had. Do something in almost the same way but slightly different to get a better result, to make life easier and more efficient. The little things you do in life count towards something much bigger. So, keep it up as the implications could be great. The manual tasks that you do in your life have importance and are never a waste of your time even if it feels like it at points. You are ridding yourself of the negativity in your life and making way for something positive. You are paving the way for a better life for yourself even if it seems like a slow process. In doing so, your actions could be making others happier too. You are moving ahead and looking toward the future.

There are issues and situations in your life that you are giving serious thought which benefit you and increase your status and power. You will have success and compensation for your hard work. You are terribly busy and focused on an issue that is allowing you to improve yourself and benefit you in some way. You should show off your skills. You are having this dream because you are learning new skills and finishing work projects that allow you to gain in some way. You have worked hard to earn something.

You are trying to gain insight into past events. You have been spending time remembering your past. You are processing negative events from the past to learn and grow. You are on a search for knowledge, and you have the ability to realize this before it's too late. You are being given spiritual guidance. You have a desire to learn more and gain new knowledge through further education. You have information that you have developed over a number of years.

You need to learn from somebody else, and you are not yet appreciated for your real value. You need to gain some experience before being able to receive an important mission. You have made good choices in your life. You have put down a solid foundation from which to stand, and even if you are not rich and successful now, you will find yourself checking off many goals from your list in the future. Your true desires of life and the Universe will manifest. You will soon become privy to some news or information. Whatever you learn is sure to be useful and important for you. You will soon meet some new and interesting individuals. This sudden expansion of your social network is likely to have multiple positive effects on your future. In particular, some of these men and women could hold the secret to improving your life or getting on the path you were destined to follow. This would eventually lead to great happiness and satisfaction for both you and them.

Look at your past experiences in order to sort out your present situation and this should be reviewed carefully before you set yourself on a course of action. There is going to be an improvement in your living conditions and home life going forward.

You have the possibility to achieve some particularly important goal you have in the near future. Put in some more effort because the success is already on the horizon. A part of your life is coming to an end. Areas of your life are changing and ending. So, make sure your prepared for this, make the right choices, and apply yourself correctly so that you are ready to take on a new challenge once this one ends. There is never a permanent ending to anything in life, things are merely changing and moving forward to the next something. You are an active participant in life. Some people are not, and these people rely on others to fix their problems in their life over and over again or having a "why me?" mentality.

You are trying to move forward with your own work but are finding it difficult to focus. There are things on your mind which you are holding onto or unwilling to change. You are showing growth and maturation. You are holding too closely to old ways of doing things and in turn, this is holding you back. You need to let go and move forward in your thoughts. You will encounter a definite period of a new phase at your work in real life. An important phase in life is now coming forward.

Self-reflect on your own personal history, past merits, accomplishments, things from your past that you like, memories that you value. Something from your past has a bearing on a present situation. You want to have what it takes to live comfortably in the future, like money. You are, by economy and industry, laying a foundation for future wealth. You will amass a fortune through industry and commercial genius.

You are making a social statement. Movement is on its way. You will feel empowered in the future. You will move in your desired directions in life. You are going to be more creative and sudden insights in life will surprise you. You are likely to encounter prosperity and wealth. You will have financial gain. You will have professional advancement in life. Many positive events will enter your life.

You are gaining a higher self-awareness, making progress toward a goal, moving in a positive direction, and you are on your way to achieving success. You are reaching toward a higher consciousness. At the moment, you are looking within yourself and searching for your life path. You have high expectations in your life. Your emotions are calm and collected. There is closure with certain struggles in your life and you are finding ways to solve specific problems. Boundaries and barriers preventing you from moving forward are torn down. Success will be yours.

In your direction and approach to life you are trying to do things that are in your best interests as quickly as possible. You are getting important things done and quickly tying up loose ends. You are catching up on things your behind on. You are attempting to keep a steady pace. You are struggling to keep motivated as you make progress with these things.

You are facing a struggle to achieve your goals. You are attempting to work against your obstacles, and you are feeling the difficulty of this situation. You are feeling that this is too much for you. You are experiencing lots of pressure to accomplish this. You need to tough it out. Patience and dedication will benefit you. Eventually it will get easier.

You will solve a financial problem. Your material conditions will improve. You have potential in your life. You will have good business. Your wealth will grow. You will have wealth, richness, gain and big joy. You will find spiritual and personal peace.

You are subconsciously looking for answers about human existence. Awaken your inner knowing and desires to go forward with your search for enlightenment. Your psyche is searching for origins in order to master life some more. You have an inner calling for spirituality and search for wisdom and enlightenment.

You will have good fortune and good luck. An incredibly happy and comfortable period will come for you. You will develop in your business. Thus, your family will never see poverty. There will be a new business opportunity. You have overcome/defeated all of your fights, struggles, conflicts, and obstacles in your life.

You have witnessed yourself making a final decision. A change has been decided on. You are aiming for a goal. You are choosing to terminate things and people who you think are working against your best interests.

You have achieved a state of mind in meditation and prayer. You are on a spiritual path to higher awareness. You have passed many stages in your spiritual awareness. You have reached a new level of achievement. You will have prosperity because of your hard work and your efforts. You are delivered down from the old life you have had. You are giving helpful assistance to those around you. You need both the physical power and mental mind to accomplish greatness. You will be successful after much struggle and obstacles.

There has been a lot of fairly difficult work that needed to be done in reality. You will be getting new ideas and putting them into action. This is a time where you challenge yourself to do better. Remember to avoid giving too much time to ideas that may not be as important as others.

You are ready to go on your mission. You will receive news about your future. Pay attention to the details in the next few days and something will be revealed to you that will be useful in making future decisions. You feel overwhelmed with your responsibilities. Remember to pay attention to the important things in your life. Stop and analyze the bigger picture to re-focus your attention on where you want to go. You need to move forward in your life and learn new abilities and skills that will help you grow as an adult.

You have an overwhelming sense of social support. You are on the same page as everyone you know on an issue. You will have overwhelming agreement. A lot of people will be interested in your ideas and goals. You are exceptionally prepared for something. You are ready to use your experience. You will be using your cultivated experience and skill. You have been training for something special for a long time. You will celebrate a final achievement with your expertise on display. You will appear the most impressive that you can in a situation. You will use your well-honed skills and experience. You will prove yourself, make a name for yourself and establish your reputation. You are exceptionally ready to impress others.

You will have money in the future and happiness. You will gain chances and opportunities in your life. You have positive signs for the future.

You will overcome your obstacles and rise to a new level of prominence and status. You are having the experience of great awareness and higher consciousness. It is a great time for you, you are truly riding in the faster and much more open lane.

You will experience a higher consciousness, newfound freedom, and greater awareness. You are experiencing a lift off for your ideas and plans. After months of preparation and planning, you are finally ready to launch your project or business. Keep a clear perspective of the ground under you and your old life, even when you have succeeded with your goals.

You are gaining a better perspective or wider view. You have bright hopes and open possibilities. You have a new start, and you are washing away the past. You have a brighter future. You have possibilities for growth in life and you are headed in the right direction. There will be a focus on yourself going forward. In life things will work out well for you. You can overcome any problems that are overwhelming you at the moment. You will encounter relief from all your problems going forward. Keep on fighting for what you believe in. God is removing contaminants from your life. God is protecting you from the people who try to harm you and stop you from reaching your highest aspirations. New energy will be entering your life that will change. Soon, you will be happier and greater in life.

You will experience a lot of luck and success in the future. You will easily achieve all of your goals. You are passing through a period of thinking and introspection. You are strong enough to overcome all obstacles in your way. Defend your own opinions and beliefs. It is time for a positive transformation and for resolving problems that have been bothering you for a long time.

The greatest chance in your life will come out. You will get what you want to achieve without too much effort. Everything you want to be will occur one by one. The doors of a new job will be opened to you. You will receive new proposals in your business life, and every feedback you give to these proposals will be in your favor. Now that you have gone through the difficult steps in life, it will be an extremely easy and happy way ahead of you. You will proceed very peacefully on this road, and you will not have any problems.

You are at the completion of a long journey. You have been working hard to see your product come into fruition and it is now time to enjoy your work. One phase has ended, and you are now transitioning to a new beginning. Be diligent and pay close attention to the complete stop of your goals and projects. Do not let your focus slip and guard down simply because it is near the end, a misstep at this final phase can have catastrophic results.

You are doing good and successful work recently. The decisions you will make in recent times will always be correct and logical decisions. In your life, you will have everything you want to have. You will be happy after every decision you make and the way you always choose in life will please you.

You will find solutions to all the complex problems that keep your head busy and create a question mark in your life. All your problems will be solved one by one, and you will start to live a calm and peaceful life.

You have done good deeds and you have forgiveness from God. You are a humble and decent human being. Although you have never committed a crime or sin, you still spend most of your time doing charity work. You will hear some surprising, good news.

A huge event will make you incredibly happy. You will have an unexpected and big promotion in your business life. Everything in your life will be perfect. I bring you peace and reassurance. Your perception of things in your natural world is changing and you are slowly losing your feelings of guilt. You are on the right path. I am reassuring you that things will turn out all right. But be wary. Do not take people or things at face value. Take the time to look deeper.

You will have success in all you try to do because you are realistic about how to reach your goals. You are sowing the seeds of the future, cultivating what you wish to bring into your life. You know that it is not usual for success to occur overnight.

You have grown due to positive energy. You have opened up to allow new people into your life which inspired your growth. You have new growth and ideas. You are growing slowly towards your dreams.

There is going to be a change of work in some fashion. You are comfortable where you are at, but you are likely to be given more responsibility. There has been a change in your values and belief system. There needs to be changes to your lifestyle and behavior. Attempt to self-improve. Change something in your life to make yourself more confident. Get rid of bad influences, bad friends, or people you feel are losers from your life.

I am reminding you of the potential that you have in life. You are being tested in a situation in waking life. A successful outcome is predicted. You are feeling vulnerable in your own ability. It is time to try and make progress in solving your problems. A choice in the future is likely to arise. This will present the best way forward. It is important, going forward, to use your skills to their maximum. Each and everything you do should be carefully thought out and then acted upon. Without this approach to life things become quite difficult. Think about your role in life and be careful you do not overdo it.

You are trying to overcome problems in an effective way. You have the potential of a successful life. Things will begin to improve over the next few months. People are going to come to you looking for advice. Lately you have been preoccupied with your past and the mistakes you have made. It is time you let your past go and forgive yourself. Forgiveness is the only way you can find your inner peace again. Do not battle with yourself. Work on improving your life.

Your emotions will finally come clear. Your uncertainty about how you really feel and what you want in life is about to change soon. There are situations which you will encounter. Through life's lessons, you will discover the situations will result in positive ideas and give you a different perspective on life. You can achieve twice what you think you can.

Progress in your objectives. Stop stalling and get back on track. You should live your life to the fullest and break free from the monotony that has been suffocating you recently. This is a sign of good luck which is awfully close to you. You will be very energetic during upcoming days. You will gain back your energy and feel like you can conquer the world.

You will have a new goal. Are you willing to learn new things to acquire more spiritual knowledge and focus on your spirituality? You will have success and abundance. You will have a spiritual awakening in waking life around emotions. You will help someone succeed and take everything in your stride.

You will have many chances in life. Try to act, instead of just talking like most people do today. Keep up the hard work. You need to review your life, cut things out, and maybe get rid of some things in your life. It is time to gain financial and spiritual independence from your relatives. It is time to earn money and solve your problems on your own. There are new beginnings. You will have goodness and liveliness. There will be a property which makes you money without any effort or people whom you do business with will make you a lot of money by making efforts for you.

Chapter 5 | 243

What message from your past should you consider at the moment? Be your own wisdom. If you are ready to examine your life, you might get access to the universal human wisdom and use it for your own benefit. Remember your own intellect and personal life experiences, and the way you know how to handle these riches. You are skillful to preserve your knowledge. The collective unconscious could open new doors for you in terms of intellectual endeavors. You will have to deal with lots of people sometime soon, and you might need good advice as per how to do that best. Success is coming your way, but only after a long period of extensive effort and work.

Your environment might deceive you, and this will increase your interest in literature and books in general. You will soon have good results regarding your career and hobbies. You feel that nothing is wrong at all with a particular issue. You have a laid-back attitude about a situation you are experiencing. You feel others are ambivalent about your health. You have a choice to make. You can have what you want if you really want it. You have to reassess an issue in your life because you are seeing things in a disoriented manner. In other words, you view the matter erroneously.

You need to pay attention to your intuition because it has an important message that you have been ignoring. You are going to push for what you want in life. It is time to think logically about why you are feeling stress or worry in waking life. You are searching for deeper wisdom within. You logically feel worried about the future but there is no need to.

You are trying to hide a situation in waking life. You want to cover up something that is important to you. You have exhausted your inner thoughts. You may be feeling drained and empty inside. Be careful that your actions stay within certain bounds. Do not go too far with something.

There is an issue or situation in your life that you are stuck in. There is an inability or unwillingness to move on or overcome a problem. Progress is intentionally not being chosen right now. A lot of brilliant ideas are born in your head that you do not want to fulfill for some reason, and they disappear. Do not scatter thoughts, they are so fleeting.

You have a curiosity to know or learn new things in life. It is time you make new goals to achieve something different and bigger in life. Find out the things that fascinate you the most and spread your knowledge to reach there.

You are in a comfort zone while someone else is running your life for you. The danger is that in the event that this person takes a wrong turn, you are doomed because you will go in the wrong direction and lose focus of what you really want in life. Wake up and take charge of your life before it is too late. You are the best person who knows your focus and where you want to drive yourself to. Get ahold of the steering wheel and start moving yourself to where you want to go. It might be tedious and tough, but at the end of the day, you will accomplish your goals and be happy with yourself. This idea of depending on others in life should stop because there is no pride in doing so. You will feel proud when you do something for yourself, and it becomes successful.

You are trying to let go of the stress, negative emotions, and things in your life. A new phase of life is emerging. Reunite the areas of your life that seem separate or disjointed. Face the difficulties you are encountering in waking life. You have got to focus on a more positive attitude which will allow you to bring great things into your life. Keep working to your full potential rather than being lazy or procrastinating. Be creative to discover more about yourself. This is a significant transition.

You will have rewards, honor, praise, and recognition for your achievements. These struggles in your life need to be addressed and resolved. You have feelings of inadequacy and being out of place. There are some aspects of your past life which you consider to be especially important, and they are always with you. It is becoming a burden to you and unless you off load your problems you might not be able to move in the future with optimism. Success and prosperity are just at the corners.

You will have good health, growth, great luck and also money. You will overcome worries. You do not want others disturbing you. Your thoughts and emotions are focused on comfort, luxury, and relaxation. You need to maintain a comfortable situation. Be careful not to let a comfortable situation to become too lazy, reckless, or neglected.

You are feeling that it is not possible to have the perfectly responsible or professional appearance that you want. You will have happiness and good changes coming into your life. You will have productivity, increase of energy and improvement of your overall well-being on your spiritual journey and life path. Your transition will be an emotional one. You are currently experiencing some difficulties in life.

You will have a meeting of your rational and emotional states of mind. You are in the middle of a transition between your physical and spiritual self. You are overwhelmed or overworked in your waking life. You have a desire to have more fun in life.

You have a fresh start in life. You are starting to feel happy in your own company. Be receptive to enjoying your achievements and relaxing with a sense of completion. Feel good about hard work completed and what you have done. You are trying to find your way through a situation that is unfamiliar, and it is unsettling because it's new. It is creating confusion and uncertainty for you.

You are doing as you please and being carefree. It feels wonderful to do whatever you want. You have few restrictions or limitations. You are experiencing a situation that allows you to exploit it for your own benefit and that allows you to enjoy yourself.

You are trying to handle a touchy situation in a careful manner. You will no longer accept no or obstacles as excuses or answers. You will do whatever it takes to reach your goals. You have a self-awareness of trying hard to be serious about something. You have a heightened sense of clarity and needing to pay attention. You are trying to be intelligent about something. There is something that is currently on your mind.

On 1/12/20 I told God I was working on everything, and I would keep doing so and that he knows that. Then I asked him to keep me healthy. This was about the time we started hearing about Covid-19 a lot in the news. When I fell asleep, I had this dream:

You are feeling very strongly about something. Be sure to examine your own health and wellness habits and make positive changes to live a healthy lifestyle. You need to become more spiritual and pay attention to your spiritual needs.

Look at all the areas of your life where you feel you could be improving and where you could put more effort into your projects. Find balance in your life. Think about what things are important to you in your life and how you can devote more time to it or them. Focus on yourself and your own powers of expression and creativity. This will bring back some balance to your busy life and allow you some emotional structure. Otherwise, the imbalance will suck the life out of you.

You are in conflict with yourself and feel concerned about what new responsibilities you have to take on. In the near future everything will go very well for you, and you will have complete confidence in yourself.

Pay attention to this! You will have success, authority, and cosmic consciousness, and abundance. Pay attention to and trust your intuition and instincts and take appropriate action. Have self-trust. Your goals are coming to fruition, and you are achieving a state of completeness. All of your wants and needs will be met. You will be rewarded for your hard work and work well done. Keep reaching for your full potential and keep your finances in check and ensure a solid foundation for yourself and your loved ones.

You will have great satisfaction in achieving your life goals as you progress on. You like showing off and you are a competitive person at heart. You are a person whom others do not like associating with in terms of business because in most instances you win.

A money windfall may also be in the offing sooner than you can imagine. You might be thinking of restarting a project which you had put on hold. You have accomplished some things in your life which are making you feel proud. You have met or set goals. You will win in life. There is a personal goal and project that you are working towards. You are working on a project which has several roles to it. You have to be ready to take in all the energies of those people who are surrounding you. Make sure you allocate duties to perform according to their qualifications and strengths in order to be successful in your project.

Things are going to be settled and you need to go back down to earth. You are ready to learn talents, rules, and you will achieve your goals. You are moving closer towards achieving your goals. All you need to do is put in more effort and everything will work out right.

FINAL THOUGHTS AND RESULTS

The purpose of writing my books was not just simply for me to publish them and make money. The real purpose was to write them so it would solidify in my mind what I was supposed to learn through each phase of my development, and to give that knowledge permanence in the world in some form of art for the inspiration of others who may need it. Each one of my books summarizes, solidifies, and completes a phase of my individuation process.

It was an obvious choice for me to become a writer. This is the art form, the vehicle, I would use to help me complete my individuation process. By publishing my books, they would be in the Universe for others who may need them, who because of their own personal journey, would be drawn to them. It is not my responsibility to force these books upon others. My only responsibility was to complete the process and give what I have learned a permanent form in the world. It is each person's responsibility to find what they need when they need it. Even though the Universe provides for us all, it is up to each individual to be responsible with what we are provided. Because of what I have learned and completed; I will be rewarded. My reward will come from me applying what I have learned to my life from here on out through the conduct of my hobbies, interests, and goals.

Things had to progress and develop in stages and in their own sweet time. This is not a fast process. It takes time to develop and unfold. Mostly because of our human minds. Our minds would not be able to comprehend, let alone handle it all, if it occurred to fast. The process is basically to learn and then apply, then learn some more and repeat until the desired form is achieved. First, the ego-conscious and unconscious are developed individually through a series of life events. Then, the mental baggage that is acquired through this developmental process must be cleansed. Once this transformation is completed, a purification occurs. This purification is completed through a series of events where the body and spirit (conscious and unconscious) are separated and modified through dreams until one's instinctual impulses are modified into a higher, more socially acceptable activity. Then when that has been completed by taking what one has learned, and then giving it permanence in the world through some type of art form, the final phase begins. This is where one lives the next part of their life receiving the rewards for completing the process and living life accordingly. It is as I mentioned previously in the book about this process being analogous to that of forging steel in a fire. You take a piece of steel and put in a fire, pull it out and beat it on an anvil, stick it back into the fire and repeat the process like a Blacksmith, until the proper form is obtained for the use it was intended.

In the final phase of the individuation process, I completely relied on and trusted my unconscious guidance. Through a series of dreams and meditations, I gleaned the messages my unconscious was providing me and then I incorporated it all into my physical life. I was being guided through this phase. That is when I wrote this book, based on my unconscious guidance, and completed this process. There are no such things as coincidences, and everything has its purpose.

As one goes through this process of Individuation, not only do transformation and evolution occur in our conscious lives by acting on, or following, our unconscious guidance, but our brain, our way of thinking, is also molded/developed by our unconscious. Our dreams are also describing to us the evolution of this process and the progress, or regression, we are making, whichever the case may be.

Each of us as individuals has our own unique, very personal path to follow to complete our own individuation process. No two paths are the same. We all may go through similar experiences and events; however, how they affect us, how we react to them, how they guide us, are different for each individual person. If that were not the case, this process would not be called Individuation, would it? We would all look and act exactly the same. Yes, we are all human beings created in much the same way; however, we all are unique in the specific path we are supposed to follow and in the work we bring into the world for the inspiration of others.

I say inspiration because it is not up to us to tell or make anyone do anything. That would alter their path. That is not up to us as individuals. Everyone has to follow their own path and be allowed to experience the events of their lives. Our only responsibility as individual human beings is to complete this developmental process and put it into some physical or material form, so that it is permanent in the world. Thus, it acts as an inspiration to others to begin and complete this process. We also inspire people by living our own individual lives as examples. Sort of like a torch lighting the way. Like I said, each person's path is unique to themselves.

The final goal of this process is to get an individual to the point where one is living life from their center through one's own unconscious guidance, instincts, intuition, and symbols that are given to them. We are not supposed to live our lives based on man-made, egocentric rules, dogmas, and creeds. These are all forms of human control. In other words, edging God out (EGO). Man did not create the Universe, world, and life. However, he can certainly affect it, and even destroy it, based on how he thinks and acts. We all must live our unconscious truth if we want to find our real paradise and eternal peace. Hence, creating a world that is guided by such principles.

Here are the six stages of development as I see them in relation to what I have been talking about.

1. Development of unconsciousness
2. Development of ego-consciousness
3. Mental cleansing
4. Integration of unconscious guidance into ego-conscious life by giving what we have learned permanent form in the world.
5. Living life as a whole self and being an inspiration to others. Finding and living life in our own paradise as a reward for completing this process and living life in the proper, intended form.

6. Rest, relaxation, recuperation, and preparation for the transition into death and a new, higher state of existence, whatever that may be.

It is my theory that if the individuation process is not completed by the time one begins the sixth stage, the person is reborn into another life, having the same sort of experiences over and over again, until a progression is made. This then keeps occurring until the Individuation process is completed. I believe this is what happened to me until I finally achieved what I was supposed to in this life. It is up to the individual on how long this takes. It depends upon how stubborn the person is and how long they *choose* to not change and develop. This, I believe, is also what my three war dreams are a symbol of. They are the story of my past lives. I have no scientific proof of this. Scientific proof would be man-made ego-consciousness. In this life, I have broken the cycle and finally completed my Individuation process. I dealt with the baggage that all of my lives had produced, and I moved on with my development. That is what I was supposed to figure out, and use, to help guide me down the proper path and complete the process. That is all that matters for me. We will see what my life brings next!

I have experienced trauma throughout my life. It was that trauma that kept me held back in life because I did not properly deal with it. Therefore, these experiences kept repeating themselves until I moved past each one by not repeating the same choices. Thereby, breaking the cycle.

Obstacles in life need to be overcome. My problems were not meant to obstruct or derail me. They were specifically given to me because I had something to learn at that specific time in my life. They taught me something very valuable that I applied to my growth and development throughout my life. I now see the problems in my life as gifts, that if used wisely, significantly enhance my life and my experiences. My purpose is to improve and develop the self. It is my sole responsibility as a human being. Then, I must share that with the world in order to inspire others.

I knew I must find the strength to fight the adversity that arose in my life. I had to find the power and energy to press on.

I had to fight. I had to overcome all of my problems, anxiety, and trauma. I had to overcome my life. I knew I would find the power to succeed at this, at life. I had survived through all of this adversity, horror, and trauma. So, because I made it through all of these experiences, I knew that I had the strength to make it through this, to develop and improve myself. I had been prepared for this moment of achievement my entire life. Then, the next step is to share it with the world. I can now be a positive example to others of what they may achieve with their own individual lives.

Through all of this, my problems disappeared, my new life is meeting my expectations. It all has brought me to a period of economic prosperity and blissful peace. I feel as though I am in tune with everything in my life. My persistence and unrelenting efforts are now beginning to pay off.

I knew my struggles had to be overcome if I was going to achieve my goals. I knew that every investment I was making would pay off in the future. I know my truth. I know I will complete my work and that will result in good, perfection, and justice to come. Early in this process, I knew I had to analyze my life in all of its entirety. I had to become a student of my life. My life became my classroom. My dreams and experiences became my professors. Through this, I learned who I really was. I obtained a physical and mental purity. I realized I was not what society, the world, and my parents had made me into, or what they all led me to believe. With this purity, I obtained a clearness of mind. This allowed me to see how my conscious and unconscious development unfolded throughout my life. I feel like I have obtained a spiritual elevation if you will.

The completion of all of this suggested to me that bigger and better things were coming into my life. The purpose of my life was to ultimately develop my unconscious, my inner and emotional mind, and then live my life accordingly. It has become obvious to me that my emotions had completely overwhelmed me because I let them. Thus, the anxieties, stresses, and trauma of life had swept me away. I now understand that the only way to come back from this, to be who I really am, was to develop my inner and emotional unconscious mind and live my truth. I analyzed all of my shocks, losses, catastrophes, struggles, fears, anger, and every other negative emotion. I attacked all of this armed with what I learned from my training as a United States Marine and as a professional Archaeologist. Then, to move forward, I had to openly express it all, instead of keeping them bottled up inside. Holding it all in sent me on this torrential course like a destructive, horrible, tsunami. I expressed this through my passion which is writing. I used my passion to carry me through this journey. As I have said many times since I healed, in my books, videos, and interviews, "Your passion is the vehicle that takes you from pain to peace!" This is what I say to people when they ask me to tell them how I did it. That is as succinctly as I can put it. I found my passion and I used it. That's how I began. That was the gift, or tool, I was given to complete this process.

For many, many years I was overcome with anxiety, feelings of frustration and confusion. I constantly felt that I just didn't fit in. I was just a face in a sea of people in a horrible, screwed up world. Now, I feel as though my life is being guided by a higher, more benevolent authority. I feel as though I am succeeding in my pursuit of knowledge and in life. I am victorious. It is as though there has been the death of the "old me."

It is as though the hard work I have been conducting throughout all of my lifetimes, has landed me exactly right at the point I am at today, both physically, mentally, and economically. It all has brought me towards serving my life's purpose, coupled with a sense of divinity. I am now consumed with passion, confidence, and enthusiasm for where my path goes moving forward. All of this has made me understand just how well blessed I am, and it leaves me in absolute awe of the universe and its seemingly magical and esoteric ways.

I am proud of myself for all of the hard work I put in building solid foundations for myself and my family. I am elated that I put in all of this hard work and effort. It is quite motivating to look back at it all now. I am now positive that the achievement of my goals will bring me my desired results. I know that I have it in me to overcome any obstacle or adversity I may encounter, while travelling down my path. My life is now back in order. It is no longer like I am a 1,000-piece puzzle scattered over a coffee table. I am better and stronger because of all of this.

It was at this point in my journey that Covid 19 hit and everything was shut down. I could not help but see how I was uniquely prepared for such an event. So, I used this time of isolation to shed all the parts and people of my life that no longer served my progression in a positive manner. I used the isolation to dig deep into my soul and search my truths. I focused on trusting my intuition and following its guidance. I spent many hours in silent meditation asking the questions I needed answered. I got rid of my ego. I studied endlessly. I focused on my book. I finished my development and this work. It all took a couple of years to complete.

Money started appearing in my life from unexpected and expected sources in miraculous, synchronistic ways. I am completely out of debt. I have a home, a nice vehicle, investments, emergency savings, retirement account, money to spend on things I desire and entertainment. I got on a healthy, new diet that's all organic and it gave me more energy and mental clarity. It boosted my immune system. I even lost some weight. I began to meet new friends who had similar interests and lifestyles as me. I began trying new things and socializing again, once Covid calmed down. That is about the time I finished my work. Kind of ironic. I was ready to throw open the doors and step out into the world with a whole new perspective.

I have a whole new life beginning. The bad and my past are finally over. It feels really good to be able to say that and know it's true. I look forward to this next phase of my life. I look forward to the richness I will experience in every aspect of my life. So, it is at this point, 3/29/2022, I release this book into the world and fulfill my personal responsibility, both physically and spiritually.

Below are the four steps I developed along my journey of healing and completing this process. After these four steps, I broke everything down even further. This became the game plan for my life going forward.

MY FOUR STEPS TO BEGIN A JOURNEY OF HEALING, DEVELOPING SPIRITUALLY, AND ATTAINING YOUR DREAMS

By
Robert Serocki, Jr.

"Without developing spiritually, there can be no development physically."

Mark Twain

1. **Release your past.**
   - Use some creative ability or art form to accomplish this. Write about it, paint, draw, sing, etc. Use whatever your passion is as the vehicle that takes you from pain to peace.
     - My book, ***A Line in the Sand*** is an example of how I began to accomplish this.
2. **Release the emotional charge from your memories so they no longer control you.**
   - This step is completed concomitantly with step #1.
     - My book, ***Chrysalis*** is an example of how I accomplished this.
3. **Build a foundation of health, both mentally and physically, to help propel you forward in your life and in the attainment of your goals.**
   - My 13-Step Foundation to healing physically and mentally was my guide.
     - My book, ***The Sword and the Anvil*** is an example of how I accomplished this, and it contains my 13-step Foundation to healing.

4. **Reconnect the mind and body by using your intuition to guide your life's work and help you attain your dreams.**
   - Life events analysis.
   - Dream Analysis.
   - Incorporate what you have learned from these two analyses into your physical life.
     - My book, *The Blacksmith* is an example of how I accomplished this.
   - Incorporate your spiritual guidance (intuition) into your physical life and let it guide you.

MY GAME PLAN GOING FORWARD

1. **Focus on your passions and purpose.**
   - The more I focus and act upon my mission, the more abundance I will attract
   - Have faith that my monetary and financial needs will be met.
   - Live my life in a manner that sets a positive example and illuminates the way for others.
2. **My life purpose.**
   - Communicating, teaching, and helping others.
   - Serve humanity in a way that suits me best.
   - Set a positive example for others.
   - Inspire others to seek their own passion and purpose in life.
3. **Further development.**
   - Learn new skills and knowledge.
   - Listen to my own inner knowledge.
   - Step out of my comfort zone to further advance and develop on all levels.
4. **Further develop my self-knowledge.**
   - Spend time sitting quietly and asking the questions I want answered.
   - Take time to focus my attention and intention to allow what I need to know to come to light.
   - Trust my answers.
   - Know that my thoughts and ideas are answering my questions and giving me intuitive guidance in regard to the next steps to take along my path.

5. **Follow up on my ideas and look for my opportunities.**
   - Discern what I would like to pursue. Then set my course of action and make it so.
   - Take the time to investigate all situations and possibilities. Choose to integrate those things that resonate with me.
6. **Recognize, acknowledge, and honor my natural talents and abilities. Use them to be an inspiration to others.**
   - Indulge in a hobby, interest, past-time, or line of study that ignites my passion and allow my natural creativity to express what's within me.
   - Express my truths in all that I do.
   - My life path is one of serving and teaching others and living my life as a positive example.
   - View situations and circumstances from a higher perspective.
   - Look to ways of expanding and expressing my values, principles, and inner truths.
7. **Manifest financial supply in order to sustain and support me along my path.**
   - My material and financial wants and needs will be met as long as I continue my proper path.
   - Build a proper financial foundation to adhere to and grow from.
8. **Prepare for big life changes that will come.**
   - As a phase or cycle ends in my life, understand that it will have a domino effect in other areas of my life.
   - Do not lament their passing or ending. Be open to receiving new into my life.
   - Understand that major life changes are around and ahead of me. This may be a time of upheaval and transition.

- Listen to my guidance and intuition during these transformational changes.
- Always maintain a positive attitude.

9. **Be prepared for new information or news that I receive.**
    - Listen to my intuition and heed its guidance.
    - This may bring some new opportunities for me to put my abilities to good use in the service of those who need it.

10. **Look to different ways to enhance my home, garden, and surroundings. This also includes within the home and family.**

11. **Be opened to receiving my well-earned rewards. Always be grateful for my blessings.**

ABOUT THE AUTHOR

Robert Serocki, Jr. was in the United States Marine Corps from 1988-92. He was a demolition expert and Scout Sniper. Robert graduated first in his Sniper School class. During his time in the Marines, he fought on the front lines of the first Gulf War. During the War, Robert was sent on a special mission to cross enemy lines under the cover of darkness. A mission that him and his fellow Marines were likely not to return from. However, Robert did. Because of his experiences, Robert developed Post Traumatic Stress Disorder (PTSD). The PTSD caused him to lose two houses, his professional job of nearly 20 years, file bankruptcy, attempt suicide twice, end up on seven different medications at once, gained 70lbs and ended up in a wheelchair for several years with nowhere to live, no way to pay bills, buy food, etc. He eventually overcame all of this. Robert suffered from, lived with, and overcame his PTSD in healthy, natural ways over the course of 20+ years.

Robert has a bachelor's degree in Anthropology, with an emphasis on Archaeology from Arizona State University. He also studied Latin, Spanish, Geology, Psychological and Social Anthropology, Philosophy, and Business. Through all of Robert's experiences, he discovered his passion for writing and how it could not only help him heal, but how it could also inspire others. This is Robert's fourth book in a series of books he has written describing his more than five-decade long journey, how he overcame it all and became successful with his new inspired life. Robert has also been in numerous newspapers, magazines, on radio, and TV. He also had his own radio show and a podcast series. He currently has a YouTube channel where he discusses what is in his books and his journey.

Robert is now a successful Entrepreneur, Author, Veteran, and PTSD survivor. His goal is to be an example to others and to inspire them by sharing his story. When he is not following

About the Author

his passions of writing and investing, Robert spends his free time camping, fishing, gardening, raising chickens, cooking, reading, working on his home, and spending time with his family and friends.

You can reach Robert by going to his website www.robertserockijr.com or by calling **1.800.410.9012** or by email at robert@robertserockijr.com

ROBERT'S OTHER PUBLICATIONS

- *A Line in the Sand: The true story of a Marine's experience on the front lines of the Gulf War.*
- *Chrysalis: A Metamorphosis has begun!*
- *The Sword and the Anvil: A definitive guide for natural, healthy healing from Post-Traumatic Stress and Trauma.*
-

Other links to Robert's books:

- Website: robertserockijr.com
- Amazon: https://www.amazon.com/s/ref=nb_sb_noss?url=search-alias%3Daps&field-keywords=robert+serocki
- Barnes and Noble: https://www.barnesandnoble.com/s/robert+serocki?_requestid=4171027

Here is a link to his YouTube channel where he discusses the information in his books:

- https://www.youtube.com/channel/UCNzGKeFN-r9WFM2_BB4lQDw

Previous TV interview:

- https://www.youtube.com/watch?v=-ReoU16UXV0

Previous Radio Interviews:

- https://soundcloud.com/robert-serocki-jr/truth-to-power-hour-10-21-06
- https://soundcloud.com/powertalk1210/marine-robert-serocki-jr-pt-1?in=powertalk1210/sets/robert-serocki-jr
- https://soundcloud.com/powertalk1210/marine-robert-serocki-jr-pt-2?in=powertalk1210/sets/robert-serocki-jr

- https://soundcloud.com/powertalk1210/marine-robert-serocki-jr-pt-4?in=powertalk1210/sets/robert-serocki-jr
- https://www.youtube.com/watch?v=M4DBaYNRH0Q&t=8s

Robert's Podcasts:

- https://soundcloud.com/powertalk1210/sets/robert-serocki-jr

Robert Serocki, Jr.
Entrepreneur/Author/Veteran/PTSD Survivor
"Inspiring people by sharing my story!"

www.ingramcontent.com/pod-product-compliance
Lightning Source LLC
Chambersburg PA
CBHW071957110526
44592CB00012B/1123